ALIENS™ OMNIBUS

ALIENS™

OMNIBUS

VOLUME 3

DARK HORSE BOOKS®

CONTENTS

cover illustration **DEN BEAUVAIS**

publisher **MIKE RICHARDSON**
series editors **RANDY STRADLEY, RYDER WINDHAM, DICK HANSOM, ANINA BENNETT, and JERRY PROSSER**
collection editor **CHRIS WARNER**
designer **JOSHUA ELLIOTT**
art director **LIA RIBACCHI**

Special thanks to **DEBBIE OLSHAN** at Twentieth Century Fox Licensing.

ALIENS™ OMNIBUS Volume 3

This volume collects material previously published as the Dark Horse graphic novels *Aliens: Rogue, Aliens: Salvation and Sacrifice*, and *Aliens: Labyrinth*; stories from issues three through five of the Dark Horse comic-book series *Dark Horse Comics*; and stories from the Dark Horse comic book *Dark Horse Presents: Aliens Platinum Edition*.

Dark Horse Books
A division of Dark Horse Comics, Inc.
10956 SE Main Street
Milwaukie, OR 97222

darkhorse.com | foxmovies.com

To find a comics shop in your area, call the Comic Shop Locator Service toll-free at 1-888-266-4226

First edition: March 2008
ISBN: 978-1-59307-872-0

10 9 8 7 6 5 4 3 2 1
Printed in China

ROGUE

script
IAN EDGINTON

art
WILL SIMPSON

colors
ROBBIE BUSCH

lettering
JOHN COSTANZA

title illustration
JOHN BOLTON

"AS MUCH AS WE HAVE COME TO FEAR THE ALIEN, IT CANNOT BE DENIED THAT IT HAS HAD A PROFOUND EFFECT ON OUR CULTURE.
"TECHNOLOGIES DESIGNED TO COMBAT IT HAVE BECOME ASSIMILATED SEAMLESSLY INTO THE MOST DOMESTIC OF OUR ENVIRONMENTS.
"DRUGS PROCESSED FROM THE ALIEN MATRIARCH'S ROYAL JELLY ARE NOW AVAILABLE COMMERCIALLY.
"NEW ECONOMIES BUILT ON THE BACK OF A CREATURE THAT USED US AS BREEDING STOCK.
"IT'S A UNIQUE INDICTMENT OF THE HUMAN CONDITION -- WE DON'T JUST CONQUER OUR FEARS, WE MARKET THEM.
"BUT IN DOING SO WE'VE LOST SIGHT OF SOMETHING..."

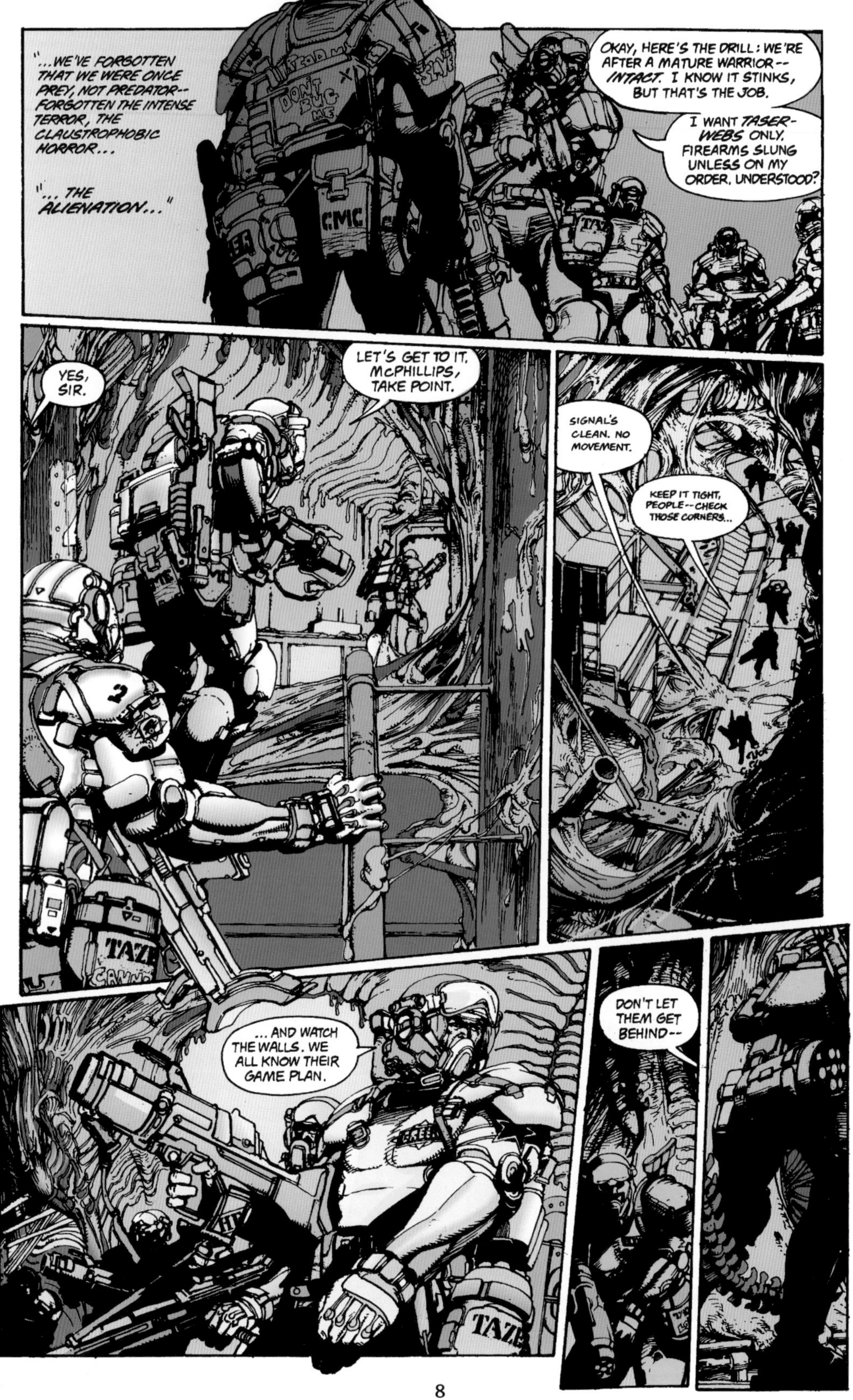
"...WE'VE FORGOTTEN THAT WE WERE ONCE PREY, NOT PREDATOR-- FORGOTTEN THE INTENSE TERROR, THE CLAUSTROPHOBIC HORROR...
"... THE ALIENATION..."
OKAY, HERE'S THE DRILL: WE'RE AFTER A MATURE WARRIOR-- INTACT. I KNOW IT STINKS, BUT THAT'S THE JOB.
I WANT TASER-WEBS ONLY. FIREARMS SLUNG UNLESS ON MY ORDER. UNDERSTOOD?
DON'T BUG ME
CMC
YES, SIR.
LET'S GET TO IT. McPHILLIPS, TAKE POINT.
SIGNAL'S CLEAN. NO MOVEMENT.
KEEP IT TIGHT, PEOPLE--CHECK THOSE CORNERS...
TAZE
...AND WATCH THE WALLS. WE ALL KNOW THEIR GAME PLAN.
DON'T LET THEM GET BEHIND--
TAZE

YEEARGH!!
BOONE! CUT IT LOOSE, MAN! CUT IT!

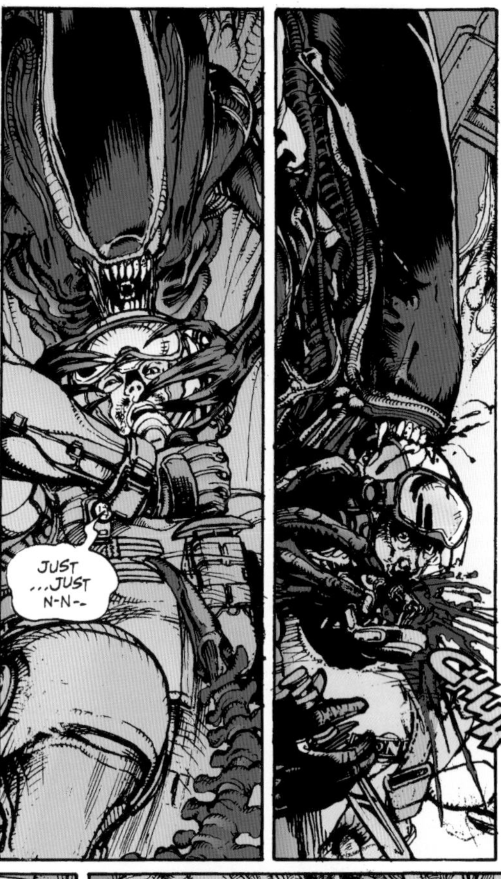
JUST ...JUST N-N--
CHUK

BASTAARRDD!!
HOLD YOUR FIRE, GODDAMMIT!

YOU DROPPED US IN PRETTY NOW, SON.
BUT YOU SAW--
OH, MAN! I GOT SIGNALS, I GOT READINGS ALL OVER!
CLICKCLICKCLICKCLICKCLIC

"WE JUST GAVE 'EM AN ALARM CALL...
"...AND NOW THEY'RE COMIN' DOWN TO BREAKFAST."

COMBAT SPACING FRONT AND REAR! HUSTLE! HUSTLE! DILLON-- THE CANNON?
PREPPED AND READY, SIR. MAX FREQUENCY, WIDE FIELD FOCUS.
STAND BY, TASER WEBS...

...'CAUSE HERE THEY COME! DILLON, FIRE ON MY MARK.

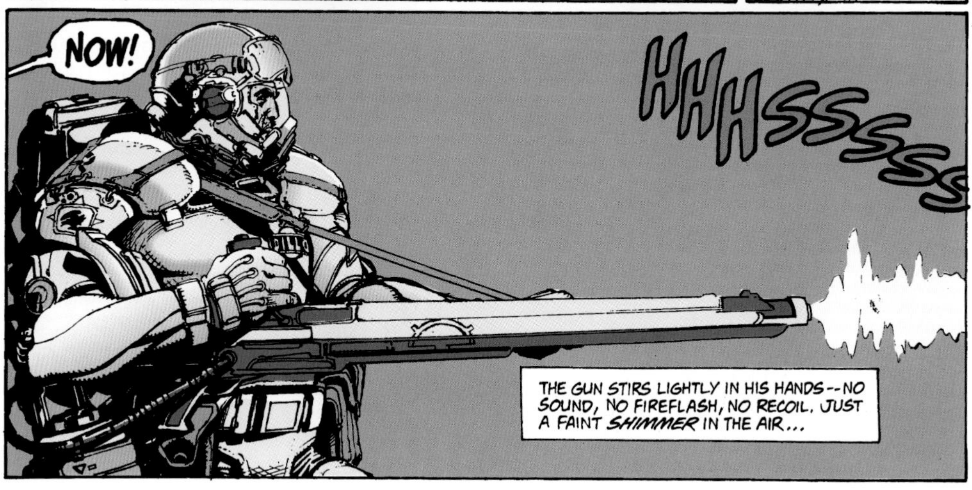
NOW!
HHHSSSSSS
THE GUN STIRS LIGHTLY IN HIS HANDS--NO SOUND, NO FIREFLASH, NO RECOIL. JUST A FAINT SHIMMER IN THE AIR...

BEATS ME HOW THIS BABY WORKS, BUT IT GETS 'EM EVERY TIME.
THAT ONE. BRING IT DOWN.
SSKREEAA
POOM

GRAB IT AND LET'S GO.

I HATE THIS PART.
MALFUNCTION? CHRIST, NOT AGAIN!
PICK IT UP, YOU GUYS-- ANOTHER THIRTY AN' THIS THING'S GOING CRITICAL!
EEP EEP EEP EEP

DOUBLE TIME, MEN. MOVE! MOVE!

SECONDS EXPAND, DISTORTED INTO SLOW, HEAVY MOMENTS.
AGONIZING.
UNENDING.

BUT NEVER ENOUGH.
GOTTA SHUT IT OFF OR SHE'LL BLOW!
CRITICAL POWER OVERLOAD 22:09 SEC.
SERGEANT REUBEN GREEN IS A THIRTY-YEAR MAN, LIKE HIS FATHER AND HIS FATHER BEFORE HIM.
A BLOODLINE OF WARRIORS BRED ON CONFLICT AND GLORY, HONOR AND SACRIFICE.
AN ANCIENT PROFESSION.
TIMES CHANGE.
COMPANIES REPLACE COUNTRIES.
THE FLAG GIVES WAY TO A DOLLAR BILL.
AN AGE-OLD PROFESSION IS SWEPT ASIDE...
...BY THE SHOCK OF THE NEW.

CONGRATULATIONS, SERGEANT-- HE LOOKS LIKE A FINE SPECIMEN. I'M DISTRESSED THAT YOU SLAUGHTERED THE OTHER ONE, HOWEVER.
HE'S DISTRESSED!!
SIR, I CAN EXPLAIN--
KLEIST, YOU SONOVABITCH! BOONE GETS TURNED INTO BEEF JERKY, AND YOU'RE PISSED 'CAUSE WE WASTED ONE OF YOUR PRECIOUS BUGS?
WE COULD'VE ALL DIED IN THAT FRIGGIN' ANT FARM OF YOURS!
MAN, YOU AIN'T PLAYIN' WITH A FULL DECK!
SERGEANT GREEN, I CAN APPRECIATE THE CORPORAL'S ANXIETY, BUT I SUGGEST HE RESTRAIN HIMSELF BEFORE HE SAYS SOMETHING HE'LL REGRET.
TAKE THE SPECIMEN TO THE DISSECTION VAT. I'LL BE ALONG SHORTLY.
YES, SIR.
JESUS! KISS HIS ASS, WHY DON'T YOU?!
DO YOURSELF A FAVOR AND REIGN IT IN, SON.
THERE'S A TIME AND PLACE FOR EVERYTHING. BESIDES, THOSE BUGS AIN'T THE ONLY THING YOU GOTTA BE WARY OF 'ROUND HERE.
HOW TRUE, SERGEANT. HOW TRUE.

SPACE--THE FORGE OF CREATION, THE LATHE OF HEAVEN.

THERE ARE A THOUSAND WAYS TO DIE OUT HERE. A THOUSAND WAYS TO LET THE HUNGRY VACUUM TEAR AWAY YOUR LIFE.

YET WE CONTINUE TO HURL OURSELVES INTO THE VOID. WRAPPED IN SHELLS OF PLASTIC AND METAL, WE CHALLENGE THE PREDATORY EMPTINESS WITH OUR MERE EXISTENCE.
WITH INTELLECT AND ARROGANCE WE CONFRONT THE DARKNESS. AFTER ALL, WE ARE NATURE'S CHILDREN...
HARLEY-DAVIDSON
COMPANY

... AND NATURE ABHORS A VACUUM.
HAGO
11 12 13 14
CHARON BASE FLIGHT CONTROL. THIS IS ZAJER/ COMM TECHNIC TRANSPORT VESSEL CALIBAN, REG # 18095774, REQUESTING LANDING CLEARANCE, OVER.
ROGER, CALIBAN. HANGAR TWELVE'S CLEAR AND READY TO RECEIVE YOU, OVER.

WE'RE IN THE TUBE, NOMINAL TO PROFILE. CUTTING THRUSTERS.
ALL RIGHT, LET'S TUCK HER IN. AND DEEGAN...
YES, BOSS?

WATCH THOSE CORNERS THIS TIME, HUH?
HEY, TRUST ME! IT'S A WALK IN THE PARK.

DEEGAN, WHEN DID YOU LAST SEE SOMEONE TAKE EIGHTY THOUSAND UGLY TONS OF METAL FOR A STROLL?

HANGAR TWELVE DECOMPRESSING. ALL CREW AND PASSENGERS, PLEASE REPORT TO DECONTAMINATION.

SO, MR. KRAY, WHAT BRINGS YOU TO SCENIC CHARON?
APART FROM US THAT IS.
CAN IT, DEEGAN-- I'M TALKING TO A NORMAL HUMAN BEING HERE.

THANKS FOR YOUR INTEREST, BUT IT'S CLASSIFIED ON A *NEED-TO-KNOW* BASIS. SORRY.
AND WE DON'T NEED TO KNOW?
GOT IT IN ONE.

FIGURES. KLEIST'S GOT THIS PLACE SEWN UP TIGHTER THAN A FROG'S BUTT.

MR. KRAY?
SPEAK OF THE DEVIL...
...AND HE SHALL APPEAR.

WELCOME TO CHARON. I'M PROFESSOR ERNST KLEIST, DIRECTOR OF THIS FACILITY.
I TRUST YOU HAD A COMFORTABLE FLIGHT?
YES, THANK YOU.

IT WAS MOST... ENLIGHTENING.
YOU WILL HAVE TO EXCUSE SOME OF OUR PILOTS. THEY CAN BE A LITTLE INDIVIDUALISTIC AND UNRULY.
I ENDEAVOR TO KEEP THEM IN LINE.

HMM... NICE ASS.
WHO? KLEIST OR THE SUIT?
NONE OF YOUR DAMN BUSINESS.

HAVE YOU GOT THE HOTS FOR HIM? HAVE YOU?
DON'T PUSH THIS ONE, DEEGAN --YOU'LL LOSE.

HA! YOU HAVE! YOU DO HAVE A HEART AFTER ALL, UNDER ALL THAT ICE AND GRANITE.

YEAH, BLOODY AND DRIPPING. BELONGED TO MY LAST WISE-ASS CO-PILOT.
HAHA HAW!
LAUGH IT UP, KID. I'M NOT THE ONE WHO'S GOTTA STRIP AND GREASE THE LOADER NEXT SHIFT.

YOU'RE ALL HEART, BOSS!

NOT MUCH TO SHOW FOR A LIFE. ONE MAN'S MEMORIES--ANOTHER MAN'S TRASH.
FACES, NAMES, NUMBERS. ALL HIS BOYS.
THE CORPS TAKES EVERYTHING YOU'VE GOT.
EVERYTHING.
BUT NEVER IN VAIN, SO LONG AS SOMEONE REMEMBERS.
SOMEONE TO KEEP THE FLAME BURNING BRIGHT.
CHOI! GIVE IT UP!
SCREW YOU!

YOU THINK BOONE WAS A WUSS? SAY IT TO MY FACE!
YOU SCI-TECH MAGGOTS AIN'T FIT TO LICK HIS BOOTS.

WHAT'S THE PROBLEM?
THE PROFESSOR WANTS US TO GIVE THIS INSUBORDINATE GRUNT THE TREATMENT, BUT WE CAN'T GET NEAR HIM. FIGHTS LIKE A MAD DOG!

I GOT JUST THE THING FOR MAD DOGS.
AW, C'MON-- GET REAL!
TAG HIM.

NYYYAAHH!!

K-K-K-KILLYUYUYOU.
DREAM ON, DOG BOY. I'M THE LEAST OF YOUR PROBLEMS! WHEN YOU SEE WHAT COMES NEXT, YOU'LL BE BEGGING ME TO SAVE YOUR FILTHY HIDE.

EYES ONLY:
PROFESSOR E. KLEIST
FROM G. DE SOUZA:
CONTROLLER—
RESEARCH AND DEVELOPMENT

HELLO, ERNST. HOW ARE YOU KEEPING? I'M SORRY ABOUT ALL OF THIS CLOAK-AND-DAGGER BUSINESS, BUT WE HAVE SOMETHING OF A SITUATION HERE AND I FELT YOU SHOULD BE BROUGHT UP TO SPEED ON CURRENT EVENTS.

AS YOU MAY ALREADY KNOW, YOUR WORK ON PROJECT CHIMERA IS GARNERING UNHEALTHY ATTENTION FROM CERTAIN QUARTERS...

...INCLUDING A NEW ASIAN-CHINESE CONSORTIUM THAT'S ATTEMPTED TO INFILTRATE Z.C.T. ON SEVERAL OCCASIONS.

ALL FUTILE EFFORTS-- UNTIL NOW.
WHEN I RECEIVED YOUR LAST PROJECT UPDATE, THE TRANSMISSION HAD BEEN INTERCEPTED AND DECODED.
A TIDY JOB, BUT CLOSE INVESTIGATION SHOWED THE DATA HAD NOT ONLY BEEN ALTERED BUT WAS INFESTED WITH VIRAL TIMEBOMBS.

POINT IS, WE CAN'T BE SURE IF THIS'S THE FIRST TIME THEY'VE CRACKED OUR TRANSMISSIONS OR THE HUNDREDTH!
WE'RE HAVING TO DEEP-CLEAN ALL OUR SYSTEMS. IT'S A NIGHTMARE, AS YOU CAN IMAGINE.

THE BOTTOM LINE IS THIS: CHIMERA'S OUR HIGHEST PRIORITY. AS OF NOW, YOU ARE TO CEASE ALL TRANSMISSIONS TO EARTH UNTIL FURTHER NOTICE.
WE CAN'T RELY ON OUR EXISTING DATA, SO I'VE SENT MR. KRAY TO COLLECT DISC COPIES OF EVERYTHING YOU HAVE, FOR PERSONAL DELIVERY TO OUR LABS.

I KNOW WHAT YOU'RE THINKING-- BUT RELAX, HE'S THE BEST OPERATIVE WE'VE GOT.

YOU HAVE HIM TO THANK FOR THAT GEL THAT REDUCES ALIEN BLOOD TO THE pH OF WATER. TOOK IT RIGHT OUT FROM UNDER THE GRANT CORPOR-ATION'S NOSE.
HE ALSO SCORED US THE SPECS FOR THOSE TASER-WEB LAUNCHERS. THERE'S NO ONE ELSE I'D TRUST ON THIS MISSION.

WHAT CONCERNS ME MOST IS HOW THEY UNSCRAMBLED THE SIGNAL. THEY DIDN'T HACK THE CODES, THEY JUST WALKED RIGHT IN.
NOW INTERNATIONAL SECURITY'S ON THE CASE, AND EVERYONE'S SCARED OF THEIR OWN SHADOW.

IT'S GOING TO BE A BAD TIME, ERNST. I ENVY YOU OUT THERE ON YOUR ISLAND. WE COULD ALL DO WITH A LITTLE PEACE AND SECURITY RIGHT NOW.

INDEED.
MESSAGE ENDS

WAKE UP, SOLDIER BOY. END OF THE LINE.
UUHHH...

WHAT THE HELL IS THIS?
KER-CHAK

YOU'VE PUSHED YOUR LUCK TOO FAR THIS TIME. IT'S GETTING OUT OF HAND. YOU MARINES NEED TO BE SLAPPED DOWN-- HARD.
DOG'S GOT TO KNOW ITS PLACE, RIGHT?
EEEVYAHH!
ONLY IT'S TOO LATE FOR YOU.

Y-YOU BUH-BUH-BASTARD...
GIVE ME YOUR BEST SHOT, TOUGH GUY.
YOU WERE A DEAD MAN THE MINUTE YOU SMEARED THAT DAMN BUG.

THE PROFESSOR DOESN'T LIKE HIS PETS BEING HURT. YOU SHOULD KNOW THAT.
N-NAAGH!

I'D LOVE TO MAKE THIS CLEAN FOR YOU, BUT IT'S NOT WORTH MY LIFE. CROSSING THE PROFESSOR IS NEVER A WISE MOVE.
PITY YOU HAD TO FIND OUT THE HARD WAY.
MAYBE IF YOU'RE LUCKY, YOU'LL BLEED TO DEATH BEFORE IMPLANTATION.
N-NO!
"LIKE I SAID..."
NAWWMPHH!!
"...IF YOU'RE LUCKY."

...HAVE SOME TIME TO KILL, I THOUGHT YOU MIGHT ENJOY A TOUR OF MY LITTLE WORLD.
THIS MIGHT INTEREST YOU. I'VE ADAPTED THE GEL YOU ACQUIRED INTO AN EFFECTIVE DISSECTION MEDIUM. NO CHANCE OF ANY UNFORTUNATE SPILLS HERE.
INGENIOUS.
THIS HAS ENABLED ME TO EXTENSIVELY ANALYZE AND CATALOGUE THE ALIEN'S MORPHOLOGY.
I DISCOVERED MORE ABOUT ITS FUNCTION AND PHYSIOLOGY THAN EVER BEFORE--BUT IT WAS AT A MOLECULAR LEVEL THAT I MADE THE MOST STARTLING FIND...
THE D.N.A. REFLEX?
YOU'VE DONE YOUR RESEARCH, MR. KRAY.
YES, TESTS HAVE SHOWN THAT AN ADULT ALIEN EXHIBITS CERTAIN PHYSICAL CHARACTERISTICS "INHERITED" FROM ITS HOST.

I GREW A SET OF "DUMMIES"-- CLONED BODY TISSUE DESIGNED TO MIMIC LIVING MATTER--FOR IMPLANTATION AND GESTATION.
THE ALIEN HAS INSPIRED MANY NEW COMMODITIES...
...BUT WHAT IF THE CREATURE ITSELF COULD BE ADAPTED-- BIOENGINEERED TO BECOME MAN'S TOOL INSTEAD OF HIS ADVERSARY?
CONSUMER BIOLOGICALS?
EXACTLY! BUT WITH THEIR INNATE HOSTILITY REMOVED BY SPLICING THEIR D.N.A. WITH THAT OF MORE PASSIVE, LESS PREDATORY CREATURES.
RESTRICTED
I EXCLUDED ALL THE MAJOR CARNIVORES AND PRIMATES. THE BEST TEST RESULTS WERE WITH DOMESTICS: SHEEP, LLAMAS, SOME CATTLE.
OF COURSE, THERE WERE A FEW SETBACKS.

I BELIEVE THERE IS AN ADAGE ABOUT OMELETTES AND BREAKING EGGS.
ALL PROGRESS HAS ITS PRICE, eh?
A NECESSARY ATTITUDE, I THINK YOU'LL AGREE. LOGIC AND TRUTH LEAVE LITTLE ROOM FOR MORAL POSTURING.
EVENTUALLY THE SUCCESSES STARTED TO OUTNUMBER THE FAILURES, AND I BEGAN TO OBTAIN A CROP OF VIABLE TEST RESULTS.

HOWEVER, I'VE YET TO BE ABLE TO PRODUCE THE EQUIVALENT QUEEN.

ROYAL JELLY ALONE DOESN'T SEEM TO BE ENOUGH. IT'S PROVING TO BE A TAXING PROBLEM IN THE EXTREME.
WE'RE GOING IN THERE?

IT'S GOOD TO RESPECT YOUR FEAR, BUT DON'T LET IT RULE YOU. ANY GOOD SOLDIER SHOULD KNOW THAT!

STAY CLOSE TO ME. NO MATTER WHAT HAPPENS, MAKE NO SUDDEN NOISES OR MOVEMENT.
DON'T WORRY!
AN INTERESTING DEVICE, THIS-- I STUMBLED ACROSS ITS POTENTIAL QUITE BY ACCIDENT. IT SOMEHOW DISRUPTS THE IMPULSES OF WHAT PASSES FOR THEIR CENTRAL NERVOUS SYSTEMS.
I'VE DEVISED A LARGER VERSION THAT'S USED IN SECURING WILD SPECIMENS FOR STUDY.
THIS ONE IS MORE LIKE A KIND OF DOG WHISTLE.
OVER THERE!
SSHH. KEEP CALM.
THEY'RE COMING.
COME ON. DON'T BE SCARED. IT'S ONLY ME...

COME TO DADDY.
THERE'S MY GOOD CHILDREN...

LOVE.
LOVE HURTS.
LOVE KILLS.
NO NO NO!!

WHY?! WHY WON'T IT WORK? WHAT ARE YOU HIDING FROM ME?

A MUTE JURY OF DEAD MOTHERS, GENE-SPLICED FAILURES. TAUNTING SPECTERS OF WHAT COULD HAVE BEEN.
THE CHALLENGE OF LIFE, FLEETINGLY GRASPED AND LOST.
TALK TO ME YOU BITCHES!
TALK TO ME!!
RESOLUTE AMBITION FRACTURING INTO FRUSTRATION-- DESPAIR--PARANOIA.
PLEASE?

I NURTURED THEM, SCULPTED THEIR GENES, CRAFTED THEIR FLESH INTO NEW VEHICLES OF MORTALITY... YET STILL THEY REFUSED MY GIFTS.
ARE ALL CHILDREN SO UNGRATEFUL?

SIR, I...
THE QUEENS. THEY'RE THE ONES-- ALWAYS DEFYING ME, BUT I'LL BREAK THEM LIKE I DID THE OTHERS. HAVE THEM RUNNING TO HEEL LIKE THE BEASTS THEY ARE.

LAST NIGHT, I DREAMED I WAS BALANCED ON THE EDGE OF A VAST ABYSS, ITS FLOOR OBSCURED BY AN OCEAN OF GREY CLOUDS.
INSTEAD OF FOLLOWING THE SAFE PATH, I DELIBERATELY STEPPED OFF--INTO THE UNKNOWN.

A RATHER BLATANT METAPHOR, DON'T YOU AGREE?
I WOULDN'T KNOW. I NEVER DREAM.
OF COURSE NOT. I'M SORRY.

WHAT'S YOUR REPORT?
IT'S THE SUBJECT SIR. HE'S ON THE MOVE.

IT TOOK TWO THOUSAND CONVICTS TO HACK CHARON OUT OF THE ROCK AND ICE.
TWO THOUSAND MEN DIGGING THEIR OWN GRAVES.
PAULIE FINN IS A GRAVE ROBBER.
ON HIS DAYS OFF FROM THE KITCHENS, HE STEALS FROM THE DEAD TO SUPPLEMENT HIS LIVING.
A SIDELINE THAT COULD TURN THE STRONGEST STOMACHS.
BUT PAULIE IS A PRACTICAL MAN.

WORKING IN THE KITCHEN HAS GIVEN HIM A HEALTHY DISREGARD FOR DEAD MEAT.
WHAT THE CHRIST IS THIS?!
S'LIKE A GODDAMN MEATLOCKER...

MMWWAAAHH!!

GAAA!!

URGHH
IT'S THE LIVE ONES YOU HAVE TO WATCH OUT FOR.

AS A CHILD HE REMEMBERS BEING TERRIFIED OF THE DARK. IT WAS WHERE THE MONSTERS LIVED, PATIENT, PREDATORY. WAITING FOR THE CARELESS TRESPASSES OF THE UNWARY.
HE FINALLY OVERCAME HIS FEAR BY EMBRACING IT.
NOW HE RELISHES THE ANONYMITY OF THE SHADOWS-- STALKING THE TWILIGHT WORLD BETWEEN COMMERCE AND CRIME.
A SILENT HUNTER.
THERE ARE STILL MONSTERS IN THE DARKNESS -- SOME OF THEM ARE HUMAN.
IS THIS A PRIVATE MOMENT OF MOODY INTROSPECTION OR CAN ANYONE JOIN IT?
BY ALL MEANS, BE MY GUEST.
SEEMS LIKE WE'RE THE ONLY ONES WHO ENJOY THE VIEW...
I LIKE TO COME HERE SOMETIMES, AWAY FROM THE GRUNTS AN' GREASERS. JUST ME AND THE UNIVERSE--HELPS PUT THINGS INTO PERSPECTIVE.
HOW'S THAT?
WELL, WE MAY BE THE SMARTEST MONKEYS ON THE ROCK, BUT OUT HERE THAT DON'T MEAN JACK.

PROFOUND, HUH?
INSPIRING. YOU HAVE THE SOUL OF A PHILOSOPHER.
...AN' A FINE LINE IN BULL. ARE YOU PUTTING A MOVE ON ME BY ANY CHANCE, MISTER KRAY?

PERHAPS, BUT PLEASE CALL ME JOHN.
I'M JOYCE.

TELL ME, WHAT BRINGS YOU OUT HERE--SO FAR FROM THE CORE SYSTEMS? ISN'T THAT WHERE MOST PILOTS PLY THEIR TRADE?

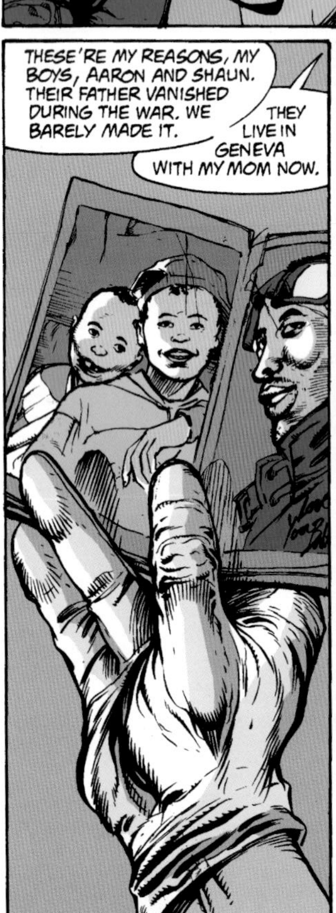
THESE'RE MY REASONS, MY BOYS, AARON AND SHAUN. THEIR FATHER VANISHED DURING THE WAR. WE BARELY MADE IT.
THEY LIVE IN GENEVA WITH MY MOM NOW.

I EARN FIVE TIMES MORE HERE THAN IN THE CORE. THAT'S WHY I TOOK THIS HAUL.
MY BOYS ARE ALL SET, BUT DON'T THINK I DON'T MISS THEM. I'M STILL THEIR MOM.

SORRY. I DIDN'T MEAN TO PRY.
NO PROBLEM. IT'S JUST THE WAY THINGS ARE. YOU LEARN TO LIVE WITH IT.

DAMN.
SOME-THING WRONG?
NO, NOT YET.
WE'RE IN ITS SHADOW-- GOT A FEW SECONDS. LISTEN, THIS ISN'T A SOCIAL CALL. I'M TAKING A CHANCE TRUSTING YOU, BUT WE NEED TO TALK.
I...
THE WHOLE BASE'S WIRED FOR SOUND AND VISION. PRIVACY'S A DIRTY WORD AROUND HERE.
WHAT I HAVE TO SAY ISN'T FOR PRYING EYES AND EARS.
MEET ME ON THE CALIBAN IN AN HOUR.
CHRIST, YOU'D BETTER BE OKAY MAN. I'M PUTTING MORE THAN MY NECK ON THE LINE HERE.

CAN I HELP YOU, SERGEANT?
I WANT TO SEE KLEIST RIGHT NOW!!
THE PROFESSOR IS IN A MEETING. HE LEFT STRICT INSTRUCTIONS NOT TO BE DISTURBED.
HE WAS MOST INSISTENT.
OUTTA MY WAY, MA'AM, OR I SWEAR I'LL...
YOU'LL DO WHAT? STRIKE A WOMAN?
UUHNN
THAT'S NOT VERY GALLANT NOW IS IT?
BUT THEN AGAIN I'M NOT A WOMAN.

REALLY, SERGEANT...
WHY CAN'T YOU MAKE AN APPOINTMENT LIKE EVERYONE ELSE?
FILTHY FREAKS AN' MACHINES IS ALL HE CARES ABOUT.
WHAT ABOUT PEOPLE, FOR CHRISSAKES?!
WHAT ABOUT THEM?
GUUHH
THAT'S ENOUGH, GRACE. I'M SURE THE SERGEANT'S LEARNED HIS LESSON.

I THINK I KNOW WHAT'S UPSET HIM.
YOU MURDERED ONE OF MY MEN, YOU BASTARD! KILLED HIM AND TRY TO CALL IT JUSTICE!!
AS YOU WITNESSED, CORPORAL CHOI DELIBERATELY DESTROYED AN EXPENSIVE SPECIMEN.

HE COULD EASILY HAVE SUBDUED IT WITH A TASER BUT CHOSE NOT TO. A CONSCIOUS ACT OF SABOTAGE.
WHAT!
AS DIRECTOR OF THIS FACILITY, I FELT OBLIGED TO AUTHORIZE THE MAXIMUM PENALTY.

MY GOD! HE WAS RIGHT! YOU ARE OUT OF YOUR MIND!!

THIS IS A SCIENTIFIC RESEARCH ESTABLISHMENT, NOT A MILITARY OUTPOST. YOU'RE UNDER MY JURISDICTION, FOLLOWING MY ORDERS!

WE'RE MARINES! NOT LAB RATS! I CAME HERE WITH A FULL PLATOON-- I'VE A HANDFUL LEFT BECAUSE OF YOU!!
I'M TIRED OF YOUR MEN'S INSUBORDINATION AND LOCKER ROOM MENTALITY. AS OF NOW, MR. LARSON WILL RELIEVE YOU OF ALL DUTIES.

GRACE WILL ARRANGE FOR YOU AND YOUR MEN'S IMMEDIATE RETURN TO EARTH.
YOU'RE AN IRRITATION I'M NO LONGER PREPARED TO ENDURE.

NOW IF YOU'LL EXCUSE ME...
...MR. LARSON AND I HAVE BUSINESS TO ATTEND TO.

A PLAGUE IS RUNNING RIOT HERE. ONE MAN'S MADNESS KILLING US ALL.
A VIRUS OF TERROR AND SUDDEN DEATH.
HOW LONG BEFORE IT'S MY TURN TO DIE?
THIS IS ABSURD.
I CAN'T TRUST THIS GUY--HE'S A COMPANY MAN, A SNAKE IN A SUIT. WHAT THE HELL WAS I THINKING OF?!
CALIBAN
FACE IT GIRL, YOU SCREWED UP ROYALLY THIS TIME.
OKAY, HERE'S THE PITCH. KLEIST'S ZCT'S GOLDEN BOY, RIGHT? A LITTLE INTENSE, BUT HE GETS RESULTS.
LET ME SHOW YOU EXACTLY HOW HE DOES IT. HOPE YOU'VE GOT A STRONG STOMACH.
FRIEND IN R&D COPIED THIS. NEXT DAY, ONE OF KLEIST'S TAME FREAKS PLAYED CATCH WITH HIS FACE.

THERE! LOOK! DO YOU SEE IT?
SEE WHAT? I... MY GOD, IS THAT... A TATTOO?
PAUSE
MEET BILLY SINCLAIR, AN OLD BUDDY OF MINE. I WAS WITH HIM WHEN HE GOT IT DONE ON SHORE LEAVE IN MELBOURNE TEN YEARS AGO.
HE SUPPOSEDLY DIED LAST MONTH. FAULTY AIRLOCK--EXPLOSIVE DECOMPRESSION. THEY SHOULD'VE HAD TO SCRAPE HIM OFF THE WALLS, BUT THERE HE IS.
ALL UTENSILS TO BE LEFT IN THE WASH
THAT MEANS YOU TOO DEEGAN!!
TAPE'S FULL OF THEM. SOME I KNOW. OTHERS--IT'S HARD TO TELL.
QUESTION IS, JOHN, WHAT'RE YOU GOING TO DO ABOUT IT?
YOU DON'T KNOW WHAT YOU'RE ASKING.
I KNOW THIS. KLEIST'S A PSYCHO, AND HE'S GOT TO BE STOPPED! YOU HAVE TO LET THEM KNOW WHAT'S HAPPENING HERE!!

IT'S NOT THAT EASY.

DO YOU KNOW WHAT IT'S LIKE TO LIVE IN FEAR TWENTY-FOUR HOURS A DAY, EVERY DAY WITHOUT END?!

THIS PLACE IS A GULAG, SIX MONTHS COMMUNICATION TIME FROM EARTH. KLEIST CAN DO ANYTHING HE LIKES HERE--ANYTHING!

WE GET A LOT OF "ACCIDENTS," UNDERSTAND? NO ONE GOES HOME--EVER!

ONLY A FEW OF US KNOW THE TRUTH. WE KEEP A LOW PROFILE. MAKE TOO MANY WAVES, LARSON'S BOYS PAY YOU A SURPRISE VISIT, AND THAT'S IT...
NUKE IT!
YOU'RE GONE.
ANOTHER "ACCIDENT."

I WANT TO LIVE TO SEE MY KIDS AGAIN. I WON'T DIE ON THIS ROCK. I'M RISKING EVERYTHING TALKING TO YOU.
JOYCE, YOU'RE NOT THE ONLY ONE TAKING A RISK...
DO NOT OPEN
TAKE OFF

THERE'S SOMETHING YOU SHOULD KNOW.

THAT'S IT! ALL UNITS CLOSE IN. SHOOT TO WOUND ONLY. I WANT THEM ALIVE.
NOBODY MOVE! KEEP YOUR HANDS WHERE I CAN SEE THEM!
YOU BASTARD! I SHOULD'VE KNOWN...
YOU DEAF, BITCH?

GLAARGH
GO AHEAD, PICK IT UP...
...PLEASE.

GEAR IS STOWED, WEAPONS RACKED. TOUR OF DUTY IS OVER.
A TIME OF MIXED EMOTIONS. JOY MUTED BY THE LOSS OF FALLEN COMRADES...
...ACCOMPANIED BY A PROFOUND SENSE OF RELIEF.
MAN, CAN YOU BELIEVE THIS?
WE'RE GOING HOME. WE'RE FINALLY GONNA SEE THE BACK OF THIS HEAP.
WHAT'S THE PLAN, SARGE?
WE'LL RENDEZVOUS WITH THE BATTLE CRUISER SAUDAKAUR, THEN DEEP FREEZE IT FROM THERE.
I HATE THOSE ICE BOXES!
PRICE YOU PAY FOR WORKING OUT IN THE BUTT END OF THE UNIVERSE.
BUCKLE IN TIGHT, GENTLEMEN. WE'RE ON OUR WAY.
THE VOICE OF GOD.
...OR AT LEAST HIS SECRETARY.

"WHOA! WHAT GIVES? WHERE ARE WE GOING?!"
I'VE GOT A BAD FEELING ABOUT THIS.
FORREST, GET THAT DOOR OPEN!
SIR, IT'S LOCKED!
RUN A BYPASS!
IT'S ON REMOTE!
IT'S A SETUP. WE'RE HEADING FOR THE ALIEN SECTOR. THAT SONOVABITCH AIMS TO DROP US RIGHT IN THEIR LAPS.
SUIT UP, PEOPLE.
WE'RE NOT GIVING UP WITHOUT A FIGHT.
A TYPICAL FUTILE GESTURE.
INITIATE SHIP AND ALIEN ZONE AIRLOCK OVERRIDES. I WANT THIS OVER QUICKLY.
I'VE BIGGER FISH TO FRY.
OH GOD.
KEEP COOL. THIS IS LIKE JUST ANOTHER BUG HUNT.
SNUB MUZZLE

GEEAHHHHH
OPEN FIRE!!
THEY'RE NOT GOING DOWN! THE GUNS ARE SCRA--

OH JESUS! THE GUNS'RE FULL OF BLANKS!!
BRRAAPP
PULL BACK! PULL BACK!
NOOO!
UUNN!

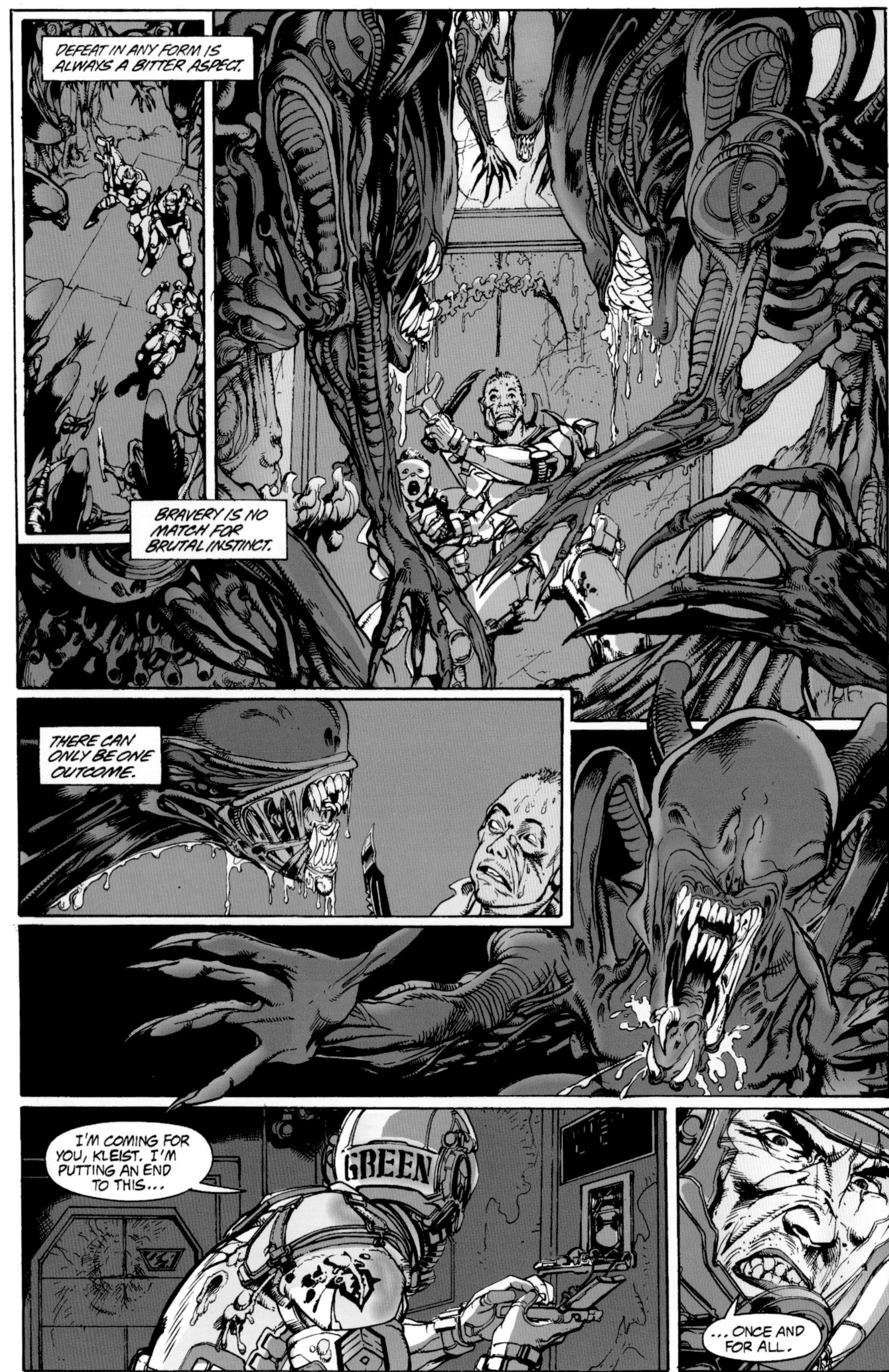
DEFEAT IN ANY FORM IS ALWAYS A BITTER ASPECT.
BRAVERY IS NO MATCH FOR BRUTAL INSTINCT.
THERE CAN ONLY BE ONE OUTCOME.
I'M COMING FOR YOU, KLEIST. I'M PUTTING AN END TO THIS...
GREEN
...ONCE AND FOR ALL.

IT WAS MEANT TO BE THE FINAL GAME. AS THE STAKES GREW, THE ODDS DIMINISHED.
HE WAS TIRED. TOO LONG IN THE FIELD. HE WANTED TO COME HOME. "JUST ONE MORE TIME," THEY SAID. "YOU'RE IN TOO DEEP TO QUIT NOW."
SO HE TOOK THE GAMBLE, PUT HIS TALENT ON THE LINE ONCE MORE...
IT WASN'T ENOUGH.
ANYTHING?
NOTHING OF WORTH. STILL DENIES EVERYTHING. WE'RE KEEPING THE WOMAN FOR LATER IF HE DIES.
WHY ARE YOU DOING THIS TO YOURSELF, EH? WE KNOW YOU'RE NOT KRAY, SO STOP PRETENDING.
TELL US WHAT WE WANT TO KNOW AND YOU'LL DIE PAINLESSLY.
CONTINUE TO TRY MY PATIENCE, AND YOU'LL SUFFER BEYOND ALL IMAGINING.
I...I...D-DON'T KNOW W-W-WHAT YOU W-W-WANT.

IT WAS AN AUDACIOUS PLAN, I ADMIRE THAT.
THE HOLO OF OLD DESOUZA ESPECIALLY. HOPING TO MAKE ME SO PARANOID ABOUT INFILTRATION THAT I'D HAND YOU THE CHIMERA DATA WITHOUT A SECOND THOUGHT.

YOU MADE ONE FATAL ERROR: ALL ZCT OPERATIVES ABOVE GRADE NINE HAVE A SECURITY CODE SURFACE COATED ON THEIR RIGHT KIDNEY.
YOU, A SUPPOSED GRADE TWELVE, DID NOT.
UH?

THAT'S RIGHT. WE'VE KNOWN YOU WORKED FOR THE GRANT CORPORATION ALL ALONG.
LET YOU FEED US THE TASER AND PH GEL DATA--WE WANTED TO KNOW WHAT YOU WERE AFTER, WHO YOUR CONTACTS WERE.

WE'VE NETTED QUITE A HAUL THANKS TO YOU, INCLUDING CAPTAIN PALMER.
NUH NUH NO. SHE'S NOT...

I MAY BE MAD AS THEY SAY I AM, BUT I'M NOT STUPID! YOU WILL TELL ME EVERYTHING YOU KNOW...

OTHERWISE YOU'LL SOON DISCOVER THERE IS SUCH A THING AS A FATE WORSE THAN DEATH.
NOOHH!

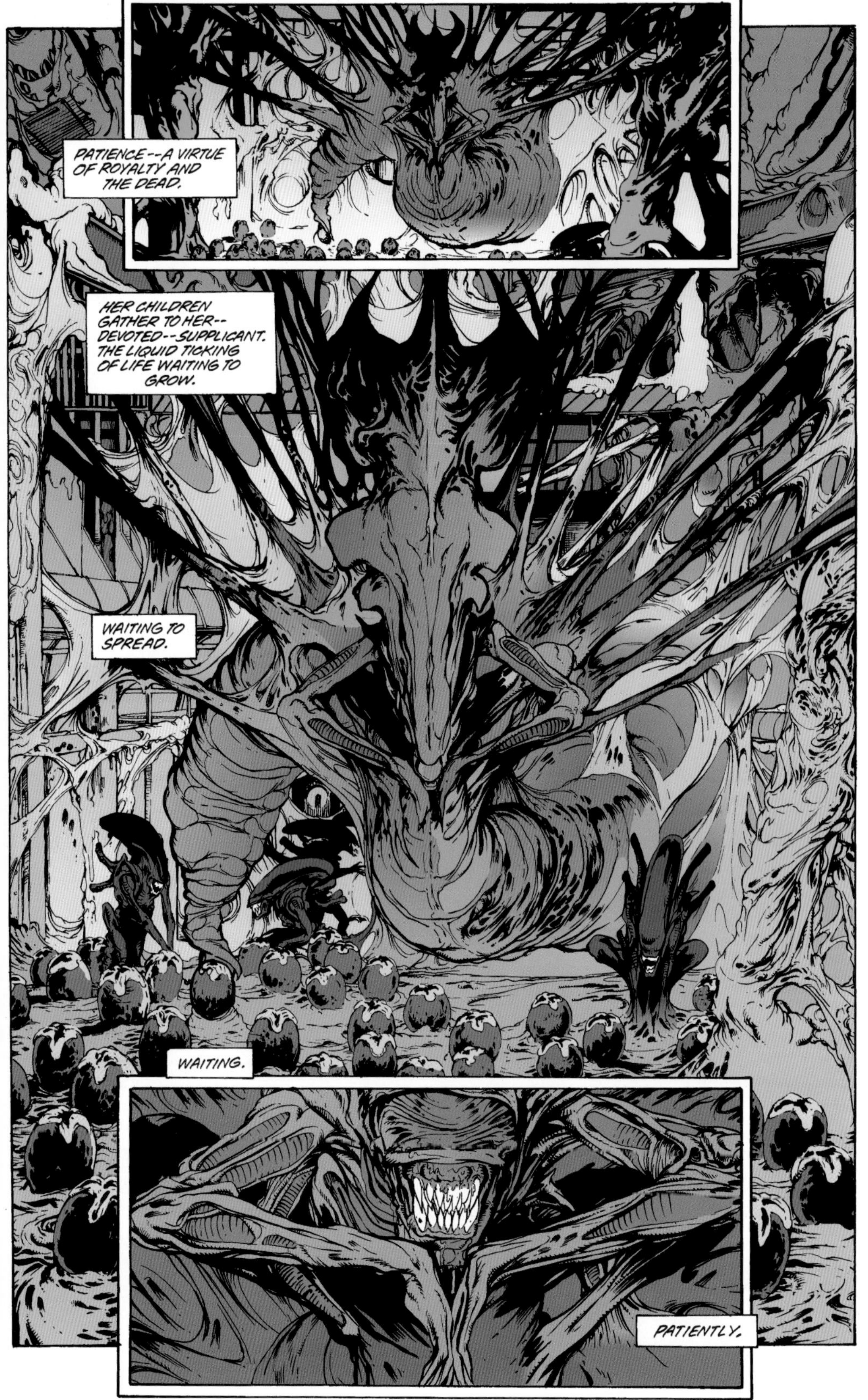
PATIENCE--A VIRTUE OF ROYALTY AND THE DEAD.
HER CHILDREN GATHER TO HER--DEVOTED--SUPPLICANT. THE LIQUID TICKING OF LIFE WAITING TO GROW.
WAITING TO SPREAD.
WAITING.
PATIENTLY.

CONTRARY TO OPINION, SCIENCE ISN'T ALWAYS A LINEAR PROFESSION. AN OCCUPATION OF THEORIES AND GOALS LACKING SOUL AND SPONTANEITY.
IT'S AN ART FORM, SUBJECT TO THE DEMANDS OF ENDURANCE AND VAGARIES OF INSPIRATION.

EVEN SO, IT WAS AN UNEXPECTED IRONY THAT THE ONE WHO WOULD STEAL MY LIFE'S WORK SHOULD YIELD MY GREATEST TRIUMPH.

CREATING A NEW ORDER FROM THE FLESH OF THE OLD DEMANDED SOMETHING RADICAL--
SOMETHING EXTREME.

THIS IS UNKNOWN TERRITORY, WHERE THE LAWS OF NATURE AND SCIENCE HAVE YET TO BE DEFINED.
KICK IN THE FLOODS.

I'M CHARTING WORLDS OF FUTURE THOUGHT.. AND THE BEASTS THEREIN.
AN ALIEN KING.
CHIMERA.
HYBRID.
USURPER.
MONARCH OF THE NEW.

PROFESSOR?
DID OUR GUEST HAVE ANYTHING FURTHER OF INTEREST TO OFFER?
NO, I'M PRETTY SURE WE'VE GOT EVERYTHING.
HE TRIED HOLDING OUT FOR A WHILE, BUT THE PROSPECT OF A KISS FROM THE FACE-HUGGER LOOSENED HIS TONGUE, YOU MIGHT SAY!
SPARE ME YOUR PATHETIC ATTEMPTS AT HUMOR.
TH-THE PILOT--PALMER. SHE'S CLEAN. KRAY'S MISSION WAS APPARENTLY SOLO. PALMER JUST GOT IN THE WAY.
THE R&D VIDEO WAS PIRATED BY A TECH NAMED SLATER.
I TRACED HIM BUT HE'S DEAD. AN ACCIDENT IN THE HYBRID PEN.
AH YES, I REMEMBER. A VERY NERVOUS YOUNG MAN--VERY CARELESS.
THE WOMAN, HOWEVER, IS ANOTHER MATTER. SHE'S MORE TROUBLE THAN SHE'S WORTH.
HMM. GIVE HER TO THE ALIENS. THE LIVESTOCK COULD DO WITH BOOSTING.
THAT WILL BE ALL.
YES, SIR.

SUCCESS AFTER SO MANY MONTHS OF BITTER FAILURE? I CAN SCARCELY BELIEVE IT.

I HAVE DONE MANY QUESTIONABLE THINGS, BUT THIS--THIS WILL BE MY VINDICATION.

I TRIED EVERYTHING. PARASITIC BONDING VIRUSES--CYBERNETIC IMPLANTS--LIVE HUMAN HOSTS INSTEAD OF CLONED BODY MASS.

ALL USELESS.

I WAS MIRED IN MY OBSESSION TO CULTURE AN ALIEN QUEEN, BLIND TO OTHER OPTIONS.

IT TOOK THE INTRUSION OF KRAY--THE ROGUE ELEMENT, THE INVADER IN OUR MIDST--TO INSPIRE WIDER BREADTH OF VISION.
GOOD EVENING, MR. KRAY.

I'M SO GLAD YOU COULD FIND THE TIME TO JOIN US.

ALLOW ME TO INTRODUCE THE LATEST ADDITION TO MY HAPPY BROOD... YOUR SON!
OH, GOD.

HE'S ONLY PARTLY YOURS ACTUALLY-- A SCRAPING OF TISSUE.
THE REST IS A COCKTAIL OF ALIEN DNA, CONCENTRATED MALE HORMONE, AND A RATHER COMPLEX BIOCHEMICAL SOUP THAT YOU WOULD HAVE KILLED TO GET YOUR HANDS ON.
UNFORTUNATELY, IT NOW SEEMS EAGER TO GET ITS HANDS ON YOU. SINS OF THE FATHER, AND SO ON.
REMARKABLE. IT HASN'T HARMED HIM IN THE SLIGHTEST. NOT A CONVENTIONAL REACTION AT ALL.
IT SEEMS TO BE MORE INTRIGUED BY HIM.
COULD THIS FINALLY BE IT?
UH UH UH
REMOVE THE MATRIARCHAL TIES... THE OVERWHELMING DESIRE TO BREED... AND THE INNATE FEROCITY BECOMES REDUNDANT?
A TRULY TAME ALIEN?

IF I CAN SUBSTITUTE A GENETIC COMMAND MATRIX OF MY OWN-- WHOLE HIVES COULD BE BIO-PROGRAMMED FOR ANY TASK!
IT WOULD REVOLUTIONIZE INDUSTRY OVERNIGHT!
ORGANIC SOFTWARE.
THE FLESH WOULD PREVAIL OVER THE MACHINE!
CONGRATULATIONS, MR. KRAY. IT WOULD APPEAR HE LIKES YOU-- ENOUGH, AT LEAST, TO LET YOU LIVE.
I, ON THE OTHER HAND, AM NOT NEARLY SO BENEFICENT, AS YOU WILL SOON DISCOVER.
AND AS FOR YOU, MY FINE FRIEND, I THINKS IT'S HIGH TIME YOU MET THE REST OF THE FAMILY.

AIR LOCK LEVEL 12
KEEP MOVING.
YOU DON'T HAVE TO DO THIS! YOU KNOW THAT HE'S INSANE!

IF WE ALL WORK TOGETHER, WE CAN STOP HIM!
NO MORE KILLING.
SHUT UP! JUST SHUT UP!!

SCREW YOU!

DAMN! WE LOSE HER AN' THE OLD MAN'LL HAVE OUR BALLS!

"RELAX, THAT'S A DEAD END. NOTHIN' BUT AN AIR LOCK AN' COLD VACUUM."

SHE AIN'T GOIN' ANYWHERE!
GUESS AGAIN, JERK.
LOOK OUT--

BRAKKA BRAKKA

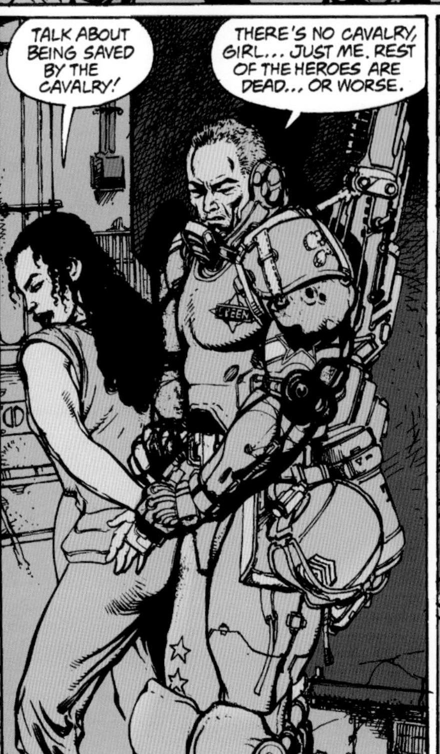
TALK ABOUT BEING SAVED BY THE CAVALRY!
THERE'S NO CAVALRY, GIRL... JUST ME. REST OF THE HEROES ARE DEAD... OR WORSE.

LISTEN, I CAN'T STAY HERE AND HOLD YOUR HAND. I'VE GOT SCORES TO SETTLE. IT'S BEST YOU'RE NOT INVOLVED.
CAN YOU TAKE IT FROM HERE?
NO SWEAT, SARGE.
I CAN HANDLE MYSELF.

CELL BLOCK H
E6

WHOA!

YOU?
HOLD IT! DON'T SHOOT!!

WE NEED TO TALK.

I'VE BEEN A FOOL, GRACE. A COMPLACENT FOOL.
YOU'RE BEING TOO HARD ON YOURSELF, PROFESSOR.
NO, I'M NOT. IN MY CONCEIT, I'VE OVERLOOKED THE OBVIOUS.
I'VE IGNORED THE PRIMARY FUNDAMENTALS OF NATURE. I IMAGINED THEY WOULDN'T APPLY TO THIS UNIQUE STRAIN.
"BUT I WAS WRONG."
SKRREEEEEEEEEEE

"MY JUDGMENT WAS INCORRECT."
"THE KING REFRAINED FROM ATTACKING KRAY NOT BECAUSE ITS NATURAL SAVAGERY HAD BEEN BRED OUT, BUT BECAUSE KRAY WAS STRAPPED DOWN... INCAPACITATED..."
"KRAY WAS SPARED BECAUSE HE WASN'T PERCEIVED AS A THREAT."
"UNLIKE NOW."
YET PERHAPS ALL IS NOT LOST.
IT'S ALL A MATTER OF PERSPECTIVE.

"WHAT WE HAVE HERE IS, IN ESSENCE, A ROGUE MALE."
"A LIVING ENGINE OF DESTRUCTION."
"SUPREMELY COMPETITIVE, IT CONSIDERS ALL OTHERS TO BE ITS RIVAL."
"NOT JUST FOR FOOD OR TERRITORY OR A MATE, BUT FOR LIFE ITSELF."
"THE PERFECT PROTOTYPE FOR ZCT'S BIO-WEAPONS ARSENAL."

BEYOND SOUND.
BEYOND CLUMSY MAMMALIAN PERCEPTION.
A SILENT SCREAM.
A PRIMAL AFFIRMATION OF LIFE--OR SURVIVAL.
ECHOING NOISELESSLY AT THE PERIPHERY OF THE SENSES.
IS HEARD...
...AND JOINED.
A CHALLENGE IS GIVEN.

SOMETHING'S WRONG.
PROFESSOR! I'VE JUST PICKED UP TWO TRANS-MISSION SIGNALS ON THE UPPER EF BAND.
TO MY KNOWLEDGE, WE HAVE NO FACILITIES FOR BROADCASTING ON THIS FREQUENCY?
CAN YOU TRACE THEIR SOURCE?
WHUP WHUP
ONE IS ON THIS LEVEL... FROM THE ALIEN SECTOR.
SPAK
THE OTHER IS...IS HERE.
IN THIS ROOM.
KRAK

K-KSSSH
RED ALERT! WE HAVE A BIO-HAZARD BREACH IN...
NO! CANCEL THAT ORDER! NOW!!
BUT PROFESSOR--
I DON'T WANT HIM SO MUCH AS SCRATCHED!
I KNOW WHERE HE'S GOING...
AND I WANT HIM IN ONE PIECE WHEN HE GETS THERE.

NOTHING. ALL FOR NOTHING.
THE WORK, THE LIVES-- ALL WASTED. CHRIST, THEY FED ME AS MUCH ROPE AS I WANTED AND WATCHED ME HANG MYSELF WITH IT.
YOU OKAY?

HM? YEAH, I'M FINE.
OLD ACCESS TUNNELS. JOINT'S RIDDLED WITH THEM. BACK FROM WHEN THIS WAS A PENAL COLONY. FEWER CAMERAS DOWN HERE.

CAN WE REACH YOUR SHIP THIS WAY?
NOT ENTIRELY, BUT CLOSE ENOUGH. I NEED DEEGAN, THOUGH. A GOOD CAPTAIN DOESN'T DESERT HER CREW.

I APPRECIATE THE RISK YOU TOOK COMING FOR ME.
FORGET IT, I WAS IN THE NEIGHBORHOOD ANYWAY. BESIDES, I OWED YOU ONE FOR CALLING YOU A COMPANY STOOGE.

YOU KNOW I'M AN AGENT FOR GRANT CORP, OR AT LEAST WAS UNTIL TODAY?
SO I HEARD. TO BE HONEST, AFTER ALL I'VE BEEN THROUGH. I COULDN'T GIVE A DAMN ANYMORE. I JUST WANT TO GET THE HELL OFF THIS ROCK.

I STOOD BY FOR TOO LONG, WATCHING KLEIST PLAY SOME SICK GAME WITH THE PEOPLE HERE.
NO ONE KNEW HIS GAME, SO NO ONE KNEW HIS RULES. YOU MAKE A WRONG MOVE, YOU DIE.
SOONER OR LATER SOMETHING HAD TO GIVE.

YOUR ARRIVAL WAS A KIND OF CATALYST FOR ME. IT WAS NOW OR NEVER. THE TRUTH HAD TO COME OUT OR I'D DIE HERE--NEVER SEE MY KIDS AGAIN.
SO YOU GAMBLED YOUR LIFE ON TALKING TO ME--A SPY?
YEAH, WELL, THINGS DIDN'T QUITE WORK OUT AS I'D PLANNED.
YOU AND ME BOTH.

AT LEAST WE'VE GOT OUR HEALTH.
YEAH, BUT FOR HOW LONG?
THAT'S WHAT I LIKE ABOUT YOU, JOHN, OR WHOEVER YOU ARE.
YOU'RE A PESSIMIST AFTER MY OWN HEART.

OOH, SUGAR.
UUUHH AHH.
BIG BOY SPECIAL
SPANG
WHAT THE F--?
C'MON DOWN, YOU MOTHER, YOU'RE GONNA BE WEARING THIS BABY FOR A HAT!
CLUD
YOU WERE SAYING?
GEE, BOSS. YOU SURE KNOW HOW TO MAKE AN ENTRANCE!
BUT YOUR TIMING SUCKS.

BETTER PUT YOUR CLOTHES ON, MISS. PARTY'S OVER.
JASON?
JUST DO AS HE SAYS, SUGAR.
I TAKE IT THIS ISN'T A SOCIAL CALL?
YOU COULD SAY THAT. YOU COULD ALSO PACK YOUR GEAR. WE'RE TEARING UP OUR CONTRACT AND SHIPPING OUT TONIGHT.
WE *ARE*?!
WOULD I LIE TO YOU? STAY HERE IF YOU WANT, I JUST THOUGHT I'D GIVE YOU THE OPTION.
NO WAY! I'M WITH YOU. LET ME GRAB MY TOOTHBRUSH AND I'M...
BWAAA BWAAA
AN ALARM!
TROUBLE.
BWAAA BWAAA BWAAA BWAAA BWAAA
DAMN! THERE'S ARMOR EVERYWHERE!
BUT... THEY'RE NOT STOPPING HERE! SO... IF THEY'RE NOT LOOKING FOR US...

"...SOMETHING REALLY BAD IS GOING DOWN!"
ALARM
AIM FOR THE LIMBS--LESS BLOOD SPLATTER!
SON OF A BITCH! LOOK AT THE SIZE OF THAT THING!
OPEN FIRE!
BUDDA BUDDA BUDDA

SKREEEE
SHISH
THOOM

OH, GOD, NO!
PULL BACK! PULL BACK!!
PUT ALL THOSE MEN ON A CHARGE, DAMMIT!
WHO INITIATED THE SECURITY ALARM?!
I WON'T HAVE MY AUTHORITY COUNTER-MANDED BY SOME GUNG-HO GRUNT!

PROFESSOR, I MUST EXPRESS MY CONCERN AT YOUR PRESENT MENTAL STATE. YOUR MANNER SEEMS SOMEWHAT IRRATIONAL.
MY DEAR GRACE. NO MATTER HOW THOROUGHLY YOU ARE PROGRAMMED--
YOU WILL NEVER EVEN REMOTELY UNDERSTAND HOW I FEEL AT THIS MOMENT.
WE SHALL SOON WITNESS THE VALIDATION OF ALL I BELIEVE.
IN A GODLESS UNIVERSE, THERE IS ONLY MAN AND THE ALIEN. ONLY ONE CAN BE THE DOMINANT SPECIES.
I HAVE TAKEN THE BRUTE CLAY OF CREATION AND RESHAPED IT INTO A SUPERIOR IMAGE.
THE ALIEN EMPIRE WILL BE DESTROYED AT THE HANDS OF ITS OWN KIND, THE KILLING STROKE BIO-PROGRAMMED BY HUMAN CUNNING... HUMAN INTELLECT.
IT BEGINS HERE... TODAY!

SSSSKK--
ELP US--PLEASE--
SOMEONE--
ANYONE--
EEAARRGGH!
WHERE THE HELL'S
LARSON?! I NEED
BACK-UP NOW!
SCOTT!
BEHIND
YOU!
--WATCH
IT!
SKREEEEEEE
EAT
THIS!
BRAKKABRAKKABRAKKG

SON OF A BITCH!
IT'S NO GOOD, SIR. WE CAN'T HOLD THEM BACK MUCH LONGER.
LAY DOWN SURPRESSIVE FIRE WITH GRENADES! WE'LL WITHDRAW TO ENGINEERING AND MAKE A STAND THERE.
BAMF
BAMF
FIRE IN THE HOLE!
BAMF
BAHWHOOOMM
FFSSSSSSSS

HOLY--! IT'S EATING THROUGH THE HULL!
FSSSSSSS
RUN! MOVE IT! DOUBLE TIME!
WHOOM
23
452

BRUMP
WHAT THE HELL...?!
HEY! WHERE'S MY BABE?
FORGET YOUR STUPID SEX SYNTH, DEEGAN.
PRESSURE SEAL'S DROPPED! MUST'VE BEEN A HULL BREACH ... A BIG ONE!

BUT HOW? THIS JOINT'S BUILT TO WITHSTAND A BATTLE CRUISER BARRAGE. I DON'T GET IT!
I DO...
MY GUESS IS IT'S THOSE THINGS. THEY'RE PROBABLY ALL OVER THIS PLACE. PRETTY SOON THEY'LL BE SWARMING OVER US TOO.
WE DON'T HAVE MUCH TIME.

SSSSSSSSSSSSSS
I'M TIRED OF THIS HIDE-AND-SEEK CRAP...

BRRAATTTTT

HURRY IT UP! WE COULD HAVE MORE OF THEM ANY SECOND!
WHERE TO NOW?

HEY! ISN'T THERE ANOTHER ACCESSWAY IN THE R&D LABS?
HELL, YES! RUNS RIGHT THROUGH TO THE HANGAR BAY. BUT IT'S USED FOR TRANS-PORTING SPECIMENS.
WHAT D'YOU THINK?

I THINK WE'RE RUNNING OUT OF OPTIONS-- FAST!

NOTHING.
I'M NOT REGISTERING A SINGLE TRACE. NOTHING'S MOVING DOWN HERE.
FASCINATING. I AT LEAST EXPECTED THERE TO BE AN INNER CADRE LEFT BEHIND TO PROTECT THE QUEEN.
THERE WAS.
THIS LOOKS LIKE WHAT'S LEFT OF THEM.
YES, YOU'RE RIGHT. SEE THE DIFFERENT CRANIAL CONFIGURATION... THE OVERSIZED MANDIBLES?
THIS WAS THE QUEEN'S ELITE, HER PRAETORIAN GUARD.
PROFESSOR, OVER HERE. I'VE GOT A TRACE.
TIK TIK TIK

TIK TIK TIK
TIK TIK TIK
STRANGE. I'M READING A LARGE SIGNAL, BUT THE FORMAT KEEPS SHIFTING. I CAN'T GET A CLEAR LOCK.
I CAN'T EXPLAIN IT...
SOME THINGS NEED NO EXPLANATION, MY DEAR.
SSSSSSSSSS

KKSSSSSSSSS
SKREEAAA
CHOK
SKREEEAAAAA

PROFESSOR, I CANNOT GUARANTEE YOUR SAFETY. WE SHOULD WITHDRAW TO A SAFE DISTANCE.
WHAT? NOW? WITH ALL I STRIVED FOR ABOUT TO COME TO FRUITION? DON'T BE ABSURD.
WHAT WE'RE WITNESSING HERE IS BIOLOGICAL ANARCHY. THE SLAUGHTER OF THE OLD BY THE NEW... EVOLUTION IN ITS MOST PRIMAL FORM...
...AND I PROVIDED THE CATALYST.
I INTEND TO SEE HIM CLAIM HIS BIRTH-RIGHT.

THAT'S IT. COME TO POPPA. DIDN'T THINK I'D LEAVE YOU BEHIND, DID YOU?
WHEN YOU BABIES HIT THE INDUSTRIAL UNDERGROUND, I'LL BE ABLE TO NAME MY OWN PRICE.
MONEY'S AS GOOD AS IN THE BANK.
SO MUCH FOR BRAND LOYALTY, EH LARSON?
YOU!
SURPRISE.
BRRAATT
AGGHH
I WANT KLEIST.
AHUHH-- DON'T KILL M--

HH... HE'S DEAD BY NOW. AAHHH! I WENT TO THE LAB... IT'S TRASHED. THE HOLDING TANK FOR HIS NEW FREAK WAS BURST OPEN... FROM THE INSIDE--
IT... IT MUST HAVE TAKEN HIM.

YOU SURE? JERK ME AROUND AN' I'LL SHOW YOU A WHOLE NEW WORLD OF HURT.
IT'S THE TRUTH. THOSE THINGS... THEY DON'T ALWAYS KILL YOU.

IF HE'S STILL ALIVE, IT'S ONLY A MATTER OF TIME BEFORE THEY FIND HIM.
HMM. PITY. STILL, I GUESS IT'LL HAVE TO DO. I'D LOVE TO CHAT SOME MORE, BUT YOU KNOW HOW IT IS.

WHERE YOU GOIN'? YOU CAN'T LEAVE ME HERE LIKE THIS. I WON'T STAND A CHANCE!
YOU'RE RIGHT...

WAIT! DON'T KILL ME, PLEASE!
DON'T WORRY. I WON'T KILL YOU...
...I'LL GIVE YOU THE SAME CHANCE YOU GAVE MY MEN.
BLAM
BLAM
BLAM
KEESH
KEESH
KEESH
OH GOD, NO!
AAAAGH!
SWEET DREAMS, LARSON.
LOCK ACTIVATED

LIGHTS ARE ON, BUT NO ONE'S HOME. KINDA REMINDS ME OF A GIRL I ONCE KNEW.
LOOKS LIKE THEY ALL TOOK OFF IN A HURRY.
MAYBE THEY DIDN'T HAVE A CHOICE.

WHICH WAY NOW?
FAR SIDE OF THE CHAMBER. AN ACCESS TUNNEL FEEDS DIRECTLY INTO THE HANGAR BAY.

WAIT! HEAR SOMETHING?
WHAT IS THAT?
SCREAMING. PEOPLE SCREAMING.

KEEP MOVING.
I'M DOWN TO MY LAST CLIP. IF WE HIT HEAVY RESISTANCE, IT'S GOING TO COME DOWN TO SOME HARD CHOICES. UNDER-STAND?

IF IT COMES TO THAT, I'LL DO US ALL, BUT HEY...

...WE'RE ALMOST HOME FREE--
KRAY!

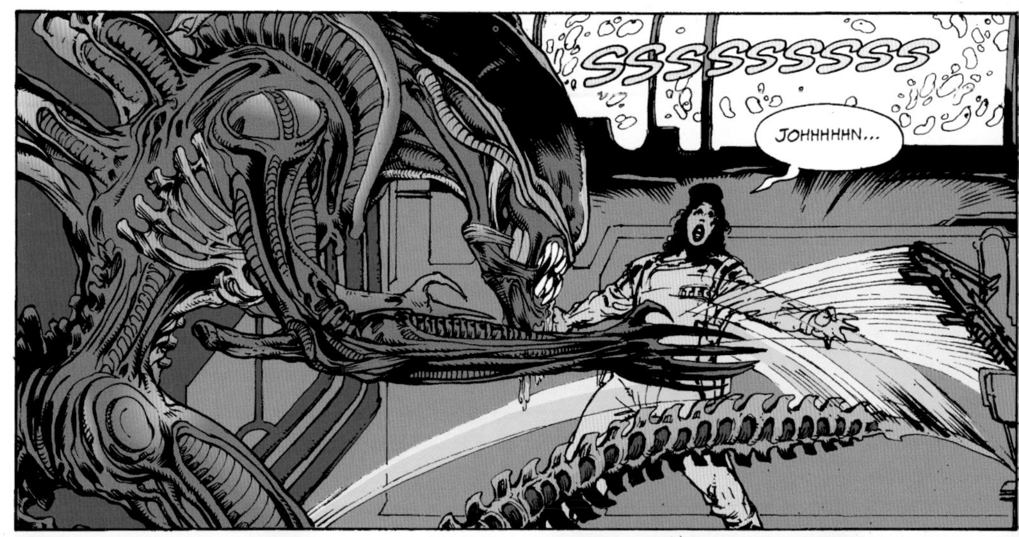
SSSSSSSSSS
JOHHHHHN...

WHAT'RE YOU WAITING FOR MAN? GREASE IT!
I CAN'T! SHE'S TOO CLOSE. IF ITS BLOOD HITS HER...
SSSSS

JOHN...KILL ME. PLEASE... FOR GOD'S SAKE...

I'M SORRY, JOYCE.

BRATTA BRATTA BRATTA

KER-RASH
SKREEEE
C'MON, YOU UGLY SONOFA-BITCH!
BRATTA
YOU ALL RIGHT, BOSS?
SURE... JUST GIVE ME A MINUTE.
I... I THOUGHT THAT... IT WAS THE END. YOU KNOW?

WE HAVE TO KEEP MOVING. HOW LONG WILL IT TAKE TO PREP THE SHIP?
A FEW MINUTES. PRIMARIES SHOULD ALREADY BE ON-LINE. COMPUTER AUTOMATICALLY RESETS THEM AFTER DOCKING.
DEEGAN?!
OVER HERE!
THE DOOR'S CODE IS SEALED, BUT NOT FOR LONG...
NO MACHINE GETS THE BEST OF JASON DEEGAN.
KERCHUNKA
SEE, WHAT DID I TELL YOU?
WALK IN THE PARK...

PRETTY SMOOTH, DEEGAN!
BLAM BLAM BLAM
GET AWAY FROM ME, YOU BASTARDS!

HOLD ON, JAY!
JOYCE! LOOK OUT!!
OH, GOD!
CLICK CLICK

DIE, YOU MAGGOTS!!
BUDDA BUDDA

WHERE'S KLEIST?
HAVEN'T SEEN HIM...

"...BUT I HOPE HE'S GOT HIS HANDS FULL!"
NO! IT WASN'T SUPPOSED TO BE LIKE THIS! YOU CAN'T DESTROY WHAT'S MINE! HE'S BETTER THAN YOU!
YOU'RE OBSOLETE!
REEEEEEEE
UKTCH
THOK
GRACE, REMOVE THAT OBSCENITY FROM MY SIGHT!
BUDDA BUDDA
SKREEEEEEEE

WHHHUP
SHRAK
SHUNG
ANIMAL!
I'LL KILL YOU!
GCK...
NNG
SSHHKT

UUUHHNN
SPLUT
CLICK
EEEEEEEEEEEEEEEEEEEEEEE
AHUH-DUH...DOES IT HURT, MY DEAR? I DO HUH-HOPE SO. UH, HAHA HA-HA...

EEP
EEP
EEP
I'LL SEE YOU IN HELL, BITCH!
EEP
EEP
EEP--
CRITICAL
CRITICAL
CRITICAL
CRIT

THANKS, FRIEND.
SEEMS I'M NOT THE ONLY ONE WHO'S ANXIOUS TO SEE THE BACK OF THIS PLACE?

WAY THINGS LOOK FROM HERE, SARGE... NONE OF US ARE GOING *ANY-WHERE.*

WHUUMM
UHH

SKREEEEEEEEEEEEEEEEEEE
WHAT'S WRONG WITH THEM?
THEY'RE ACTING LIKE THEY'VE BEEN HIT WITH A SOUND CANNON...
...EXCEPT WE DON'T HAPPEN TO HAVE ONE!
TEC

WHO CARES?! WE GOT LUCKY, SO LET'S HAUL ASS WHILE WE CAN!

I'M JUST SORRY WE DIDN'T RUN INTO KLEIST!

MAN, OH MAN, I THINK WE'RE GONNA MAKE IT!
INTO THE SHIP!

BAY DOOR OVERRIDE INITIATED. DITCHING GRAVITY COUPLERS. READY FOR MANEU-VERING THRUSTERS ON YOUR MARK...
SCREW THAT...

...JUST PUNCH IT!
BUH-ROOM

WE MAINTAINED ORBIT FOR THREE DAYS, MONITORING TRANS-MISSIONS, AND WATCHING FOR SURVIVORS.
THE ONLY THING WE PICKED UP WAS STATIC.
IN HINDSIGHT, OUR FAILURE WAS INEVITABLE. MANKIND'S PRIZED INTELLECT HAS BECOME OUR GREATEST CONCEIT.
WE DRESS OURSELVES IN TECHNOLOGY AND THINK IT MAKES US OMNIPOTENT.
THE ALIEN FUNCTIONS ON A BASER, PURER LEVEL. ITS PURPOSE IS THE SIMPLEST... REPRODUCE AND SURVIVE.
WE CANNOT CONTROL THEM, OR CALL THEM EVIL...
...YET WE ALLOW MEN LIKE KLEIST TO ASSUME POWER.
I'VE SET COURSE FOR EARTH. WE'LL RENDEZVOUS WITH MORENO STATION IN EIGHT MONTHS.
THIS IS CAPTAIN PALMER OF THE TRANSPORT VESSEL CALIBAN SIGNING OFF.

SACRIFICE

script
PETER MILLIGAN

art
PAUL JOHNSON

lettering
ELLIE DE VILLE

title illustration
PAUL JOHNSON

THE DEVIL BITES INTO ME AND I WAKE UP IN HELL.
SCREAMING. ON FIRE. IN HELL.

THEN HE HOLDS ME AGAIN AND THE FIRES STOP BUT I'M STILL SCREAMING.
AND THEN SLOWLY THE SCREAMING STOPS AND IT'S OVER ONCE MORE.
AND THEN THE MAN WITH THE BEARD PRETENDS HE WASN'T REALLY HOLDING ME.
CALM DOWN, IT'S JUST A NIGHTMARE. MY NAME'S JOHN MASTERS.
DO YOU REMEMBER THE ACCIDENT?

AN ACCIDENT. THE SHIP CRASHED. EVERYONE DEAD. FIRE ...
THAT'S RIGHT. I'VE BROUGHT YOU SOMETHING TO EAT. SOMETHING IN HERE TO MAKE YOU SLEEP AS WELL. GIVE US ALL SOME PEACE.

YOUR INJURIES ARE VERY SLIGHT, CONSIDERING WHAT YOU'VE BEEN THROUGH.
YEAH, I'M... I'M LUCKY TO BE ALIVE ...

I WOULDN'T GO THAT FAR.

IT'S NICE TO FEEL THE SEDATIVE SWIM THROUGH YOUR SYSTEM, TO KNOW THAT PEACE IS APPROACHING.
I HAVE BEEN HERE JUST TWO DAYS.
FEELING WARM NOW, FURRY AND WARM, MY MIND WANDERS BACK TO THE SHIP, AND BECAUSE I'M WARM IT DOESN'T HURT TO THINK ABOUT IT...
THE CAPTAIN'S MESSAGE, SAY-ING THERE WAS A PROBLEM...
THE CRACK OF AN EXPLOSION AS SOME-WHERE AN ENGINE BLEW AND THEN THE LURCH AS THE SHIP DROPPED.
MY FACE PRESSED AGAINST THE WINDOW, THE NOISE, THE AMOUNT OF IT ALL AROUND ME.
I NEVER KNEW THERE COULD BE SO MUCH NOISE.
I WENT TO PRAY BUT PHYSICALLY COULDN'T BRING MYSELF TO DO IT.

THERE MUST HAVE BEEN AN EXPLOSION BUT I DON'T REMEMBER THAT, JUST WAKING, SCREAMING, IN HELL, IN THE FLAMES, ALREADY RUNNING, THE NOISE EVEN LOUDER...
I MUST HAVE BEEN THROWN CLEAR, OR JUMPED, OR WAS JETTISONED, BEFORE THE EXPLOSION.
THE SMELLS WERE LOUDER THAN THE NOISE NOW, FIRE, BURNING METAL, FUEL, WOOD, PLASTIC, DEATH.
I WORKED MY WAY AROUND THE FIRES BUT THERE WAS NO ONE BUT ME. EVERYONE ELSE WAS PART OF THE FIRE NOW.
I WAS THE ONLY SURVIVOR.
AND SO I WALKED, HALF MAD, HALF DEAD, THROUGH THE JUNGLE.
I'D SEEN THE SETTLEMENT FROM THE WINDOW AND KNEW MY ONLY HOPE WAS TO FIND IT.
I CAME ACROSS SOME STONES THAT REMINDED ME OF THE STANDING STONES I SAW ONCE IN SCOTLAND, EARTH.
I TOUCHED THE CENTRAL STONE AS THOUGH IT WERE AN OLD FRIEND.
IT WAS VERY COLD AND DIDN'T FEEL LIKE A FRIEND. IT HAD A STAIN, LIKE A PORT-WINE BIRTHMARK.
AND THEN I HEARD THE NOISE BEHIND ME.

I RAN UNTIL I FELL AND SLEPT, DREAMING OF DRAGONS AND MY MOTHER AND DISTANT FATHER, AND WHEN I WOKE I STARTED RUNNING AGAIN.
I FOUND THE SETTLEMENT SHORTLY BEFORE DARK. HOW DID I FIND IT? WAS I GUIDED? DID I FOLLOW AN INVISIBLE STAR THAT SHONE THE WAY TO THIS LITTLE BETHLEHEM?
BETHLEHEM? I THOUGHT. KNOWING *MY* LUCK IT WILL TURN OUT TO BE *CALVARY*.

LET ME IN! OPEN UP!
WHY DON'T YOU OPEN UP?
THANK YOU...
AH... MY NAME'S ANN... ANN MCKAY...
THE SHIP I WAS ON...
IS THERE SOME KIND OF PROBLEM? I DON'T HAVE ANYTHING CONTAGIOUS.
WHY WON'T SOMEONE TALK TO ME?
WHERE ARE THE OTHERS? ARE THEY STILL OUT THERE?
THERE ARE NO OTHERS. ALL DEAD. I'M THE ONLY ONE.
YOU'RE LYING! THERE MUST BE OTHERS. WHERE ARE THE GUNS? THE MARINES?
MARINES? I...

AND AS I LIE HERE IN BED, IN AND OUT OF DREAMS, I SEE THAT TERRIBLE FACE AGAIN.
AND I IMAGINE THAT IT HAS EYES.
HOW DARK WOULD THEY BE? EXACTLY HOW TERRIBLE?
WHAT WOULD A PERSON SEE IN THEM, BESIDES HIS OR HER OWN DEATH?
THERE ARE SOFT NOISES OUTSIDE.
A WHISPER. FOOTSTEPS.

AT THAT MOMENT MASTERS MAKES AN APPEARANCE ...
THERE'S A MONSTER, ISN'T THERE? AN ALIEN. OUT THERE.
YOU SAW IT?

BRIEFLY. YOU SMELL OF ALCOHOL.
I DAMN WELL HOPE SO. I'VE BEEN DRINKING ALL DAY AND I'D HATE TO THINK IT DIDN'T NOTICE.
YOU SEE ANYTHING ELSE OUT THERE?

UHH, NO. NOTHING ELSE.
HOW LONG HAS IT BEEN OUT THERE?
LOOK, I'D RATHER NOT TALK...

HOW LONG, MASTERS?
ABOUT NINE MONTHS, OKAY? IT LANDED ON A CARGO SHIP.
NATURALLY, IT HAD SLAUGHTERED EVERYONE ON BOARD. IT'S ALONE, POSSIBLY WOUNDED, POSSIBLY MAD.

YOU'VE BEEN TERRORIZED BY THAT THING FOR NINE MONTHS?
WHY HASN'T SOMEONE COME TO HELP YOU?

WE'VE TRIED ASKING FOR HELP. WE'RE A LONG WAY FROM ANYWHERE OUT HERE AND ONE SOLITARY ALIEN DOESN'T SEEM TO CUT MUCH ICE NOWADAYS.
LOOK, I CAN'T STAND AROUND TALKING, I'VE GOT THINGS TO DO.
LIKE WHAT, MISTER MASTERS? MORE DRINKING?
WHO WAS THAT MAN WITH THE SCARRED FACE?
YOU REALLY ARE INSUFFERABLE, AREN'T YOU? YOU'RE REFERRING TO MAD RICKETTS. HE WAS HOPING YOUR SHIP WOULD BRING SUPPLIES. WEAPONS. MARINES. WE ALL WERE.
TO BE BLUNT, WE'RE ALL DISAPPOINTED THAT YOU'RE ONLY YOU. WE HOPED FOR A LITTLE MORE.
TO BE BLUNT, SO DID I.
I SLEEP ALMOST ALL THE NEXT DAY AND WAKE IN THE EVENING FEELING BETTER.
IN THE SETTLEMENT, THE MONSTER IS EVERYWHERE, A FOG, A CLOUD.
IN EVERY CORNER, EVERY HOME, EVERY GAZE...

I WONDER IF, IF YOU LIVED HERE, THAT AFTER A WHILE YOU WOULD THINK OF NOTHING BUT THE ALIEN.
WOULD EVERYTHING BE BOILED DOWN TO WHEN IT MIGHT STRIKE AGAIN? EVERYTHING REDUCED TO THE SHAPE OF ITS JAWS?
WOULD THERE BE SOMETHING ALMOST... ATTRACTIVE ABOUT THAT?
LATER I FIND A SMALL BUILDING THAT SEEMS DIFFERENT FROM THE REST. THE DOOR WON'T BUDGE.
I CAN HEAR SOMETHING INSIDE, A KIND OF HUM, LIKE A GENERATOR...
WHAT'S TO HIDE?
WHAT ARE YOU DOING?
AAH, NOTHING. JUST LOOKING AROUND.
DON'T PLAY WITH KNIVES OR YOU'LL CHOP YOUR FINGERS OFF.
AHH... NO, OF COURSE. ABSOLUTELY...
THAT'S ENOUGH, RICKETTS.

MIND YOUR OWN BUSINESS, JOHN.
LET'S NOT GET ALL BORING ABOUT THIS. SHE DOESN'T KNOW ANY-THING. THERE'S NOTHING SHE COULD DO IF SHE DID.

GO TO SLEEP.
I DON'T SLEEP.
ALL RIGHT. THEN JUST DO WHATEVER YOU DO TO GET THROUGH THE NIGHT. PLEASE?

WHAT WAS ALL THAT ABOUT? WHAT DON'T I KNOW?
NOTHING. HOW DO YOU FEEL?
CURIOUS AS HELL. WHAT DON'T I KNOW?

I'LL EXPLAIN IT ALL LATER. BELIEVE ME. LATER
YOU SEEM DIFFERENT. ARE YOU A LITTLE MORE SOBER?
YEAH, OR A LITTLE MORE DRUNK. I'M NOT SURE WHICH. IT GETS HARD TO TELL THE DIFFERENCE AFTER A WHILE.

WHAT IS IT? WHAT ARE YOU LOOKING AT?
YOU.
OH.

YOU'LL PROBABLY THINK THIS IS LUDICROUSLY FORWARD, BUT I NEED TO SAY SOMETHING. IT MIGHT BE A LONG TIME BEFORE WE'RE OFF THIS PLANET. YEARS, MAYBE.
DON'T, MASTERS. WHATEVER YOU'RE THINKING OF SAYING, DON'T.

IT CAN BE VERY LONELY, AND THE OPTIONS ARE SOMEWHAT LIMITED, IF YOU KNOW WHAT I MEAN.
I'D LIKE TO... I'D LIKE YOU TO CONSIDER LIVING WITH ME.

ARE YOU INSANE? IS EVERYONE INSANE HERE? I'VE ONLY KNOWN YOU A FEW DAYS, DURING WHICH TIME YOU'VE BEEN A BORING, OBNOXIOUS DRUNK.
THE OPTIONS ARE SOMEWHAT LIMITED? THANK YOU VERY MUCH.

I'M SORRY I DIDN'T MEAN IT LIKE THAT.
GOOD NIGHT, MASTERS.
ANN, FOR GOD'S SAKE, I'M NOT JUST MAKING A PASS.

I'M JUST TOO OLD... TOO MISERABLE AND TOO OLD FOR GAMES.
WE MIGHT ALL BE DEAD TOMORROW. AND IF WE'RE ALIVE, WHAT LIFE IS THERE HERE, ALONE?

PLEASE DON'T SAY ANYTHING ELSE. YOU'LL ONLY FEEL EVEN MORE STUPID LATER.
WHAT'S THAT SUPPOSED TO MEAN?

WHY DON'T I TELL HIM? AM I ASHAMED?
AND WHY DIDN'T I TELL HIM ABOUT THE STONE?

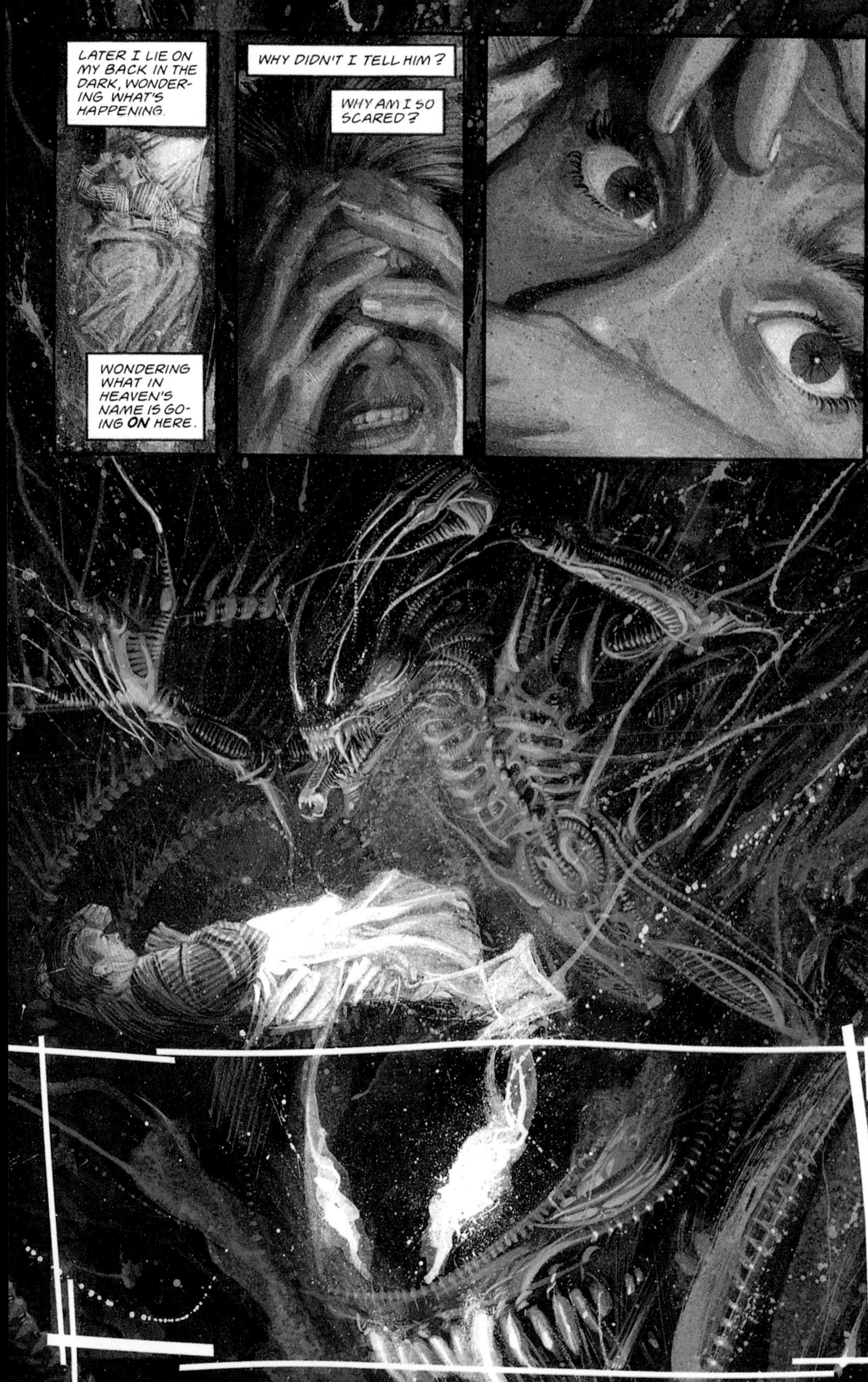
LATER I LIE ON MY BACK IN THE DARK, WONDERING WHAT'S HAPPENING.
WONDERING WHAT IN HEAVEN'S NAME IS GOING ON HERE.
WHY DIDN'T I TELL HIM?
WHY AM I SO SCARED?

THE LOVELINESS OF THE MORNING SEEMS A LITTLE OFFENSIVE, UNDER THE CIRCUMSTANCES.
DID I DREAM LAST NIGHT?
RICKETTS RAMBLING ON ABOUT KNIVES.
AND MASTERS, SUDDENLY PROPOSITIONING ME LIKE THAT.
MASTERS, DOES THE SETTLEMENT HAVE A CHURCH?
OF COURSE IT DOESN'T. WHAT'S THE PROBLEM, GUILTY CONSCIENCE?
NO, I WAS GOING TO OFFER TO GIVE A SERVICE.
A SERVICE?
IT'S SUNDAY, ISN'T IT?

I REMEMBER WHAT SEEMS LIKE SEVERAL LIFE TIMES AGO, MOTHER SAYING,
YOU WANT EVERYTHING, THAT'S YOUR PROBLEM. YOU EXPECT TOO MUCH. YOU'LL NEVER BE HAPPY IF YOU EXPECT TOO MUCH.

PERHAPS YOU THINK OUR ANCESTORS SHOULD HAVE STAYED IN THE SWAMP? OR MAYBE YOU'RE JUST SORE BECAUSE DADDY'S LEFT YOU.
I MEAN, WHAT ON EARTH IS TOO MUCH?

MY GOD, WHAT A TERRIBLE CREATURE I WAS.
MORE THAN YOU CAN GET, THAT'S TOO MUCH. MORE THAN YOU CAN POSSIBLY GET.

SHE HAD SUCH NICE WHITE TEETH. I REMEMBER THEM, EVEN FROM THAT DAY.
THAT DAY. WHAT IS IT NOW, TWENTY YEARS AGO?

THAT DAY. A STRANGE LOOK OF FEAR AND BEAUTY TEARING ACROSS MOTHER'S FACE AS SHE SAYS,
OH GOD, STAY HERE, STAY RIGHT HERE...
WHY, WHAT'S WRONG?

BE QUIET! JUST DO AS YOU'RE TOLD AND STAY HERE.
IT'S IN THE HOUSE!

YOU SHOULD HAVE TOLD ME.

I LIKE TO LET PEOPLE GET TO KNOW ME FIRST.
WHEN THEY KNOW I'M A PRIEST FROM THE BEGINNING THEY TEND TO CLAM UP.

IS THAT THE REAL REASON? WEREN'T YOU REALLY JUST ENJOYING NOT BEING A PRIEST?
SO YOU ACTUALLY BELIEVE IN THAT STUFF? YOU BELIEVE THERE'S A GOD?

OF COURSE I DO.
AND YOU GUYS STILL TAKE THOSE VOWS, DON'T YOU?

OF CELIBACY, YES. IT'S A LITTLE SACRIFICE WE MAKE TO GOD. IT BRINGS US CLOSER TO HIM.
SO WHAT ARE YOU DOING HERE? SAVING OUR SOULS? YOU'D BE WASTING YOUR TIME.

I WAS ON A MISSIONARY SHIP. WE WENT OFF COURSE.
JOHN, WHAT'S WRONG WITH THIS PLACE? THERE'S SOME-THING ROTTEN ABOUT IT. NO. NOT ROTTEN.
SOME-THING EVIL.

I'VE HEARD THAT WORD A MILLION TIMES, BUT THIS IS THE FIRST TIME I'VE EVER REALLY **FELT** IT.
DO YOU BELIEVE IN THE **DEVIL**, JOHN?

JOHN?

HUH.
HEAR NO EVIL, SEE NO EVIL...

'AFTERNOON, PRIEST.

OUT FOR
A STROLL?

I SAID, OUT FOR A STROLL?
OH, JOHN, YES. JUST GETTING SOME AIR.
GOOD FOR YOU. WANNA DRINK?
SHOULD I MENTION THE STRANGE PROCESSION? CAN I TRUST HIM?
AHH, NO, NO THANK YOU. I DON'T DRINK.
OF COURSE, YOUR VOWS.
MY CYSTITIS, ACTUALLY. ALCOHOL SETS IT OFF. YOU OUT HERE FOR ANY PARTICULAR REASON?
YEAH. I WANTED YOU TO KNOW I WON'T GIVE UP. YOU MIGHT BE HERE A LONG TIME AND THIS PLACE MIGHT JUST MAKE YOU LOSE YOUR FAITH.
IF YOU HAVEN'T STARTED LOSING IT ALREADY.
JOHN, CAN I TRUST YOU?
NO.
I DIDN'T THINK SO...
NO. NO, I'M SORRY...
I CAN'T...

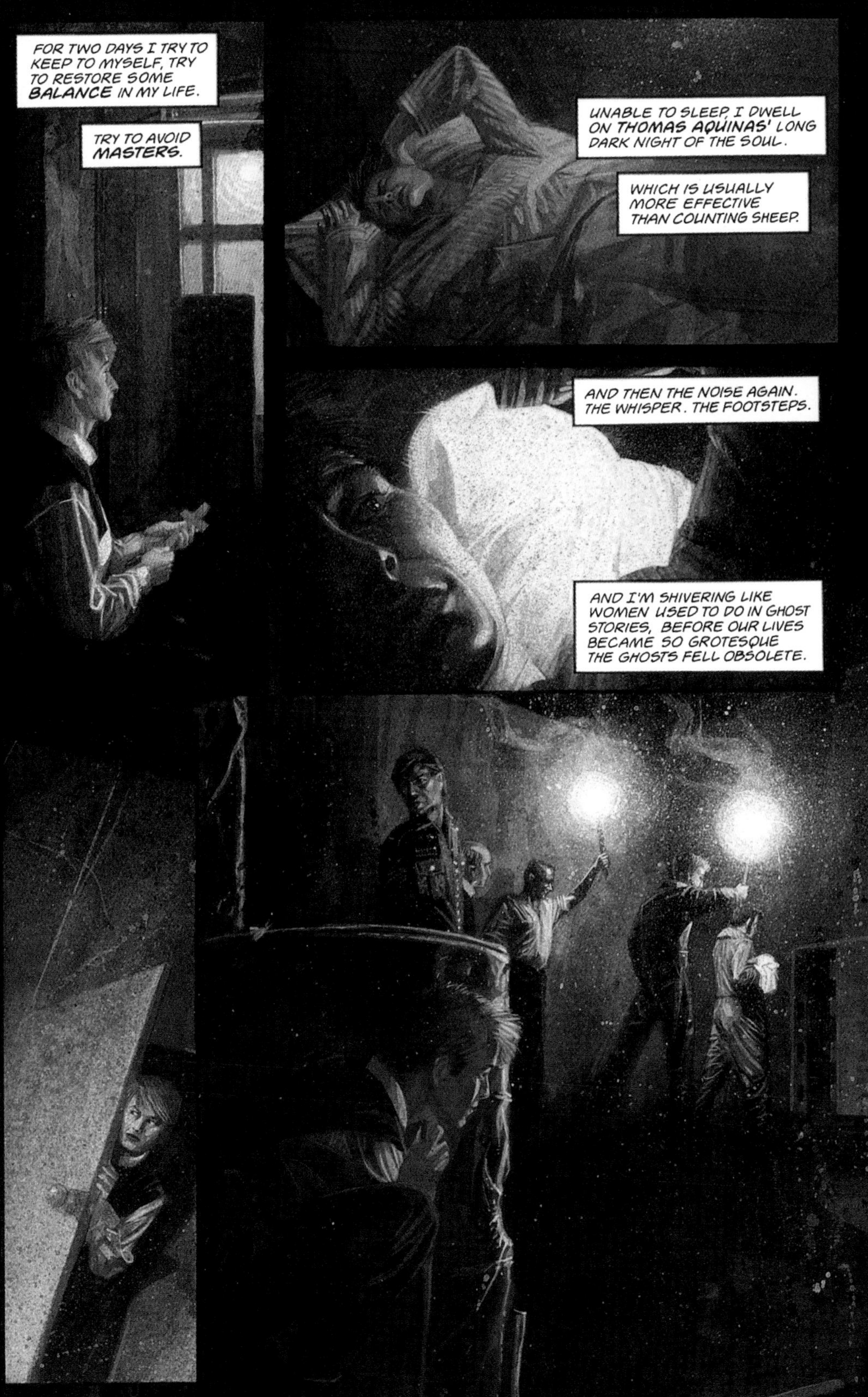
FOR TWO DAYS I TRY TO KEEP TO MYSELF, TRY TO RESTORE SOME BALANCE IN MY LIFE.
TRY TO AVOID MASTERS.
UNABLE TO SLEEP, I DWELL ON THOMAS AQUINAS' LONG DARK NIGHT OF THE SOUL.
WHICH IS USUALLY MORE EFFECTIVE THAN COUNTING SHEEP.
AND THEN THE NOISE AGAIN. THE WHISPER. THE FOOTSTEPS.
AND I'M SHIVERING LIKE WOMEN USED TO DO IN GHOST STORIES, BEFORE OUR LIVES BECAME SO GROTESQUE THE GHOSTS FELL OBSOLETE.

SOON THE JUNGLE IS SWALLOWING US. I STAY AS CLOSE AS I CAN.
I CAN'T EVEN BEGIN TO WONDER WHAT THEY'RE DOING.
AFTER TWENTY MINUTES THEY STOP AT THE STONE. THE STONE I TOUCHED.
WHAT ARE THEY GOING TO DO NOW?
DANCE NAKED AROUND IT?

THEY'RE MOVING AWAY, QUICKLY. I DON'T UNDERSTAND, I ...
WAIT. THEY'VE LEFT SOMETHING. ON THE STONE.
THEY'RE RUNNING NOW. I'VE ONLY A FEW SECONDS.
MUSTN'T LOSE THEM. NEVER FIND MY OWN WAY BACK IN THE DARK.
MY HAND IS SHAKING. THE PORT-WINE STAIN. STONE NO FRIEND.
SHE DOESN'T KNOW ANYTHING. NOTHING SHE COULD IF SHE DID...
OH, JESUS.
SSSSSHHHHHHHHHAAAAHHH

IT'S BEHIND ME, RIGHT BEHIND ME, HOT STINKING BREATH ON MY NECK...
JAWS OPENING BEHIND ME, READY TO SNAP...
AIEEE!
AHHH!

AAAEEEEEEKEEEEEEEEEEEEEEE

THIS IS THE STONE, THE DEVIL'S ANVIL, SMOOTH TO THE TOUCH, STRAIGHT AS A CHURCH.
MY GRAVESTONE, MY DEATH BED. ALTAR OF MY LAST EUCHARIST, WHERE BLOOD WILL TURN INTO PORT WINE.
EARLIER, WHILE I DRIFTED IN BLACK WATER, AN ALARM SOUNDED IN THE SETTLEMENT.
WHOOAA
WHOOWAA
WHOOAA
THE MAIN GATE... GO CHECK THE MAIN GATE...

GHUUUUU

I AWOKE TO BLUE. THE SOUND OF BIRDS AND RUNNING WATER.
I HOPED SO MUCH THAT I HAD DIED AND GONE TO HEAVEN.
I'M ALIVE? HOW AM I ALIVE?
BABY?
BABY!
WHERE'S THE BABY?
OH, GOD.
WHY DIDN'T YOU LET HER LIVE?
WHY COULDN'T YOU LET ME SAVE HER?
ARE YOU THERE? IS ANYBODY THERE?
IS ANYONE AT HOME?

I DON'T REMEMBER MUCH ABOUT THE JOURNEY BACK.
SHIELDED BY A LACK OF CONCERN, I SEEMED TO BE SAFE FROM DANGER.

GOOD GOD, YOU'RE ALIVE!

WHERE HAVE YOU BEEN? WHEN THE ALIEN ATTACKED, WE THOUGHT...
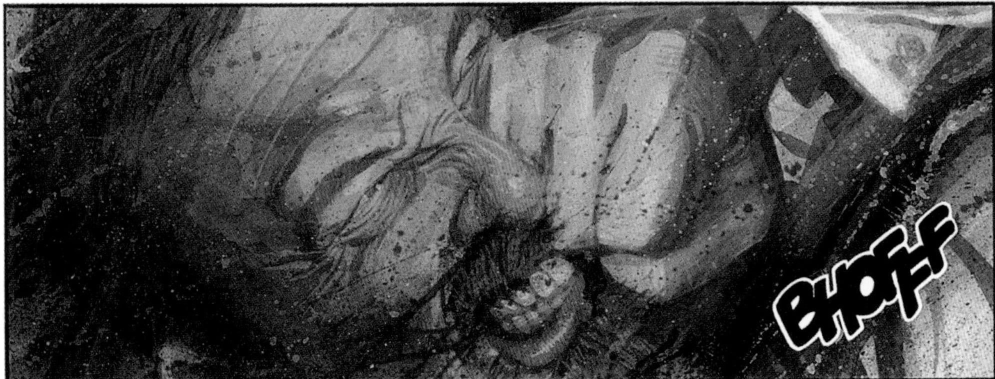
BHOFF

I FOLLOWED THEM. I SAW WHAT THEY, WHAT YOU, GIVE TO THE ALIEN. IT'S NOT THE MONSTER, YOU ARE.
ANN, I'M SORRY. I WANTED TO TELL YOU...

WHAT DID YOU DO?
DID YOU TOUCH THE OFFERING?

THE OFFERING? THE OFFERING? YOU MEAN THE BABY?
YES, I TOUCHED IT. I TOOK IT AWAY, I TRIED TO SAVE IT...

I FAILED. I LOST IT IN THE RIVER.
BUT AT LEAST THAT MONSTER DIDN'T GET IT.
MURDERER!
UHHGH!
SEE WHAT YOU'VE DONE! BECAUSE OF YOU THE ALIEN ATTACKED.
IT WAS DEPRIVED OF WHAT IT WAS EXPECTING. SO IT KILLED TWO OF US AND WOUNDED THREE MORE.

I TOLD YOU! WE SHOULD HAVE TURNED HER AWAY. I TOLD YOU SOMETHING LIKE THIS WOULD HAPPEN!
MASTERS, IS THIS TRUE? THE ALIEN...

IT CAME LAST NIGHT. GOT THROUGH THE OUTER WALL. I THOUGHT IT HAD TAKEN YOU AWAY TOO.
YOU SHOULDN'T HAVE TOUCHED THE... THE BABY, ANN. YOU DIDN'T KNOW WHAT YOU WERE ***DOING.***

OH YES I DID. I KNEW EXACTLY WHAT *I* WAS DOING. I WAS TRYING TO SAVE THE LIFE OF AN INNOCENT CHILD.
YOU'RE THE ONES WHO NO LONGER KNOW WHAT YOU'RE DOING.

YOU'RE NO BETTER THAN ***DEVIL WORSHIPPERS,*** SACRIFICING CHILDREN TO SATAN.
IT'S NOT LIKE THAT. FOR A START, ***OUR*** DEVIL IS ***REAL.***
SECONDLY, THOSE BABIES... AREN'T ***REAL*** BABIES.

WHAT ARE YOU TALKING ABOUT? I ***FELT*** IT. IT WAS WARM. IT WAS BREATHING, JUST. IT WAS A ***HUMAN BABY...*** AND YOU WERE... FEEDING IT TO THAT ***CREATURE.***

YOU'D BETTER COME WITH ME.

WE DIDN'T WANT TO SHOW YOU STRAIGHT AWAY, UNTIL YOU'D BEEN HERE A WHILE AND UNDERSTOOD A LITTLE OF WHAT WE'VE ALL GONE THROUGH.
IT WOULD BE EASY TO HAVE A KNEE-JERK REACTION.
BUT NO ONE CAN UNDERSTAND UNTIL THEY HAVE LIVED UNDER THE SHADOW OF THE ALIEN.
MY GOD. OH, MY GOD...
I KNOW, I KNOW, SOMETIMES I CAN'T BELIEVE IT MYSELF.
BUT THIS IS THE ONLY WAY...
NO, NOT LIKE THIS.
I'M SORRY, BUT YOU'RE WRONG. THEY JUST ABOUT KEEP THE ALIEN AWAY FROM OUR DOOR. WITHOUT THEM WE'D BE DEAD.
YOU SAW WHAT HAPPENED WHEN YOU TOOK THE LAST OFFERING AWAY. IT ATTACKED US.
HOW...OFTEN?
ONE EVERY TWO DAYS. IT PROBABLY LIVES OFF ANIMALS THE REST OF THE TIME.
THE OFFERINGS SEEM TO SATISFY HIS TASTE FOR *HUMAN* BLOOD.

I SAY HUMAN, BUT IT'S NOT AS IF THEY'RE REALLY HUMAN.
WHAT... ARE THEY... THEN?
GENETIC CREATIONS. TOO YOUNG TO THINK OR FEEL PAIN OR FEAR.

I MEAN, THEY WOULDN'T EVEN BE HERE UNLESS WE MADE THEM FOR THIS PURPOSE. THEY CAN'T SURVIVE MORE THAN A FEW HOURS AWAY FROM THE MACHINES.
IT'S NOT AS THOUGH WE DRAGGED BABIES OFF THE STREET AND FED THEM TO THE ALIEN, IS IT?

CARRY ON TRYING TO CONVINCE YOURSELF. YOU DON'T CONVINCE ME. I DON'T THINK YOU CON-VINCE YOURSELF EITHER.
IF YOU DID, WHY DO YOU HAVE TO DRINK EVERY WAKING HOUR?

WHAT ABOUT THEIR SOULS, HUH? WHAT ABOUT ALL THE FUTURES YOU'RE DESTROYING?
WHAT ABOUT WHAT YOU'RE DOING TO YOURSELF, ALLOWING YOURSELVES TO TAKE PART IN THIS... THIS SLAUGHTER.

CAN'T YOU SEE WHAT THIS ALIEN HAS DONE TO YOU? WHAT HAVE YOU BECOME?
I MEAN, WHAT'S THE POINT OF LIVING... IF THIS IS THE ONLY WAY YOU CAN LIVE?

THIS WHOLE PLACE STINKS OF DEATH AND DECAY. YOU'RE NO LONGER HUMAN.
YOU'VE DETERIORATED INTO A BUNCH OF PARANOID INDIVIDUALS, EATEN AWAY BY GUILT AND FEAR. YOU'RE POSSESSED, ALL OF YOU.
CLAP CLAP
CLAP
CLAP
CLAP

NICE WORDS— BUT YOU HAVEN'T HAD TO LIVE WITH THAT THING FOR ALMOST A YEAR.

MORALITY IS A LUXURY WE CAN'T AFFORD OUT HERE. THERE'S NO RIGHT OR WRONG, JUST SURVIVAL OR DEATH.
SO DON'T LECTURE US, GOD-WOMAN. DON'T GIVE US ANY OF YOUR SOUL TALK.

MY WIFE WAS KILLED BY THE ALIEN. IT TOOK HALF MY FACE OFF ON THE SAME DAY.
IF WE'D HAD THE OFFERINGS BACK THEN, MY WIFE WOULD STILL BE ALIVE.

ARE YOU SAYING THAT THIS MINDLESS CREATURE IS WORTH MORE THAN MY WIFE? MORE THAN ANY OF US HERE?
RICKETTS, PUT IT DOWN.

WHAT RICKETTS SAYS IS TRUE.
I'VE NO RIGHT TO LECTURE YOU.

SO I'LL PUT MY MONEY WHERE MY MOUTH IS. THAT'S THE OLD EXPRESSION, ISN'T IT?
I'LL GO TONIGHT INSTEAD OF THIS BABY.

DON'T BE INSANE. **YOU** CAN'T GO!
WHY NOT? IF I REALLY BELIEVE IN WHAT I'M PREACHING, IN **GOD**, IN THE **SANCTITY OF LIFE**, ANY HUMAN LIFE, THEN IT'S WHAT I **SHOULD** DO.
IT'S WHAT I SHOULD **WANT** TO DO.

ANN, COME BACK, WE HAVE TO **TALK** ABOUT THIS...
LET HER GO. IT'LL BE A GOOD THING.

HUH?
I MEAN, SHE'S MUCH **BIGGER** THAN THE BABIES. WE WON'T NEED TO MAKE ANOTHER TRIP FOR A **WHOLE WEEK**.

EVEN AS MY MOTHER SCREAMED AT ME, THE WALL CAVED IN.
TWENTY YEARS AGO, AND I STILL SEE IT, AS THOUGH IT WERE HAPPENING IN FRONT OF ME NOW.

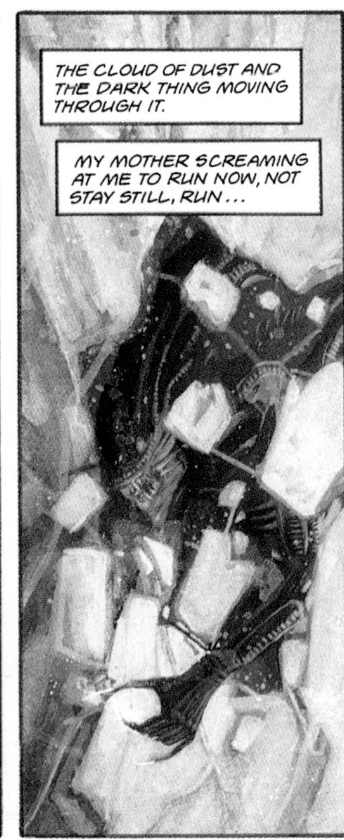
THE CLOUD OF DUST AND THE DARK THING MOVING THROUGH IT.
MY MOTHER SCREAMING AT ME TO RUN NOW, NOT STAY STILL, RUN...

SHE ALWAYS SAID THAT I WAS TOO DISSATISFIED, THAT I WANTED TOO MUCH, THAT I WOULD NEVER BE SATISFIED.
I WANTED **CERTAINTIES**, SHE SAID, AND THERE WERE NO CERTAINTIES IN THE REAL WORLD.

SHE PUSHED ME TOWARDS THE WINDOW...
RUN!

AND AS I FELL I LOOKED BACK AND SAW HER...
I SAW HER...

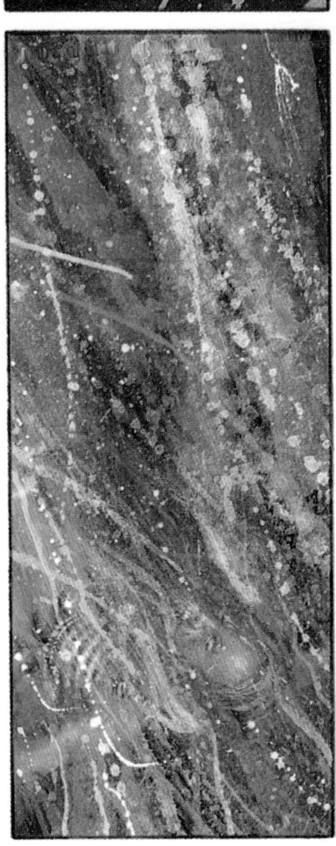

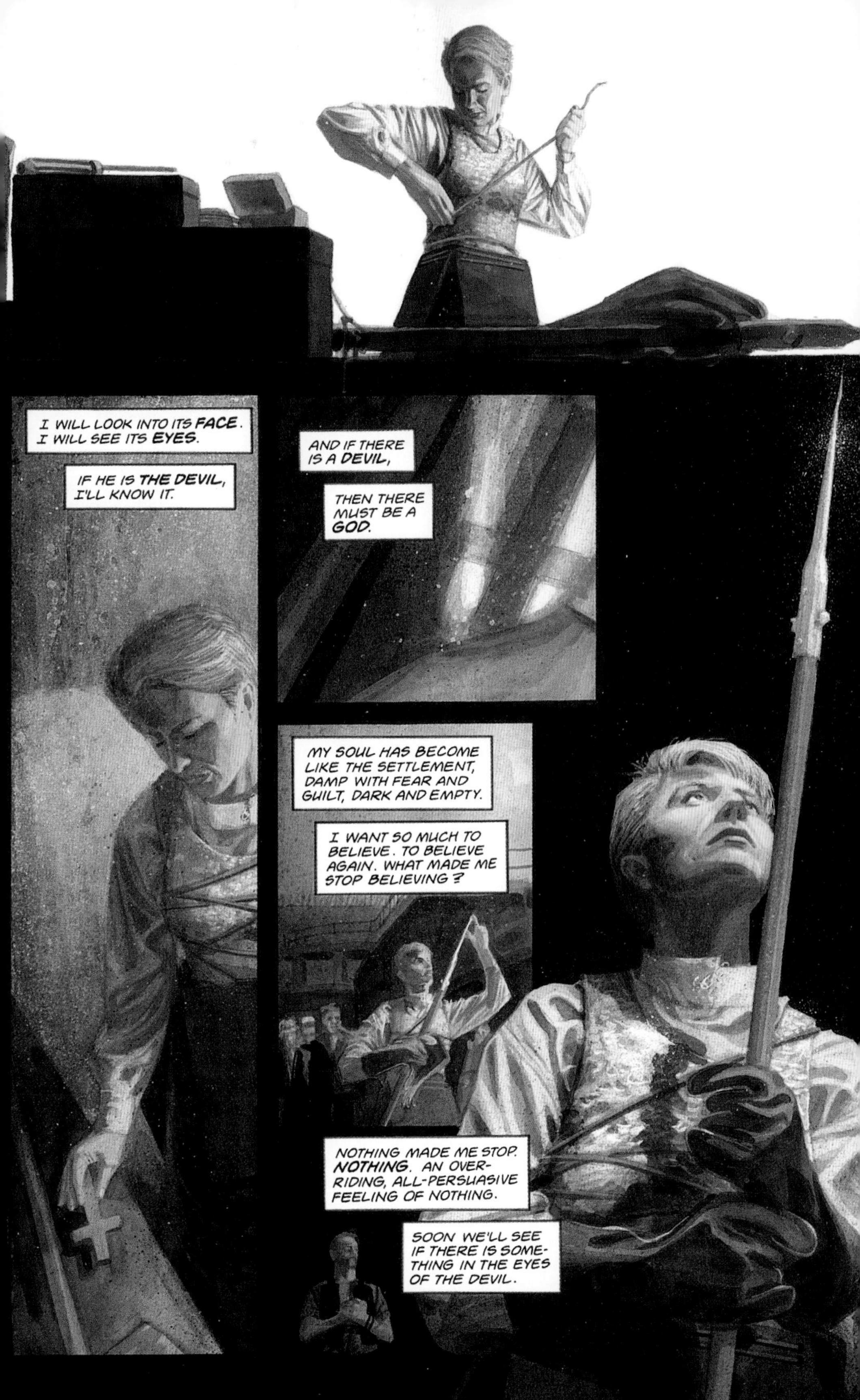
I WILL LOOK INTO ITS FACE. I WILL SEE ITS EYES.
IF HE IS THE DEVIL, I'LL KNOW IT.
AND IF THERE IS A DEVIL,
THEN THERE MUST BE A GOD.
MY SOUL HAS BECOME LIKE THE SETTLEMENT, DAMP WITH FEAR AND GUILT, DARK AND EMPTY.
I WANT SO MUCH TO BELIEVE. TO BELIEVE AGAIN. WHAT MADE ME STOP BELIEVING?
NOTHING MADE ME STOP. NOTHING. AN OVER-RIDING, ALL-PERSUASIVE FEELING OF NOTHING.
SOON WE'LL SEE IF THERE IS SOME-THING IN THE EYES OF THE DEVIL.

YOU'RE ACTUALLY GOING THROUGH WITH THIS?
YES.
THERE'S NOTHING I CAN DO TO STOP YOU?
DO YOU HAVE THE COURAGE TO TAKE MY PLACE?
NO.
TAKE THIS. IT'S A GRENADE. ABOUT THE LAST WEAPON WE HAVE LEFT HERE. YOU'LL HAVE TO GET REAL CLOSE TO USE IT THOUGH ...
I INTEND TO GET CLOSE ...
THANK YOU, JOHN.

NOW HERE I AM. IT TOOK ME HALF AN HOUR TO FIND THE STONE.
WRONG. IT TOOK ME TWENTY YEARS.
TIME PASSES. HOURS. I'M SICK THREE TIMES.
I TRY TO BREATHE SLOWLY, TRY TO STOP MY-SELF HYPER-VENTILATING.
WHERE IS IT?

O...OKAY...
O...KAY...
COME ON...
COME ON, THEN...
COME ON...
SHHHH
SHWCK!

OPEN YOUR EYES... OPEN YOUR EYES...
MOTHER, HELP ME OPEN MY EYES...
SKKK
AIEEEII!

WHAT'S... HAPPENING?
WE'RE FIGHTING BACK. WE'RE HUMAN AGAIN, THANKS TO YOU.
YOU CAN'T BEAT IT... LIKE THIS...
WE KNOW. WE'VE BEEN BUSY.
WHEN YOU LEFT TO FACE THE CREATURE ALONE YOU... YOU MADE US ALL FEEL... SO ASHAMED... WE REALIZED...
UGHGHGH!
NO... NO...
AAEIAEEEEE
OH, JESUS... BACK AWAY!
NOW! NOW! RUN!

WHY ARE WE STOPPING? IT'S TOO STRONG...
HUMAN INGENUITY. AND THAT OLD COMMUNITY SPIRIT.
WE WERE STRONG ENOUGH TO PULL DOWN MAMMOTHS, TO FACE SABRE TOOTH TIGERS. BUT ONLY BY WORKING TO- GETHER. BY OURSELVES, WE HAD NO CHANCE.
COME ON, YOU UGLY BASTARD! COME CLOSER...
KKH! KKKR
SKRAR

GOT IT! WE'VE STUCK IT!
WE'VE WON!
YEE HARR! HOORAYYY!
UHHH?
ANN!
AIEEEII!

I HEAR IT MOANING BEHIND ME...
THE MONSTER IS SLOWLY WORKING ITS WAY OFF OF THE PIKES.
IT ISN'T DEAD YET. THIS ISN'T OVER YET.
I CAN SMELL ITS BREATH. IT'S LIKE A GAS, PARALYZING ME...
ANN! NOW! WHILE YOU HAVE A CHANCE!
START CLIMBING!
NO.
I HAVE TO LOOK INTO ITS EYES.
I HAVE TO SEE...
IF THEY'RE THE EYES OF THE DEVIL...

I SAW MY MOTHER RUN TOWARDS THE ALIEN.
SAW AND FULLY REALIZED FOR THE FIRST TIME HOW UNCONDITIONAL, HOW ABSOLUTE, HOW **CERTAIN** HER LOVE WAS FOR ME.

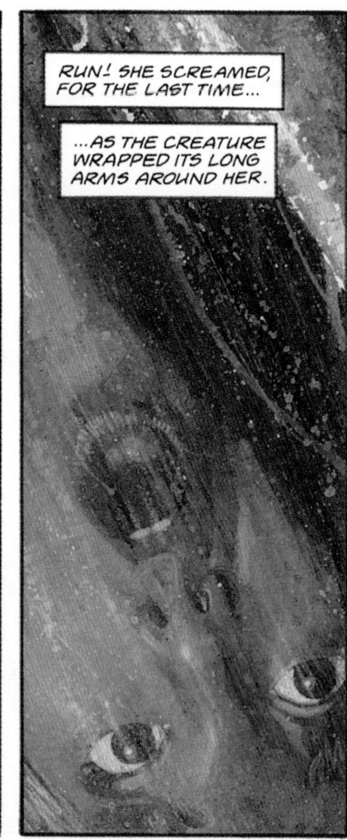
RUN! SHE SCREAMED, FOR THE LAST TIME...
...AS THE CREATURE WRAPPED ITS LONG ARMS AROUND HER.

I RAN, SCREAMING MY-SELF NOW, UNABLE TO SHAKE FROM MY MIND THE PICTURE OF MY MOTHER...
...FALLING INTO THE ALIEN'S ARMS. THE MOUTH OPENING. MY MOTHER...

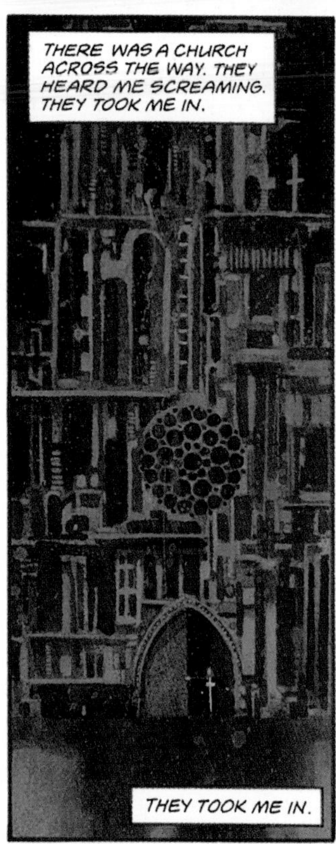
THERE WAS A CHURCH ACROSS THE WAY. THEY HEARD ME SCREAMING. THEY TOOK ME IN.
THEY TOOK ME IN.

I HID IN THE CHURCH. FOR TWENTY YEARS, I HID.

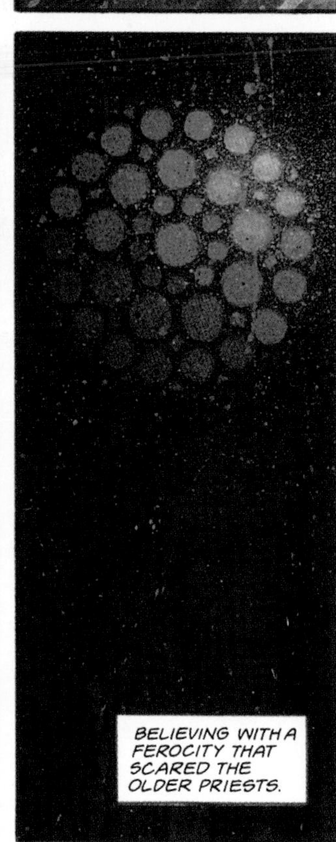
BELIEVING WITH A FEROCITY THAT SCARED THE OLDER PRIESTS.

AND NOW, BLACKNESS. I OPEN MY EYES BUT THERE IS ONLY BLACKNESS. AND A VOICE I RECOGNIZE AS MASTERS' SAYING...
ANN, YOU'RE OKAY. YOU'RE BACK AT THE SETTLE-MENT.
MASTERS? ...THE ALIEN?
YOU KILLED IT.

I... KILLED IT?
YOU PUSHED THE GRENADE RIGHT INTO ITS MOUTH. BLEW THE ROOF OF ITS SKULL OFF. BUT THE EXPLOSION... THE EXPLOSION...
YOUR EYES...

I'M BLIND, AREN'T I?

YES.

I IMAGINE HIM ABOVE ME. HIS EYES WILL BE RED.
HE'LL BE FULL OF PITY FOR ME. I CAN LIVE WITH THAT.

BLIND. OF COURSE.
I STARED INTO THE SUN AND IT BURNT OUT MY EYES.

I STARED INTO THE SUN. I STARED INTO THE CREATURE'S EYES.
AND WHAT DID I SEE?

NOTHING.
IT HAS NO EYES. NEITHER OF US HAVE NOW.

I SAW NOTHING.

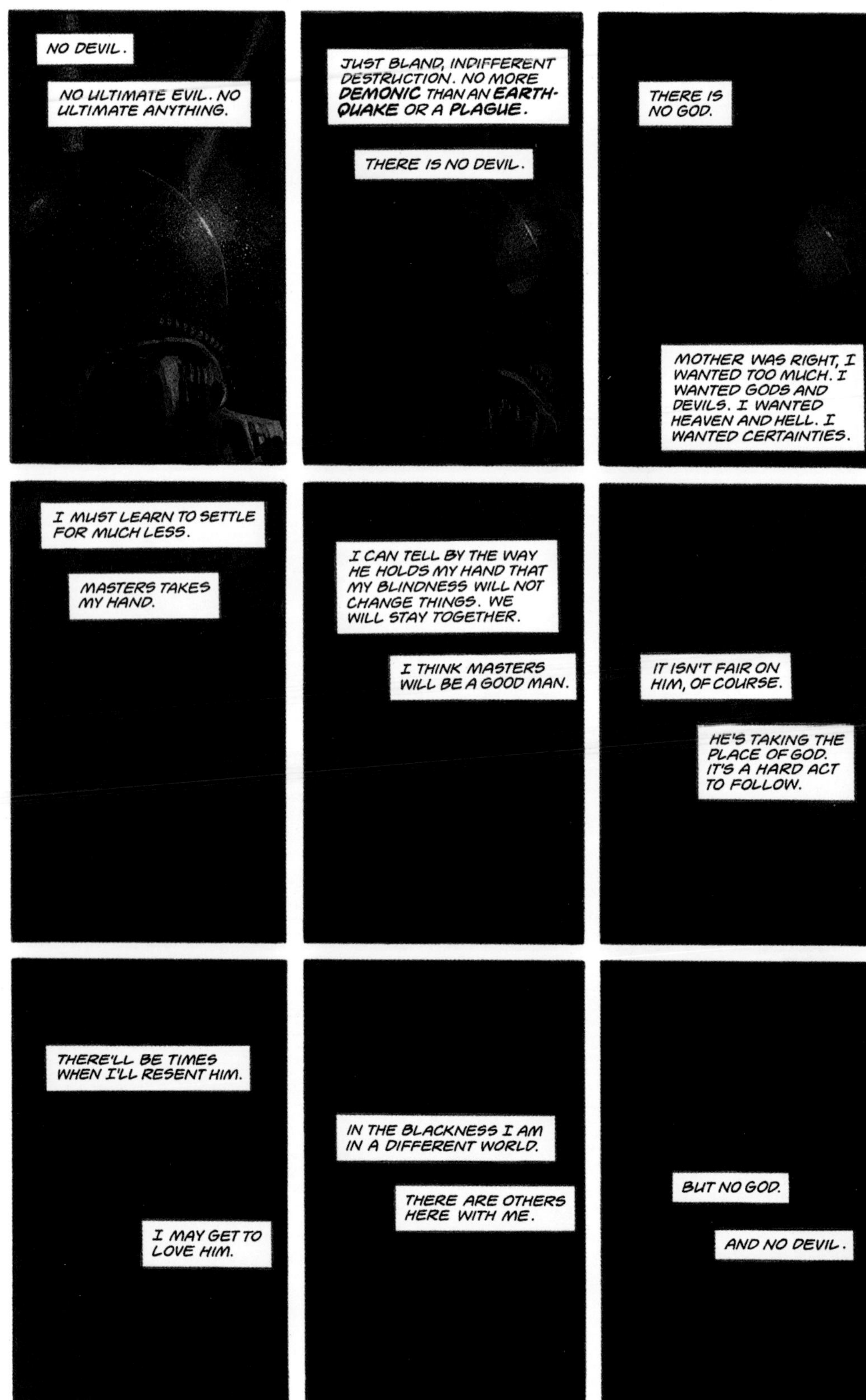
NO DEVIL.
NO ULTIMATE EVIL. NO ULTIMATE ANYTHING.
JUST BLAND, INDIFFERENT DESTRUCTION. NO MORE DEMONIC THAN AN EARTHQUAKE OR A PLAGUE.
THERE IS NO DEVIL.
THERE IS NO GOD.
MOTHER WAS RIGHT, I WANTED TOO MUCH. I WANTED GODS AND DEVILS. I WANTED HEAVEN AND HELL. I WANTED CERTAINTIES.
I MUST LEARN TO SETTLE FOR MUCH LESS.
MASTERS TAKES MY HAND.
I CAN TELL BY THE WAY HE HOLDS MY HAND THAT MY BLINDNESS WILL NOT CHANGE THINGS. WE WILL STAY TOGETHER.
I THINK MASTERS WILL BE A GOOD MAN.
IT ISN'T FAIR ON HIM, OF COURSE.
HE'S TAKING THE PLACE OF GOD. IT'S A HARD ACT TO FOLLOW.
THERE'LL BE TIMES WHEN I'LL RESENT HIM.
I MAY GET TO LOVE HIM.
IN THE BLACKNESS I AM IN A DIFFERENT WORLD.
THERE ARE OTHERS HERE WITH ME.
BUT NO GOD.
AND NO DEVIL.

LABYRINTH

script
JIM WOODRING

art
KILIAN PLUNKETT

background inks
MONTY SHELDON

colors
MATT HOLLINGSWORTH

lettering
ELLIE DE VILLE

title illustration
KILIAN PLUNKETT

REGULATIONS SAY YOU'RE HERE AS BACK-UP FOR THE LEAD TEAM AND TO PROVIDE A RETREAT ESCORT IF NECESSARY.
BUT WHAT YOU'RE REALLY GOING TO DO IS SIT BACK, RELAX ...
... AND WATCH RUPP AND HOLLISTER HERE LIQUIFY EVERY ALIEN IN THIS CAVERN WITH THESE NEWLY-DEVELOPED PARTICLE-PLASMA PROJECTORS.
MAKE IT A CLEAN SWEEP, MEN. I WANT THIS PLACE STERILIZED!
AYE AYE, SIR!

OVER THERE!
TUN
TUN TUN TUN
HOLY TOLEDO!
OFFHAND I'D SAY THIS REPRESENTS THE END OF THE ALIEN THREAT.
NO DUH, SHERLOCK!
KINDA TAKES ALL THE SPORT RIGHT OUT OF IT, DON'T IT?

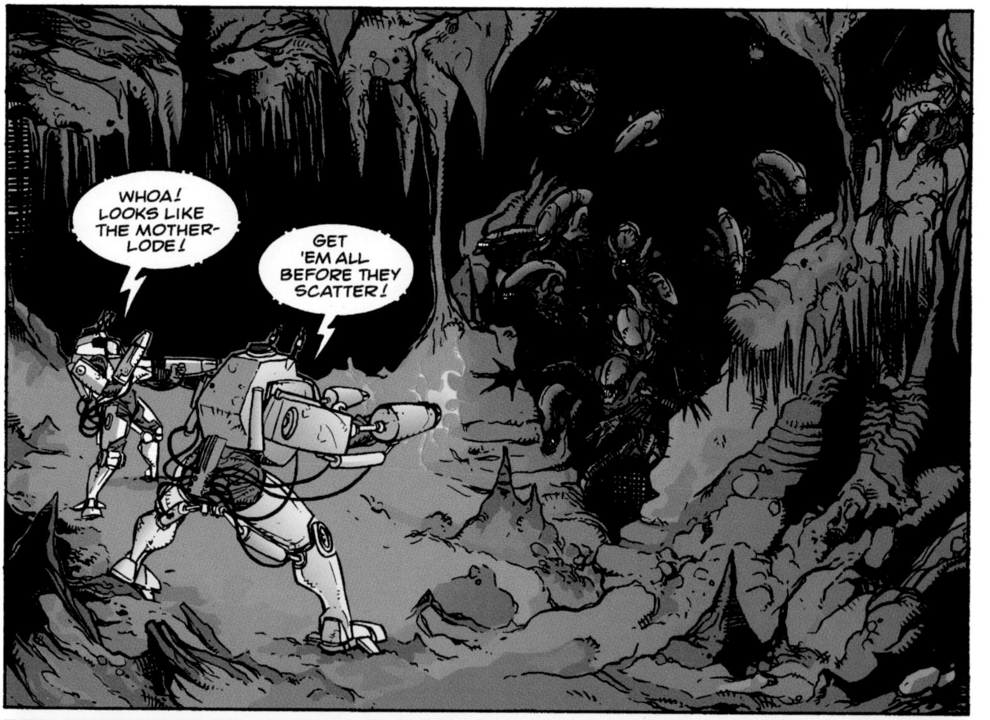

WHOA! LOOKS LIKE THE MOTHER-LODE!
GET 'EM ALL BEFORE THEY SCATTER!
TUN 
SPLUUUUUURNCH!

OH--
FUH!
SPLOOONSH

WHAT HAPPENED?

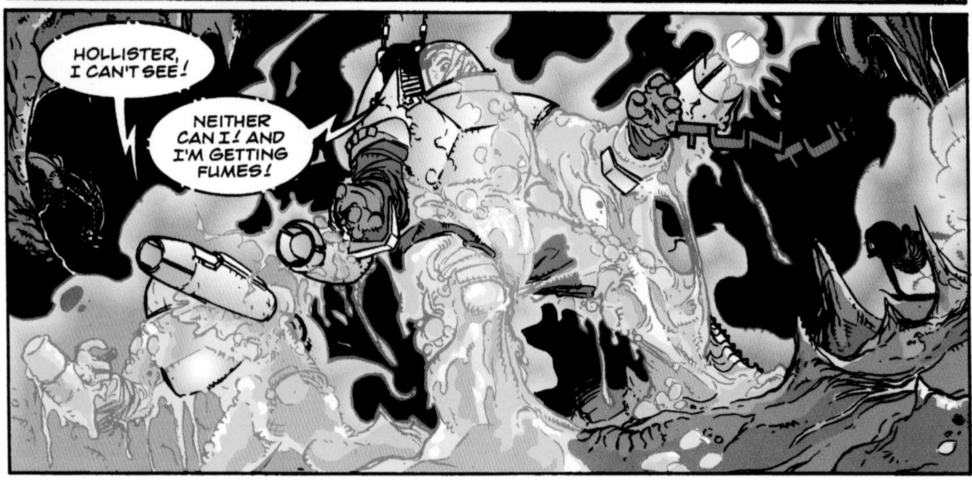
HOLLISTER, I CAN'T SEE!
NEITHER CAN I! AND I'M GETTING FUMES!

THE STUFF'S GETTING IN! HOW? THESE SUITS ARE ACID-PROOF!
NO, JUST ACID-RESISTANT... THIS CONCENTRATION... HELP ME! I CAN'T BREATHE!
ZZZZT
THE TRANSPORT IS DISSOLVING!
GET THIS STUFF OFF ME!
AAAAAAH
CRESPI! BLOW THE BOLTS ON THAT ESCAPE HATCH!
MY EYES!
I CAN'T... HUALK!
YESSIR!
WHOOM!
YAAAAAAH!
THE SUIT IS BURNING INTO ME! OH GOD! OH GOD!
SKRUTCH!

FIGHT! FIGHT! KILL THEM, COLONIAL MARINES!
THEY'VE GOT HOLLISTER!
THEY'VE GOT US ALL, YOU DUMB SON OF A BITCH! FIGHT! FIGHT!
MOTHER, I NEED HELP.
AIEEEEYAUGH!!!
HUMPFULKCH!
MERCIFUL GOD, NOOOO!
THIS ... IS HOPELESS ...
KEEP FIGHTING ...

WHAT'S HAPPENING?

THE LEDGE IS DISSOLVING!

KERRAAASH!

HISSSSSSSK
CHOUGHSK!
ZZZZZT... ATTVIO3, COME IN! ATT ZZT V ZT O3, COME IN! WHA ZZZZZZZZZZZZT ZZT OING ON IN THERE? OV ZZZZT!
TUNCH
SSSSSSSK!
HURN!
CHUSK
ULLLNNN...
ATTVIO3, WHAT ZZZZZT -OING ON? COME IN ATTVIO3! OVER!
WE'RE COMPLETELY SCREWED! THE CAR IS DESTROYED, EVERYONE'S DEAD, THERE ARE ALIENS EVERYWHERE! GET US OUT OF HERE!
HRIIIEEEENK
GRENADE RIGHT, CRESPI!
DO YOU HAVE A CODE RED, REPEAT, CODE RED? OVER?
CODE RED!? YES, I'D SAY SO, GOD FRIGGIN' DAMN IT!
CHIEEEK

ATTVIO3, WE MAY NOT COMPROMISE SHIP SAFETY IN RESPONSE TO CODE RED. SORRY. CAN YOU GET OUT INTO THE OPEN ?
NO, WE'RE COMPLETELY SURROUNDED!
CRESPI!
OOF!
GET DOWN!
WHOOOM!

COME ON!

GOD, IT'S DAYLIGHT!

WATCH YOUR HEAD!

THE SHIP! COME ON, WE CAN MAKE IT!
WHY DON'T THEY BRING IT CLOSER TO US?
YOU KNOW THEY CAN'T! HURRY, CRESPI!
I'M TRYING, DAMMIT!
YAAAAH! GOD, NO!
HISSSSK!

HURRRRRRSK!
GHACK!

GOD ALMIGHTY!
SLISH
CLICK

BRRAAAPPP
SPLOTCH
SPLOTCH
SPLOTCH
NIEEENCH!
GAH!
YOU ALL RIGHT?
NO.
COME ON, LET'S GO.
WE'VE GOT TO GET IN THE CLEAR. THEY WON'T OPEN THE LOCK FOR US IF THERE'S ANY CHANCE OF ALIENS GETTING ON BOARD.

AAAAAAAAAAAH!
GIBBS!
NO!
SCRUNCHCHCH
SSSSPLURCHLE
SCLURINCHERUNCINCH

HURRARRSSSSSSSK!
CHANK!
SPLUNC
GNG!

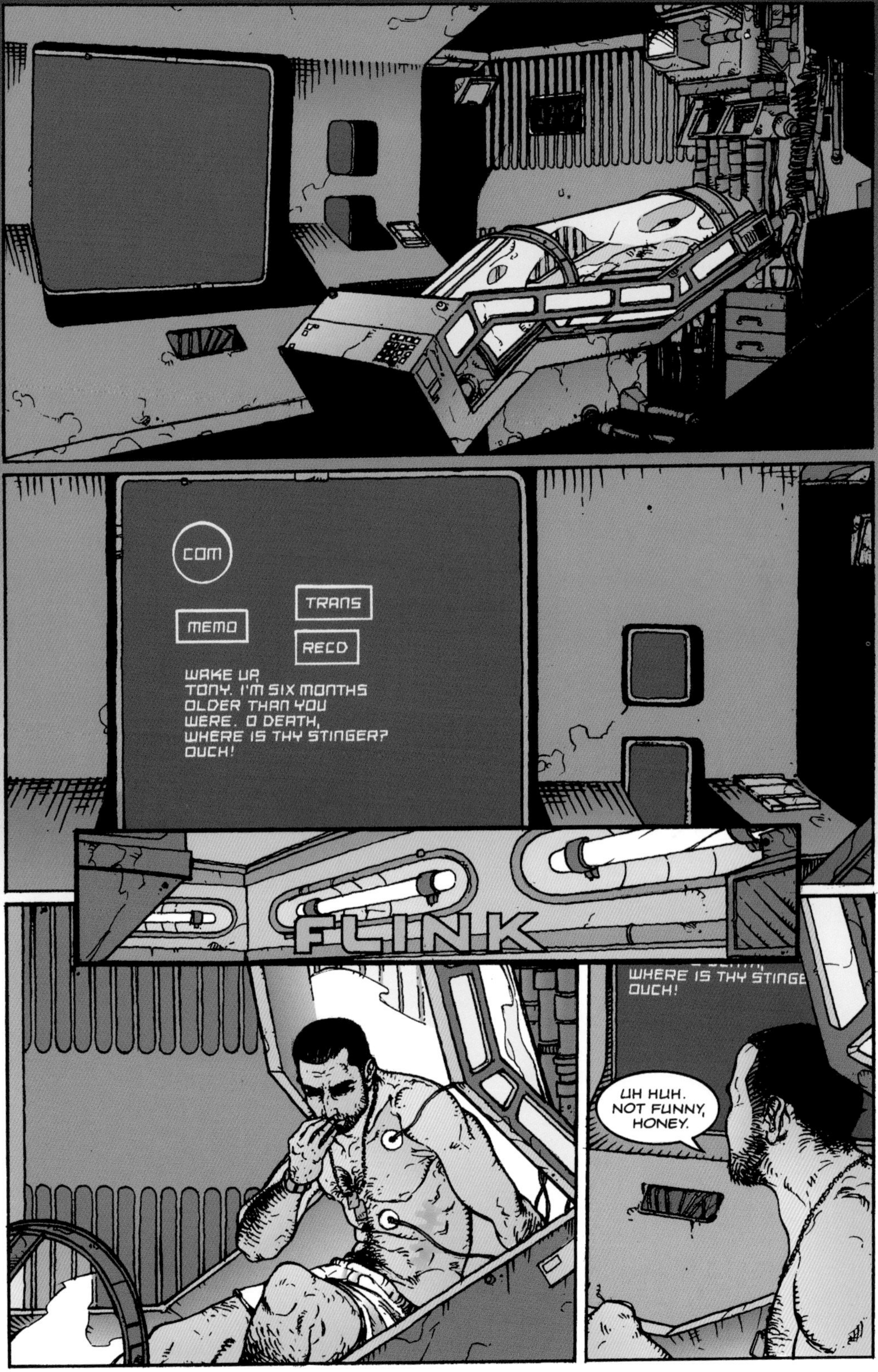

COM

TRANS

MEMO

RECD

WAKE UP,
TONY. I'M SIX MONTHS
OLDER THAN YOU
WERE. O DEATH,
WHERE IS THY STINGER?
OUCH!

FLINK

WHERE IS THY STINGE
OUCH!

UH HUH.
NOT FUNNY,
HONEY.

TRANS
RECD
THIS IS COLONEL DOCTOR CRESPI. HOW ARE WE ?
TRANS

THIS IS LIEUTENANT COLONEL HELLER. WE'RE FINE, SIR.

WE DOCK AT THE INNOMINATA AT 09:00 HOURS. HOW DID YOU SLEEP, SIR?
LIKE PLASTIC. ANYTHING TO RELEASE ?

YES, SIR, THERE IS ONE. I WILL RELEASE IT NOW.

CODED ENTRY
COL. DR. ANTHONY CRESPI
EYES ONLY
CONTRACT FEL
NNGLIKP

THANK YOU, UH, LIEUTENANT COLONEL. I'LL SEE YOU ON THE BRIDGE IN ABOUT TWENTY MINUTES, AFTER I GET CLEANED UP.
VERY GOOD, SIR.

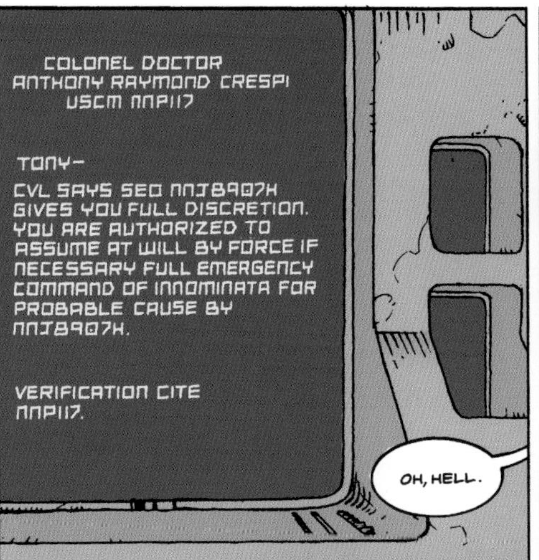
COLONEL DOCTOR
ANTHONY RAYMOND CRESPI
USCM NNP117
TONY–
CVL SAYS SEO NNJB907H GIVES YOU FULL DISCRETION. YOU ARE AUTHORIZED TO ASSUME AT WILL BY FORCE IF NECESSARY FULL EMERGENCY COMMAND OF INNOMINATA FOR PROBABLE CAUSE BY NNJB907H.
VERIFICATION CITE NNP117.
OH, HELL.

WHUFF.
VIZP

GREETINGS, ALL.
GREETINGS, SIR.

SO, THAT'S SHE WHO CANNOT BE NAMED.
HAVEN'T YOU BEEN BEFORE, SIR?
NOPE ... NOPE ...

SIR, I KNOW WE'RE NOT SUPPOSED TO KNOW WHAT GOES ON THERE, BUT I WONDER IF YOU COULD DE-BUNK SOME UGLY RUMORS ...
UGLY RUMORS?

WELL, SIR ... WE'VE HEARD THAT CREW MEMBERS THERE ARE CONSIDERED EX-PENDABLE, AND USED IN CLANDESTINE EXPERIMENTS, AND THAT--

THAT'S ENOUGH, HELLER. I WOULDN'T CONCERN MYSELF WITH RUMORS, IF I WERE YOU. A MAN DOESN'T WANT TO BE KNOWN AS A GOSSIP.

COFFEE, SIR?
NO, THANK YOU. SEE YOU AT LANDING, MEN.
YES, SIR.

SIR!
AT EASE, ALL. AS YOU WERE.
I DON'T FEEL WELL AT ALL, SIR.

NEITHER DO I, MCGUINNESS. I THINK I MUST FEEL AS BAD AS YOU LOOK.
I...

YES, SIR. I'M FEELING FINE NOW, AND I HOPE YOU SOON WILL BE TOO.
NO QUESTION, LIEUTENANT. YOUR RECOVERY HAS BEEN AN INSPIRATION TO US ALL.

WILL I BE WORKING UNDER YOU ON BOARD THE INNOMINATA, SIR?
NOT LIKELY MCGUINNESS. NOT IF YOUR LUCK HOLDS. I EXPECT TO BE DEEPLY INVOLVED IN SOME EXCRUCIATINGLY BANAL SERIES TESTS.

SOUNDS GOOD TO ME. THE INNOMINATA IS A LITTLE TOO HUSH-HUSH, TOO NEVERWAS, TOO DIDN'THAPPEN, TO SUIT MY TASTE.
GOOD QUESTION.
IF THAT'S THE CASE, WHY DID YOU VOLUNTEER FOR THIS TOUR?

COLONEL DOCTOR CRESPI, SIR. COLONEL THOMPSON WISHES TO SEE YOU ON THE UPPER BRIDGE BEFORE LANDING.
VERY GOOD.

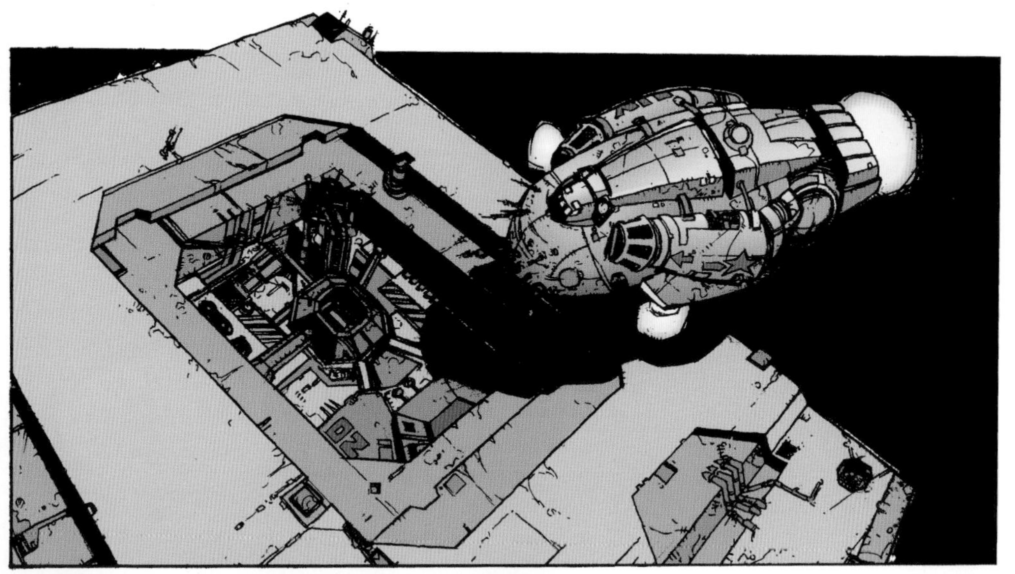

COLONEL DOCTOR CRESPI? I'M ADMIRAL THAVES.

COLONEL DOCTOR ANTHONY CRESPI REPORTING FOR DUTY, SIR.

AT EASE UNTIL FURTHER NOTICE, CRESPI. WELCOME ABOARD THE INNOMINATA.

YOU MUST HAVE SOME VERY INFLUENTIAL FRIENDS BACK HOME, CRESPI. A LOT OF GOOD MEN WERE IN LINE FOR THIS POST.

NO INFLUENTIAL FRIENDS I'M AWARE OF, SIR. MY EXPERIENCE--

NO NEPOTISM IMPLIED, CRESPI. YOUR RECORD SPEAKS FOR ITSELF. WHAT I'VE SEEN OF IT. MUCH SUB ROSA, EH?

TO A CERTAIN EXTENT, SIR. INTELLIGENCE WAS NEVER MY--

YES, MOST IMPRESSIVE. A GOOD THEORETICAL ANALYST IS ALWAYS VALUABLE. COLONEL DOCTOR CHURCH MAY WELL FIND A USE FOR YOU.

OF COURSE, I EXPECT TO BE WORKING CLOSELY WITH COLONEL DOCTOR CHURCH.

WELL... NOTHING IS CARVED IN STONE.

SIR, I HOPE THERE HASN'T BEEN A MISUNDERSTANDING. MY ASSIGNMENT IS TO SUCCEED COLONEL DOCTOR LENNOX AS COLONEL DOCTOR CHURCH'S RESEARCH PARTNER.
THERE'S YOUR QUARTERS, A-89. THERE'S A BRIEFING CARD IN THE PLAYER. GET FAMILIAR WITH THE FLOOR. YOUR ORDERLY IS ON CALL.
A 89
ADMIRAL THAVES, I AM HERE TO WORK WITH COLONEL DOCTOR CHURCH, AM I NOT?
THAT HAS TO BE WORKED OUT. WHY DON'T YOU BRIEF YOURSELF AND HAVE YOUR ORDERLY SHOW YOU AROUND? WE HAVE A LOUNGE THAT MIGHT SURPRISE YOU!
I WOULD PREFER TO MEET COLONEL DOCTOR CHURCH AND GET BROUGHT UP TO SPEED RIGHT AWAY, SIR.
CRESPI, YOU HAVE AT YOUR DISPOSAL THE BIGGEST RESEARCH AREA ON THIS STATION. YOU'LL HAVE PLENTY OF TIME TO SET UP AND RUN ANY OPERATION YOU WANT. FOR NOW, THOUGH, WHY DON'T YOU RELAX?
PERHAPS YOU'LL FIND THIS A BIT BLUNT, BUT I'VE FOUND A LITTLE BOY-GIRL ACTION TAKES THE EDGE OFF A LONG COLD SLEEP. NOW, UP IN THE LOUNGE, YOU'LL FIND—
TO BE A BIT BLUNT MYSELF, SIR, ALL I WANT TO DO IS MEET COLONEL DOCTOR CHURCH AND GET TO WORK.
WELL, I'M SORRY TO HAVE TO INFORM YOU THAT CHURCH HAS DETERMINED THAT HE DOESN'T NEED A NEW SECOND-IN-COMMAND. BUT DON'T WORRY! YOU'LL HAVE EVERY—
SIR, I RESPECTFULLY REQUEST THAT I MEET WITH COLONEL DOCTOR CHURCH IMMEDIATELY.

OH, WELL.
REQUEST DENIED.

ADMIRAL THAVES, I HAVE MY ASSIGNMENT, AND I INTEND TO PERFORM IT. IF I MUST PETITION SUPERCEDING AUTHORITY TO DO SO, I WILL.
OH, MY GOLLY. A TOUGH GUY. ISN'T THAT FINE? WHY DON'T YOU GO RELAX IN YOUR QUARTERS WHILE I GO DISCUSS THIS WITH COLONEL DOCTOR CHURCH?

COLONEL DOCTOR CRESPI?
YES?

COLONEL DOCTOR CHURCH REQUESTS YOUR COMPANY IN L67, SECTOR D.

TELL HIM THANKS FOR THE LOUSY BUGGY RIDE.

ZEEEEEEEEN

COLONEL DOCTOR CRESPI? I'M PAUL CHURCH. WON'T YOU COME IN?
THANKS.
PLEASE, SIT DOWN, DO.
THANKS.
PLEASANT JOURNEY?
UNEVENTFUL AS ONLY COLD SLEEP CAN BE.
NO, I DON'T MEAN YOUR TRIP HERE. I MEAN THE MONTHS AHEAD. SHALL THEY BE PLEASANT... OR OTHER-WISE?
THINGS ARE PRETTY WELL ESTABLISHED IN THEIR COURSE HERE, CRESPI. IT'S ALL ROUTINE AT THIS POINT. IT WASN'T NECESSARY FOR YOU TO BE SENT TO REPLACE LENNOX. I TOOK STEPS TO PREVENT IT, YOU KNOW.
IF HE HADN'T DIED WHEN HE DID, HE WOULD HAVE BEEN TRANSFERRED. NOTHING FOR HIM TO DO HERE. NOTHING FOR YOU TO DO EITHER.
MY RESEARCH HAS BEEN DOWN-SIZED. HARDLY ENOUGH TO KEEP ME ENGAGED. SPACEBORNE VIRUS TYPING...
...DULL STUFF.
I UNDERSTAND ONE OF YOUR VIRUSES PUSHED COLONEL DOCTOR LENNOX'S BRAIN OUT THE BACK OF HIS HEAD.
OH, NO, CRESPI. WHAT A MACABRE NOTION. VIRUSES ARE LITTLE TEENY THINGS.

CHURCH, MY TOLERANCE FOR BALONEY IS PRACTICALLY NIL. IF YOU WON'T SHOOT STRAIGHT WITH ME, YOU CAN EXPLAIN WHY TO A BOARD OF REVIEW.
THE OTHER BOYS WON'T PLAY FAIR AND NOW YOU'RE GOING TO CALL DAD. I'M DISAPPOINTED BY YOUR LACK OF RESOURCEFUL-NESS.
YOU'RE OUT OF YOUR LEAGUE, CRESPI. YOUR SUPERIORS HAVE TOSSED YOU INTO THE INNOMINATA LIKE CAVE MEN THROWING A DOG INTO A POND TO FETCH THEIR REFLECTIONS.
WELL...
COME ON, LET'S GO. I'LL SHOW YOU MY SETUP.
AUTHORIZED PERSONNEL ONLY
BEYOND TH
O'HARA, LAWLESS, THIS IS COLONEL DOCTOR CRESPI. HE'LL BE WORKING WITH ME IN G LAB.
I'LL NEED TO BE PUT ON THE BIOSCAN ASAP, OF COURSE.
HMMMMM? OH, THERE'S NO HURRY...
WE'LL SEE HOW THINGS WORK OUT.
LET ME REMIND YOU, CHURCH, THAT YOU ARE NOT MY SUPERIOR OFFICER. ALL THIS LATERAL OBSTRUCTION IS GOING TO SERVE YOU VERY POORLY.
CAN YOU STILL GET GOOD CHOCOLATE ON EARTH? I HEARD THEY'D STOPPED MAKING IT.

SHHH! DON'T WAKE THE BABY.
YOU HAVE ONE HELL OF A LOT OF NERVE, CHURCH.
I ACCEPT THE COMPLIMENT, CRESPI.
HOW LONG DO YOU THINK YOU COULD GET AWAY WITH THIS?
HAVE YOU EVER HAD TO TESTIFY AGAINST A PERSONAL FRIEND? I COULDN'T MAKE MYSELF DO IT.
WHAT?
LOOK.

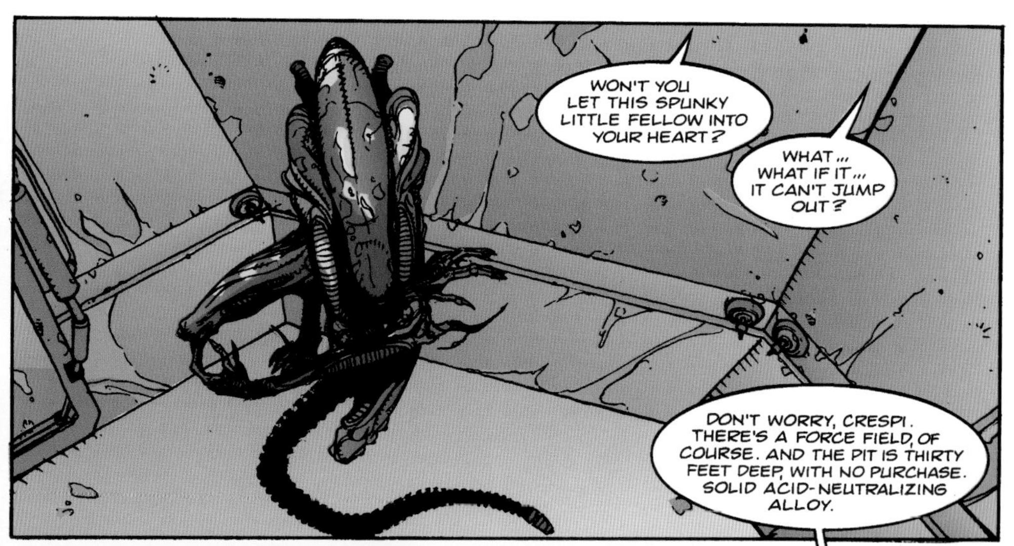
WON'T YOU LET THIS SPUNKY LITTLE FELLOW INTO YOUR HEART?
WHAT... WHAT IF IT... IT CAN'T JUMP OUT?
DON'T WORRY, CRESPI. THERE'S A FORCE FIELD, OF COURSE. AND THE PIT IS THIRTY FEET DEEP, WITH NO PURCHASE. SOLID ACID-NEUTRALIZING ALLOY.

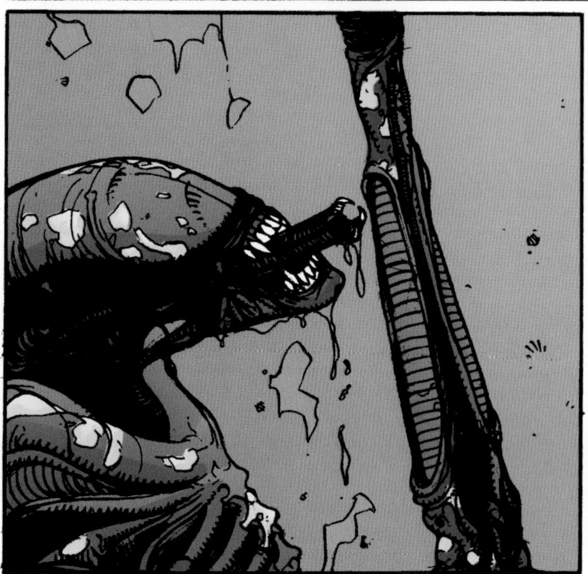

SEE THE ELECTRODES ON THE WALLS? THEY'RE MOTION-ACTIVATED. IF AN ALIEN ATTEMPTED TO JUMP, IT WOULD NOT ONLY BE ELECTROCUTED...

...BUT ROASTED ALIVE.
SEE HERE.

THIS WILL GIVE YOU AN IDEA OF THE EXTENT OF THIS OPERATION.

THIS MUST UTILIZE HALF THE INNOMINATA'S NONRENEWABLE RESOURCES.
MORE LIKE FIVE-EIGHTHS.

WHY ARE YOU SO EAGER TO HELP ME SHUT YOU DOWN?
ASK ME LATER. HEADS UP.

BZZZZT!
SKREEEEEELLK

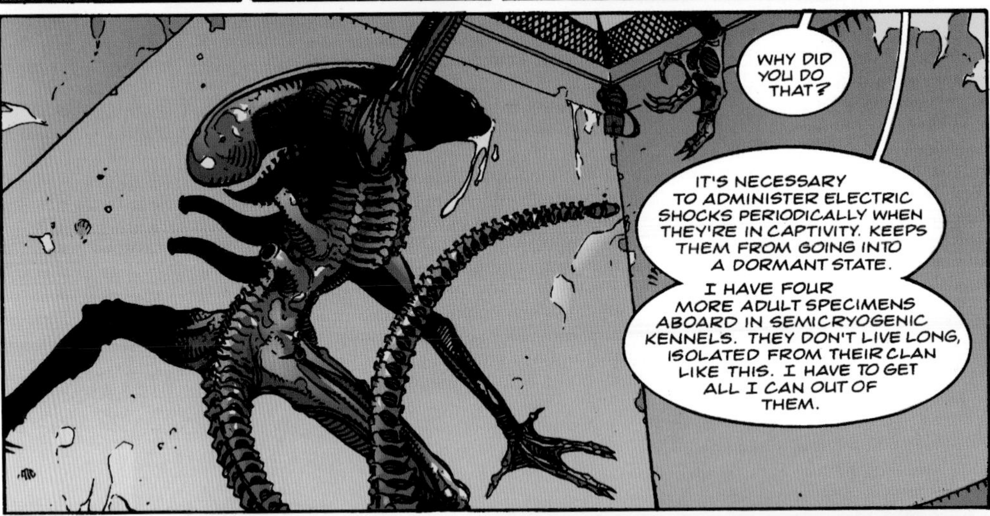
WHY DID YOU DO THAT?
IT'S NECESSARY TO ADMINISTER ELECTRIC SHOCKS PERIODICALLY WHEN THEY'RE IN CAPTIVITY. KEEPS THEM FROM GOING INTO A DORMANT STATE.
I HAVE FOUR MORE ADULT SPECIMENS ABOARD IN SEMICRYOGENIC KENNELS. THEY DON'T LIVE LONG, ISOLATED FROM THEIR CLAN LIKE THIS. I HAVE TO GET ALL I CAN OUT OF THEM.

TO TELL YOU THE TRUTH... WELL, I WOULDN'T MIND GIVING THAT THING A SHOCK OR TWO FOR AULD LANG SYNE MYSELF. I HAD A RUN-IN WITH A FLOCK OF THOSE MONSTERS ONCE.
YOU DON'T SAY.

YES... NINE YEARS AGO ON SOLANO'S MOON. THEY ATTACKED MY SQUADRON. KILLED EVERYONE BUT ME.
WE KNEW THEY WERE DANGEROUS, OF COURSE, BUT I DIDN'T KNOW HOW THEY... HOW THEY WERE.

ALL I REMEMBER IS THAT SKIN, THAT STINK, FLASHES OF TUBES AND DROOL, AND THOSE TEETH. AND BLOOD. MY CAPTAIN HAD HIS HEAD CORED LIKE AN APPLE.
DEAR ME. HOW AWFUL FOR YOU.
SAY, DIDN'T I READ THAT YOU SURVIVED AN ENCOUNTER AS WELL?
SIR, THE SYSTEM IS READY.
VERY GOOD. HAWKS, THIS IS COLONEL DOCTOR CRESPI. HE'S HERE TO UNCOVER OUR ILLEGAL OPERATION.
HOW DO YOU DO, SIR. ILLEGAL OPERATION? I DON'T UNDERSTAND.
THAT'S ALL RIGHT, HAWKS. NEITHER DOES HE. JUST STEP OVER HERE, CRESPI.
THAT DOOR LEADS TO A MAZE. ONCE INSIDE, THE CREATURE WILL BE CONFRONTED WITH CHOICES.
LET'S SEE IF YOU CAN SECOND GUESS ITS BEHAVIOR.
THERE'S A MAN IN THERE!
YES. ALIENS DON'T HAVE EYES. THEY CAN'T BE FOOLED BY HOLOGRAMS.
BUT DON'T WORRY; I'VE TAKEN EVERY PRECAUTION. WHEN THE ALIEN ATTACKS, THE AUTOMATIC SENSORS WILL ACTIVATE THE ELECTRODES.
NOW, CRESPI, THAT ALIEN IS STARVING, AND AS YOU MAY KNOW, ALIENS ARE VERY FOND OF PIG. WHAT WILL IT DO?

I KNOW IT WON'T RETREAT, BUT... I THINK IT'LL ATTACK THE PIG, EAT, AND THEN ATTACK THE MAN.
WRONG, CRESPI. R-O-N-G, WRONG.

HRUSK

SKRIEEEEE

AS YOU SAW, IT DIDN'T HESITATE. IT WILL STARVE TO DEATH BEFORE IT WILL NEGLECT AN OPPORTUNITY TO ATTACK AN ENEMY.

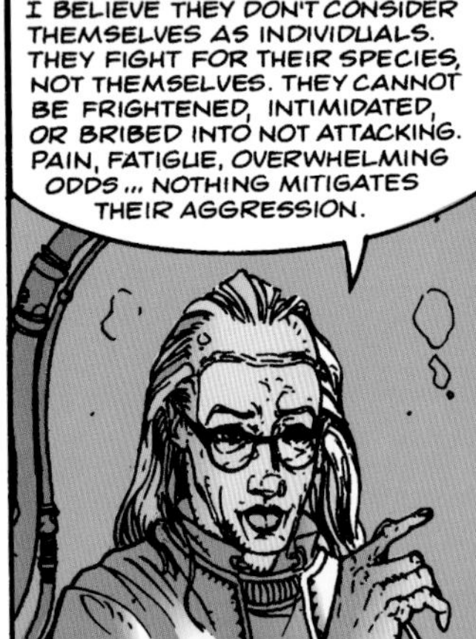
I BELIEVE THEY DON'T CONSIDER THEMSELVES AS INDIVIDUALS. THEY FIGHT FOR THEIR SPECIES, NOT THEMSELVES. THEY CANNOT BE FRIGHTENED, INTIMIDATED, OR BRIBED INTO NOT ATTACKING. PAIN, FATIGUE, OVERWHELMING ODDS... NOTHING MITIGATES THEIR AGGRESSION.

AS YOU CAN SEE, IT'S UP AND AT 'EM AGAIN.

AND IN A MINUTE IT WILL HAVE TO MAKE ANOTHER CHOICE.

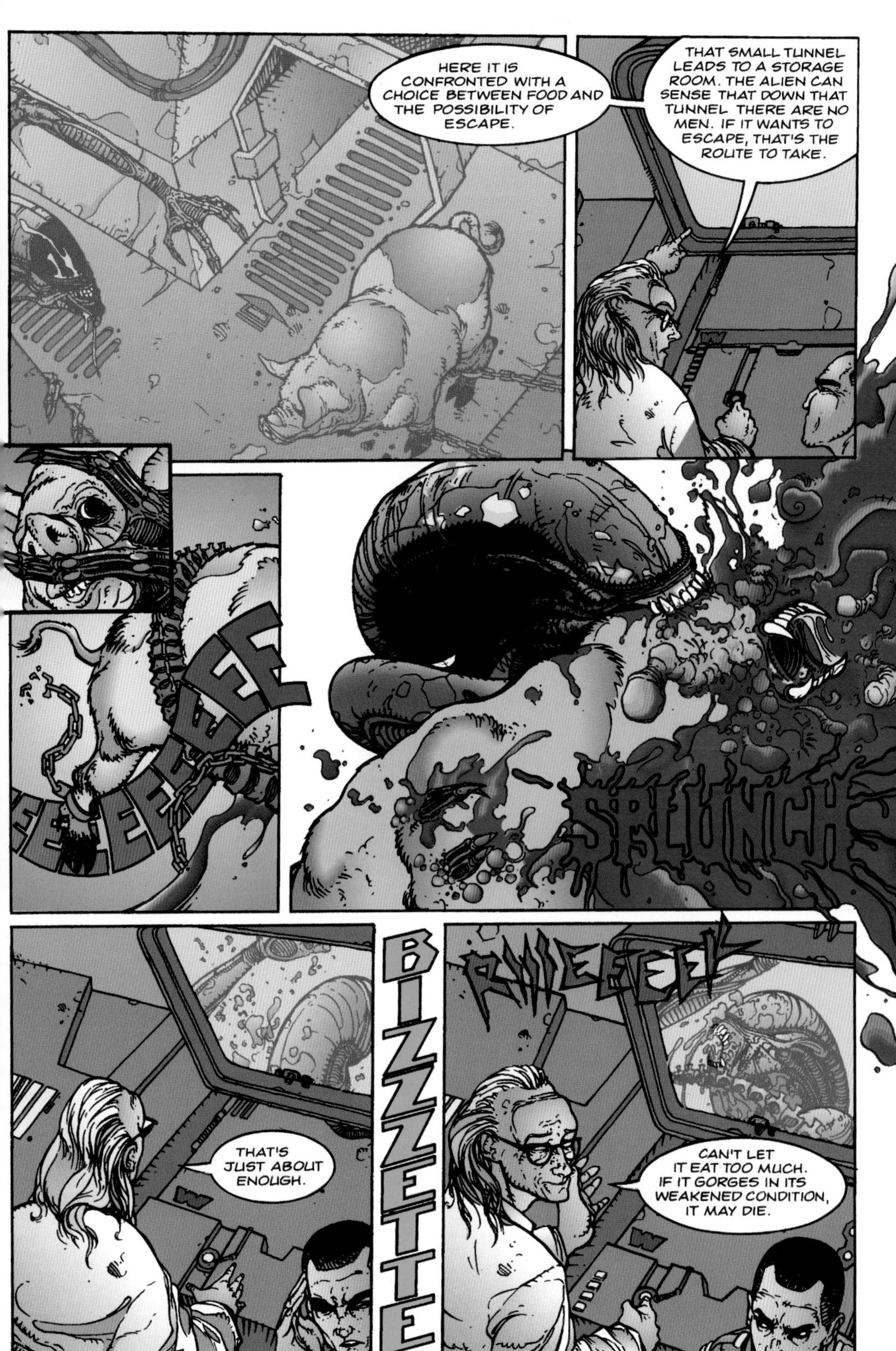
HERE IT IS CONFRONTED WITH A CHOICE BETWEEN FOOD AND THE POSSIBILITY OF ESCAPE.
THAT SMALL TUNNEL LEADS TO A STORAGE ROOM. THE ALIEN CAN SENSE THAT DOWN THAT TUNNEL THERE ARE NO MEN. IF IT WANTS TO ESCAPE, THAT'S THE ROUTE TO TAKE.
SPLUNCH
BIZZETTE
RIIEEEE!
THAT'S JUST ABOUT ENOUGH.
CAN'T LET IT EAT TOO MUCH. IF IT GORGES IN ITS WEAKENED CONDITION, IT MAY DIE.

I'M SURE YOU NOTICED THAT IT DIDN'T JUST KILL THAT PIG. IT PRACTICALLY SWAM IN IT. FEARFUL PREY SEEMS TO ATTRACT ALIENS AND STIMULATE THEM TO MAKE ESPECIALLY MESSY KILLS.

I DON'T THINK IT'S A FORM OF PLAY, EXACTLY, BUT THEY DO SEEM TO ENJOY IT.

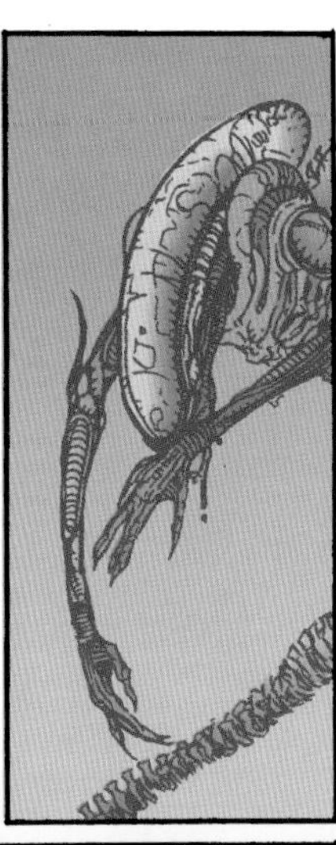

CARE TO GUESS WHICH ONE IT'LL ATTACK?
UH... THE ARMED MAN?

BIZZZISSST
HSSSS
HRRRSSSSK
HAH! GOOD CALL, CRESPI! AN ALIEN WILL ALWAYS ATTACK A PERCEIVED THREAT.

OUT OF THE HUNDREDS OF SIMILAR TESTS I'VE RUN ON DOZENS OF ALIENS, THERE HAS NEVER BEEN A SINGLE DEVIATION FROM THIS RULE.

HUNDREDS OF TESTS? DOZENS OF ALIENS? WHAT YOU'RE TELLING ME IS TANTAMOUNT TO A CONFESSION, CHURCH.

BUT LET'S OVERLOOK THAT FOR THE TIME BEING. YOU'VE DETERMINED SOME EXTREMELY SIMPLE BEHAVIOR PATTERNS. WHAT IS THE POINT OF SO MUCH REPEAT EXPERI-MENTATION?

IT'S NOT REPETITIOUS. EACH TIME THE MAZE IS SET UP, NEW SEN-SORY EQUIPMENT IS BUILT INTO IT. I'M COMPILING A DATA OVER-VIEW THAT WILL SET A NEW STANDARD OF BIOANALYSIS.
NOW YOU'LL SEE SOMETHING INTEREST-ING.

NEITHER MAN IS ARMED, BUT THE ONE IN THE BACK IS FULL OF *FITR*, A TELEPATHINE THAT INDUCES A SENSE OF IN-VULNERABILITY AND INCREASED MENTAL STRENGTH.

THE OTHER MAN IS COLD SOBER AND, AS YOU CAN SEE, SCARED WHIZLESS.

AIEYAAAAAH!

THERE, CRESPI! DID YOU SEE THAT!?
I'M NOT SURE WHAT I SAW. THE ALIEN STARTED TO ATTACK BUT THEN ACTED AS IF IT CHANGED ITS MIND.

NOT QUITE. FIRST, IT WENT FOR THE SCARED MAN. WHAT CAUSED IT TO PAUSE WAS THE WILL OF THE DRUGGED MAN.

ALIENS COMMUNICATE WITH EACH OTHER TELEPATHICALLY. THEY CAN SENSE FEAR IN OTHER ANIMALS. MY WORKING HYPOTHESIS IS THAT THEY CAN PSYCHICALLY "SEE" THE MINDS OF MEN, BUT CANNOT UNDERSTAND THEM.
I SUPPOSE THAT'S PLAUSIBLE, BUT--
BUT WHAT? YOU JUST SAW THAT ALIEN WAVER DURING AN ATTACK. HAVE YOU EVER HEARD OF SUCH A THING BEFORE? NO, YOU HAVEN'T. BUT THAT MAN UNDER THE INFLUENCE OF *FITR* WAS WILLING THE ALIEN TO STOP ITS ATTACK ... AND IT DID!

THIS AND PREVIOUS EXPERIMENTS INDICATE THAT A WEAKENED ALIEN CAN HAVE ITS ACTIONS INFLUENCED BY A HUMAN MIND IN AN EXALTED STATE.
IF WHAT YOU'RE SAYING IS TRUE ... THE IMPLICATIONS--
IF IT'S TRUE, I'LL PROVE IT. THIS RESEARCH HAS JUST BEGUN. SYNTHETIC E WAVES! ALIENS REDUCED TO FAWNING PUPPIES AT THE TOUCH OF A PAD! ENTIRE HIVES TURNED TO PETTING ZOOS!
A BIT TOO ESOTERIC FOR TRADITIONAL VENUES OF RESEARCH, EH? RISKY, MESSY, INCONCLUSIVE, POSSIBLY IMMORAL. PROFOUND POTENTIAL FOR MISUSE... A PEARL BEYOND PRICE. SECRETS COUNTERMANDING SECRETS. OFFICIAL SMOKESCREENS...
...TOP INVESTIGATIVE MEN SENT TO SEE HOW MUCH CAN BE FOUND OUT.
WHAT ARE YOU SAYING?
WHY DON'T WE HAVE YOU CODED INTO THE BIOSCAN LOCK NOW?
HOW MANY CREW MEMBERS HAVE DIED DURING THE COURSE OF YOUR RESEARCH?
IT DEPENDS ON WHO YOU ASK.
I'M ASKING YOU.
NONE.

EXCUSE ME, COLONEL DOCTOR CHURCH— WAS THE SPECIMEN IN KENNEL 4 TRANSFERRED?
TRANSFERRED? NO.

SOMETHING'S WRONG, THEN, SIR— THE DOOR TO KENNEL 4 IS OPEN AND THE ALIEN IS GONE.
WHAT?!

WILLIAMS, SECURE THE FLOOR, THEN GET TO THE SYSTEMS MONITORS. BRIGGS, INFORM ADMIRAL THAVES. WEBSTER, GET ME A HEAD COUNT.
YES, SIR!

SECURE THIS DOOR. GET REINFORCEMENTS AND COVER THE LAB PERIMETER!
YESSIR!

THE ALIENS ARE ALL WEARING TRACKING DEVICES, SO IT'S JUST A MATTER OF...
COLONEL DOCTOR CHURCH, ALL PERSONNEL ARE ACCOUNTED FOR EXCEPT LIEUTENANT MORTENSON.
GET MORTENSON ON CAMERA! I'LL FIND THE ALIEN.

THERE ARE THE KENNELED ALIENS...
...AND THERE'S MORTENSON. WHAT THE DEVIL IS HE DOING?
O, WHERE, O, WHERE HAS MY LITTLE DOG--
THERE! IN THAT BREAKER ROOM!
SHALL I PUT MORTENSON ON COM, SIR?
LET ME DO IT. THAT ALIEN IS ONLY TWENTY YARDS AWAY FROM HIM. IF MORTENSON PANICS, THAT THING WILL BE ON HIM LIKE A DOWAGER ON A PATTY MELT.
MORTENSON, THIS IS COLONEL DOCTOR CHURCH.
HUH?!
YES, SIR, COLONEL DOCTOR CHURCH.
I WANT YOU TO GO DIRECTLY TO THE COMPRESSOR ROOM IN SJ 12.
RIGHT AWAY, SIR?
YES, IMMEDIATELY. I WANT YOU THERE IN SIX SECONDS.
WHAT IS THAT NITWIT DOING FUTZING AROUND WITH THOSE SUITS?
AU
SJ 12
I'M HERE, SIR. DO YOU COPY?
BIG AND BOLD, MORTENSON. SHUT THE DOOR BEHIND YOU AND LOCK IT, PLEASE.
YES, SIR. ANYTHING ELSE?
YES. GIVE THANKS. YOU JUST HAD A CLOSE SQUEAK.

WHAT'S THE PROBLEM, SIR?
THIS IS ADMIRAL THAVES. WHAT THE *HELL* WERE YOU DOING WITH THOSE DE-CON SUITS?
I WAS CHANGING THE FILTERS, SIR.
ON WHOSE AUTHORITY?
STATION'S ORDERS, SIR. IS THERE A PROBLEM?
MY GOD!
MORTENSON! GET OUT OF THERE!
BUT, SIR, I WAS JUST--
YAAAAAH!
HAWKINS. YOU AND STOCKDALE, SUIT UP AND SUBDUE THAT CREATURE.
YES, SIR!
WHAT WAS THAT MAN DOING DOWN THERE IN THE FIRST PLACE? STATION'S ORDERS, MY ASS!
SIR, IF I MAY RESPECTFULLY SUBMIT...

...WHATEVER HE WAS DOING THERE IS NOW A MATTER OF SECONDARY IMPORTANCE.

CHURCH, I EXPECT THE RESULTS OF A COMPREHENSIVE INVESTIGATION IN MY HANDS IN TEN HOURS.

YES, SIR.

BLACKMAN, YOU AND... UH, WHO ARE YOU?
SHARON MCGUINNESS, TFC, SIR.

MCGUINNESS... BLACKMAN, YOU AND MCGUINNESS CONFIRM THAT THE ALIEN HAS BEEN RE-CONFINED, AND THEN I WANT YOU TO CORDON OFF SECTOR SJ AND BEGIN A SURFACE ANALYSIS.

WILLIAMS, CLEAN AND CLOSE THE LAB. I WANT LIVE GUARDS AT THE KENNEL.
YES, SIR.

CRESPI, I'LL MEET YOU IN THE LAB IN TWELVE HOURS.
CERTAINLY. I'LL BE IN MY QUARTERS.

ZEEEEN
YES?
IT'S LIEUTENANT MCGUINNESS, SIR.
COME IN, MCGUINNESS.

MAY I SIT DOWN, SIR?
YES, OF COURSE.

I THOUGHT YOU'D STILL BE AT THE ACCIDENT SITE.
WE DID SOME PRELIM AND SPECIFICATION, AND NOW THE SWEEPS ARE DOWN THERE.
FIND ANYTHING?
THE TRACKING DEVICE ON THE ESCAPED ALIEN HAD BEEN CUTOFF. CUT, AS WITH A BLADE. IT WAS IN THE BREAKER ROOM. NO ALIEN RESIDUE.
OH, BOY.
IN THE GENERATOR ROOM WE FOUND A SUBSTANCE SMEARED ON THE PIPES WHERE THE ALIEN WAS HIDING. SMELLED LIKE PHEROMONE.
I DON'T THINK I WANT TO HEAR THIS.
IT GETS WORSE. MORTENSON WAS THERE CHANGING THE DE-CON SUIT FILTERS ON STATION'S ORDERS, ALL RIGHT. THE KENNEL DOOR LOCK WAS OPENED BY THE STATION TOO.
YOU'RE SAYING THIS WAS A DELIBERATE KILLING?
IT SURE LOOKS THAT WAY.
YOU'RE A CLASS THREE SYSTEMS TECH. CAN YOU UNSCRAMBLE THE STATION CODE AND TRACE THAT ORDER ON THE MAINLINE?
NOT WITHOUT AUTHORIZA-TION.
YOU HAVE IT. SUB-ROSA, MCGUINNESS. DON'T GET CAUGHT. REPORT ONLY TO ME. DO YOU UNDERSTAND?
YES, SIR.
I WANT THIS TO BE OUR LITTLE SECRET.

I, UH, CAN'T SAY I KNEW MORTENSON WELL, OR THAT I REALLY WANTED TO. I THINK MOST ANYONE WOULD AGREE THAT WE WERE VERY UNLIKE ONE ANOTHER.

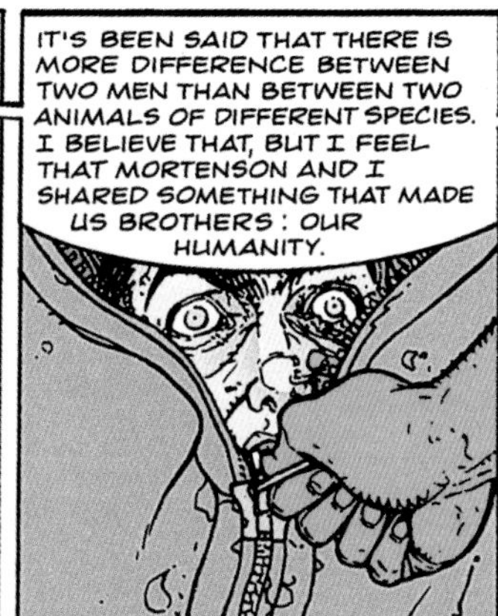
IT'S BEEN SAID THAT THERE IS MORE DIFFERENCE BETWEEN TWO MEN THAN BETWEEN TWO ANIMALS OF DIFFERENT SPECIES. I BELIEVE THAT, BUT I FEEL THAT MORTENSON AND I SHARED SOMETHING THAT MADE US BROTHERS : OUR HUMANITY.

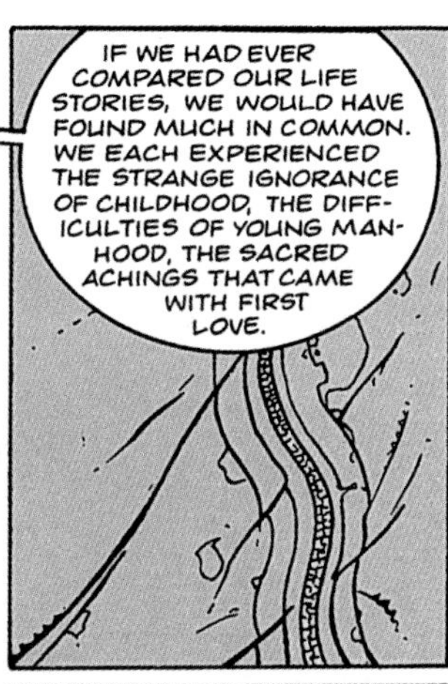
IF WE HAD EVER COMPARED OUR LIFE STORIES, WE WOULD HAVE FOUND MUCH IN COMMON. WE EACH EXPERIENCED THE STRANGE IGNORANCE OF CHILDHOOD, THE DIFF-ICULTIES OF YOUNG MAN-HOOD, THE SACRED ACHINGS THAT CAME WITH FIRST LOVE.

709
NOW EVERYTHING THAT WAS A MAN IN HIM IS AT AN END. NO MORE SATISFACTION FOR HIM, NO MORE FRUSTRATION, NO MORE JOY, NO MORE FEAR.
ED

WE CONSIGN HIS REMAINS TO THE VOID. THERE IS NOTHING MORE TO BE SAID. GOOD-BYE, MORTENSON.

TAKE THE BODY TO THE DISCHARGE BAY.
HOLD ON JUST A MINUTE, COLONEL DOCTOR CHURCH.
MORTENSON SIGNED AN ORGAN DONOR RELEASE. YOU MIGHT WANT TO KEEP THE BODY FOR... RESEARCH, SPARE RETINAS...

THAT'S UNNECESSARY, ADMIRAL THAVES. PROTOCOL DICTATES --
DON'T YOU DARE RECITE THE DAMN RULE BOOK TO ME!

I BEG YOUR PARDON, SIR.
IT'S YOUR CALL, CHURCH. I JUST THOUGHT THE DUMB DEAD BASTARD MIGHT BE OF SOME USE. GOD KNOWS IT'S ABOUT TIME HE WAS.
I RESPECTFULLY SUBMIT THAT BURIAL IN SPACE WITH MILITARY HONORS IS APPROPRIATE.
FINE, FINE. SHOOT HIS ASS FULL OF DIAMONDS WHILE YOU'RE AT IT.
MILITARY HONORS ... WHAT A LOAD OF CRAP!
BRING HIM TO THE DISCHARGE TUBE. I'LL JETTISON HIM MYSELF.
YES, SIR.
YOU'VE HAD A COUPLE OF FULL SHIFTS, CRESPI. WHY DON'T YOU GO HAVE YOURSELF SOME R AND R?
THANKS. I THINK I'LL HIT THE GYM.
OH, COLONEL DOCTOR CRESPI, BEFORE YOU GO, I WONDER IF I COULD HAVE A WORD WITH YOU ... ABOUT THE TRUNK LINE.
CERTAINLY, MCGUINNESS.

WE CAN TALK IN PRIVATE OVER THERE.
I'VE FOUND OUT SOME DISTURBING THINGS, SIR, BUT BEFORE I TELL YOU, I HAVE TO COME CLEAN.
ON THE TRANSPORT SHIP, YOU ASKED WHY I VOLUNTEERED FOR DUTY ON THE INNOMINATA. I DIDN'T TELL YOU, BUT THERE IS A REASON.
THE MAN YOU WERE SENT HERE TO REPLACE, DAVID LENNOX, WAS MY ... FIANCE, I GUESS YOU COULD SAY. HE HAD BEEN CHURCH'S RESEARCH PARTNER FOR SIX YEARS WHEN WE MET.
DAVID TRIED REPEATEDLY TO HAVE HIMSELF TRANSFERRED, BUT COULD NEVER GET THE ORDERS. SOMETHING WAS HAPPENING HERE.
HE TRIED TO SEND ME A CODED MESSAGE BUT IT ARRIVED SCRAMBLED. THEN I WAS TOLD THAT HE HAD DIED OF A HEART ATTACK ... ON BOARD THE INNOMINATA.
SHORTLY AFTER, MY APARTMENT WAS BURGLARIZED. EVERYTHING HE'D EVER SENT TO ME WAS TAKEN. EVERYTHING, EVEN LOVE LETTERS. I WANT TO ... NO, I NEED TO KNOW WHAT HAPPENED HERE.
I'M CERTAIN DAVID DIDN'T DIE OF A HEART ATTACK.

LENNOX WAS STUPID TO SEND YOU CODED INFORMATION. AND YOU'RE SUPREMELY STUPID TO BE HERE ON YOUR OWN LITTLE FACT-FINDING MISSION.
I'VE DONE THE LITTLE FACT-FINDING FOR YOU, DON'T FORGET. ARE YOU INTERESTED IN WHAT I'VE FOUND OUT?
EASY, NOW. GO ON.
WELL, FIRST OF ALL, I COULDN'T TRACE THE STATION ORDER THAT RELEASED THE ALIEN THAT KILLED MORTENSON. THERE'S A CODED MASTER RECORD, OF COURSE. I'M TRYING TO CRACK IT, BUT I DON'T KNOW IF I CAN. IT'S REAL DIRTY.
SECOND, I FOUND THAT ALL THE CREW MEMBER MEDICAL RECORDS HAVE BEEN ALTERED. NO TELLING WHY 'TIL I BUST THAT CODE.
DO YOU HAVE A NUMBER FOR CREW MEMBER FATALITIES?
HOLD ON TO YOUR HAT. THIRTY-FOUR DEATHS IN THE LAST THREE YEARS.
IMPOSSIBLE!
DON'T I JUST WISH.
ELEVEN DEATHS A YEAR? AND ONLY ONE SHUTTLE HERE AND BACK PER YEAR? IT DOESN'T ADD UP! WHERE ARE REPLACEMENTS COMING FROM?
PERHAPS THEY'RE COMING IN ON THE THREE UNSCHEDULED SHUTTLES THAT HAVE BEEN ARRIVING HERE EACH YEAR FOR THE PAST FIVE YEARS.
WHAT?!
IT'S ALL IN THE STATION MAINLINE. WHATEVER'S GOING ON HERE HAS SUPPORT FROM HIGH UP.
I... I CAN'T BELIEVE IT!

SON OF A --!
DO YOU WANT ME TO CONTINUE, IN MY SUPREMELY STUPID WAY, TO TRY TO GET INTO THE CODED MASTER RECORD, SIR?
I APOLOGIZE FOR THAT. YES, BY ALL MEANS CONTINUE.
THANK YOU, SIR.
I DON'T NEED TO TELL YOU TO BE DAMN CAREFUL WHEN YOU'RE DIGGING INTO THE STATION SYSTEM. BUT IF YOU'RE CAUGHT, I'LL BACK YOU.
THAT'S GOOD TO KNOW-- OH!
MORTENSON.
DON'T GET CAUGHT, MCGUINNESS.
CENTRAL? THIS IS CRESPI. I'LL BE IN THE GYM FOR THE NEXT TWO HOURS.
VERY GOOD, SIR.
URNT
...EACH PLANT PRODUCES PER PELOPSIAN YEAR A SINGLE FRUIT UP TO EIGHT METERS IN DIAMETER. THE FLESH OF THIS FRUIT YIELDS A BRIGHT YELLOW OIL WHICH...

EEEEEEEEEEEEEEEEE
WHAT NOW?!
EEE
OH MY GOD!
RUN! RUN!
AAAGH!
WHAT THE FONG...?
GOOD MORNING, NEIGHBORS!
GET IT AWAY FROM ME! OH GOD, KEEP IT BACK!
OH, DON'T BE AFRAID OF TRIXIE, MA'AM. HE WON'T BITE!
352

SHAME ON YOU FOR SCARING THAT NICE LADY, TRIXIE! BAD DOGGIE!
BIZZZZZT
COME ALONG, TAFFY. DON'T STOP AT EVERY HYDRANT.
BIZZZZLE
HRRR
CHURCH, WHAT IN THE HOLY HELL ARE YOU DOING?!
JUST TAKING LITTLE TOODLES FOR A WALK.
A... A WALK?! I... I SHOULD ARREST YOU ON THE SPOT!
ARREST ME? WHAT FOR?
WHAT FOR? HOW ABOUT IMPROPER HANDLING OF CONTRABAND LIFE FORMS, RECKLESS ENDANGERMENT, FELONY JEOPARDIZATION, BIO-TERRORISM, CONDUCT UNBECOMING TO AN OFFICER, AND CRIMINAL INSANITY?!
YOU MEAN NO ONE APPRECIATED MY DEMONSTRATION?
I... I WAS MERELY TRYING TO MAKE A POINT.
WHAT IN THE NAME OF BUDDHA COULD *THAT* BE?

THAT I HAVE THESE CREATURES UNDER MY COMPLETE CONTROL. THEY OFFER NO THREAT.
TELL THAT TO MORTENSON.
MORTENSON WAS A FOOL WHO GOT HIMSELF KILLED BY BEING WHERE HE HAD NO BUSINESS BEING. BLACKMAN, PREPARE THE HOLDING CELL.
YESSIR.

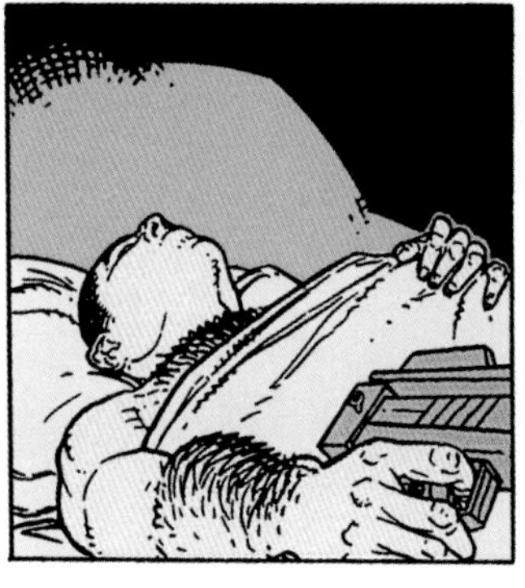

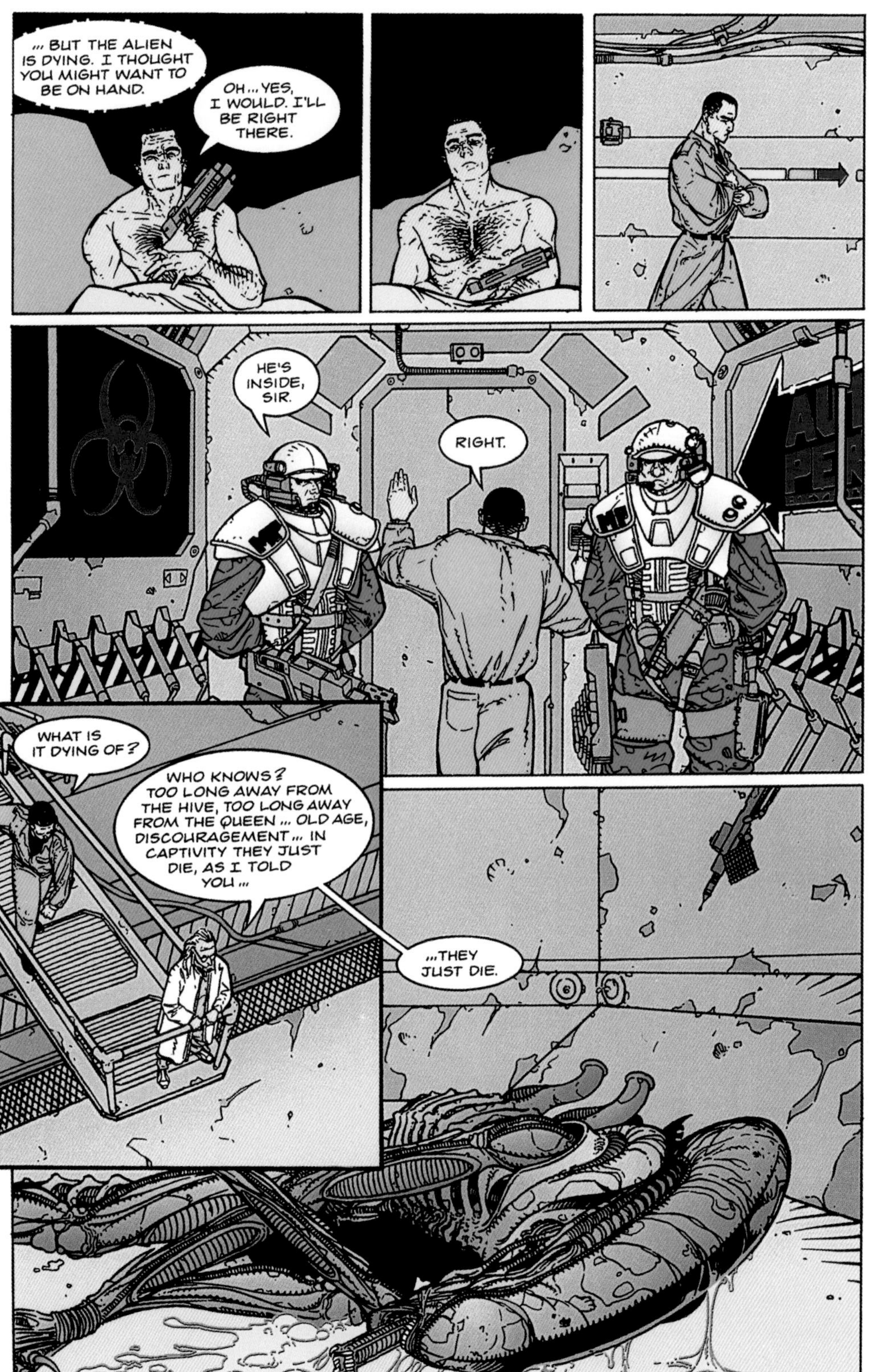

... BUT THE ALIEN IS DYING. I THOUGHT YOU MIGHT WANT TO BE ON HAND.
OH ... YES, I WOULD. I'LL BE RIGHT THERE.
HE'S INSIDE, SIR.
RIGHT.
WHAT IS IT DYING OF?
WHO KNOWS? TOO LONG AWAY FROM THE HIVE, TOO LONG AWAY FROM THE QUEEN ... OLD AGE, DISCOURAGEMENT ... IN CAPTIVITY THEY JUST DIE, AS I TOLD YOU ...
... THEY JUST DIE.

LOOK AT IT, CRESPI. DOES YOUR HEART KNOW THIS MONSTER? DO YOU SEE THE DESPERATE FEAR OF YOUR FATHERS IN ITS BLIND, DESTROYER'S HEAD?
WHEN MEN FIRST LOOKED INTO THE OUTER VOID, INTO SPACE, THEY LOOKED INTO THE SOUL OF THIS SOULLESS CREATURE. WHEN MEN KILL EACH OTHER, AND HURT THEIR CHILDREN, AND CLOSE THEIR EYES SO THAT GOOD WILL NOT DISTRACT THEM, THEY ARE WORSHIPPING THAT CREATURE.
IN THEIR HEARTS, ALL MEN WOULD LIKE TO BE LIKE THIS ONE : HIDEOUSLY STRONG, UNCHAINED BY CONSCIENCE, CHARGED BY THE BLACK HEART OF THE COSMOS TO GO FORTH AND ANNIHILATE.
CRESPI
GOOD-BYE, YOU DARK THING.
EEEEEEEEEEEEEEE
IT'S A FLATLINER, SIR.
THANK YOU, STOCKDALE. HAVE THE BODY BROUGHT TO B LAB, PLEASE.
NOW WHAT?
NOW COMES THE DISSECTION.

ITS BODY ACIDS HAVE BEEN DRAINED AND REPLACED WITH NEUTRALIZING AGENT. STILL, WE NEVER KNOW WHAT WE MIGHT RUN INTO. A LITTLE POCKET OF HOT JUICE, A SPURTING GLAND.
I HOPE THIS PROTECTIVE GEAR ISN'T TOO CUMBERSOME, CRESPI.
ON THE CONTRARY, IT'S AMAZINGLY UN-CONFINING. YOUR OWN DESIGN?
YES. THE WELL-KNOWN MOTHER OF INVENTION WAS MY MUSE. STOCKDALE, HAND ME THE BRETZ SAW, PLEASE.
YESSIR.
EVER SEEN INSIDE ONE OF THESE, CRESPI?
ONLY FRESHLY BLASTED.
HOW VERY GUNG HO OF YOU.
THIS ORGAN IS WHAT INTERESTS ME MOST.
WHAT IS IT?

THE SURFACE IS LINED WITH COMPOUND CELLS OF FULLERITE-ENCASED HURLANTIUM. THE INTERNAL STRUCTURE IS SOLID NEURONS IN TWO BINARY FANS. VERY, VERY DENSE.
MMM HMM.
I THINK IT'S THE ALIEN PSYCHIC RECEIVER. THE FULLERITE AND HURLANTIUM PICK UP E-WAVES AND THE BINARY FANS CREATE INTERFERENCE PATTERNS FROM ELECTRO-MAGNETIC FIELDS.
SO IT WOULD NOT ONLY RECEIVE BRAINWAVES BUT ENABLE THE ALIEN TO ASSESS AN-OTHER ANIMAL'S PHYSICAL CHARACTERISTICS BY SEEING ITS SUBTLE BODY.
EXACTLY! THAT'S WHY STRONG ELECTROMAGNETIC FIELDS REALLY AFFECT ALIENS ... GIVES 'EM THE EQUIVALENT OF AN ICE-CREAM HEAD-ACHE.
I'LL REMEMBER THAT.
NOW, YOU CAN SEE THAT THIS THING HAS WITHERED. IN HEALTHY SPECIMENS IT'S MORE BULBOUS, FILLS THE CAVITY TIGHTLY. BUT IN A LANGUISHING CAPTIVE, IT ATROPHIES.
WHICH COULD EXPLAIN WHY THE CREWMAN UNDER THE INFLUENCE OF THE TELE-PATHINE WAS ABLE TO AFFECT THE ALIEN'S BEHAVIOR!
EXACTLY.
AND THIS ... RECEIVER IS WHERE THE CREW-MAN TUNED IN. THAT IS, IF YOUR SURMISAL IS CORRECT--
WAIT! FULLERITE AND HURLANTIUM CAN BE SYNTHESIZED!
IT SEEMS SO OBVIOUS, DOESN'T IT?

HAVE YOU TRIED TO RE-CONSTRUCT IT IN A COLD TANK? OR IN A COMPUTER MODEL?
NOT YET. THE MOLECULAR STRUCTURE IS TOO COMPLICATED TO BE DUPLICATED THROUGH TRADITIONAL GEL-IDIFICATION.
HOW ABOUT A COMPUTER MODEL?
SO FAR I DON'T HAVE SUFFICIENT STRUCTURAL DATA.
WELL, LET'S GET THAT MISSING DATA AND BUILD ONE OF THESE THINGS!
YOU JUST SAID "LET'S," CRESPI. DOES THAT MEAN YOU NO LONGER CONSIDER THIS AN ILLEGAL OPERATION?
IT MEANS I CONSIDER THIS RESEARCH TOO IMPORTANT NOT TO RECEIVE FULL ATTENTION.
OF COURSE, THIS PSYCHIC SENSE ORGAN IS ONLY PART OF THE PICTURE. THIS STRUCTURE HERE IS VERY LIKE A CEREBELLUM, BUT I DON'T THINK IT IS.
THERE IS AN ENORMOUSLY COMPLEX NEUROLOGICAL STRUCTURE IN THE DORSAL REGION THAT I SUSPECT IS WHAT THE ALIEN HAS INSTEAD OF A BRAIN.
MY GOD! WELL, LET'S SEE IT.
THIS IS AN ARTICULATION. WE HAVE TO CUT AROUND IT. THOSE WHITE SACS FORM A RECEPTOR BODY. WE WANT TO REMOVE IT INTACT.
YOU MAY AS WELL PREPARE YOURSELF FOR THE LONG HAUL, CRESPI. THIS MAY TAKE HOURS.
NO PROBLEM, BOYS. I'LL WAIT.

IS COLONEL DOCTOR CHURCH IN THERE?
YES, SIR. HE AND COLONEL DOCTOR CRESPI HAVE BEEN WORKING TOGETHER FOR THE PAST SIX HOURS.
WORKING TOGETHER, YOU SAY? WELL, THAT'S FINE!
IF WE CAN USE ONE MORE SPECIMEN I CAN GET SIXTEEN DIFFERENT MODELS ON RE-QUAD, NO PROBLEM.
WE'LL START ON THE NEXT SHIFT IF YOU LIKE.
EXCELLENT, EXCELLENT. THE IMPLICATIONS OF THIS PROJECT ARE... MIND-NUMBINGLY SIGNIFICANT.
I QUITE AGREE, CRESPI, AND IF I MAY SAY SO I THINK IT TAKES A SPECIAL KIND OF SCIENTIST TO APPRECIATE THAT.
WHY DON'T YOU GO GET SOME REST, EH? YOU LOOK ALL IN.
RIGHT, THOUGH I DON'T KNOW IF I'LL BE ABLE TO SLEEP. SEE YOU IN EIGHT HOURS.

COLONEL DOCTOR CRESPI! I NEED TO SPEAK WITH YOU. I'VE FOUND OUT SOMETHING IMPORTANT ABOUT CHURCH.
SO HAVE I, MCGUINNESS.

I'VE JUST SPENT SIX HOURS WATCHING COLONEL DOCTOR CHURCH IN ACTION AND THE MAN IS, TO USE A MUCH-ABUSED TERM, A GENIUS.
CRES

HE HAS OPENED DOORS TO TECHNOLOGICAL INNOVATION THAT BORDERS ON THE MYSTICAL. THE WORK HE IS DOING HERE WILL CHANGE THE FACE OF SCIENCE FOREVER.
BUT--

I REALIZE YOU HAD PERSONAL MOTIVATIONS, BUT CHURCH IS A TOTAL PROFESSIONAL. AS OF THIS MOMENT, YOU WILL DESIST SPYING AROUND. UNDERSTOOD?
SIR, I'VE BEEN PIRATING THE STATION SURVEILLANCE SYSTEM. I'VE FOLLOWED CHURCH'S EVERY MOVE FOR THE PAST EIGHTEEN HOURS. I WATCHED YOU AND HIM DISSECT THE ALIEN.

HE'S TOYING WITH YOU, SIR. THE ALIEN RESEARCH IS ONLY A SMALL PART OF WHAT HE'S DOING HERE. THE STATION RESOURCE REQUIREMENTS DON'T JIBE WITH CONSUMPTION RECORDS.

SOMETHING ON BOARD THE INNOMINATA IS USING ALMOST A THIRD AGAIN AS MUCH POWER AS ALL KNOWN SYSTEMS, INCLUDING THE ALIEN LAB, COMBINED.

CHURCH HAS A HIDDEN OPERATION ON BOARD, SIR. SOMETHING BIG. SOMETHING HE DOESN'T WANT YOU TO FIND. HE'S ENGAGED YOUR INTEREST IN THE ALIEN RESEARCH TO THROW YOU OFF THE TRACK.

THE BASTARD.

MCGUINNESS, YOU'RE A GOOD SOLDIER. DO YOU KNOW WHERE THIS GHOST FACILITY IS?
I THINK SO, SIR. I BELIEVE IT'S LOCATED IN K LAB. IT'S DESIGNATED AS A ZERO-G TEST FACILITY...

... BUT THAT'S WHERE THE THIRTY PERCENT POWER OVERAGE IS GOING. CHURCH HAS HAD THREE DOUBLE-CODE SINGLE-ACCESS LOCK DOORS INSTALLED AND IT'S NOT ON THE STATION MAINLINE AT ALL.

OKAY. YOU'VE CONVINCED ME. HOW DO WE GET IN?
CHURCH HAS A CODE SLATE. IF WE CAN GET THAT, I CAN EXTRACT THE KEY. HE KEEPS IT IN HIS UNITY STATION. ON MY PIRATE MONITOR, I SAW HIM LEAVE IT ON THE CONSOLE.
AND WHERE'S CHURCH NOW?

HE'S ASLEEP. TOOK SOMETHING AND HE'S OUT LIKE A LIGHT.
CAN YOU GET THAT SLATE?

THE BIOSCAN WON'T LET ME INTO CHURCH'S UNITY HOLE. YOU'LL HAVE TO DO IT.
I'LL BE RIGHT BACK. USE MY PRIVATE COM LINE IF ANY-THING COMES UP.

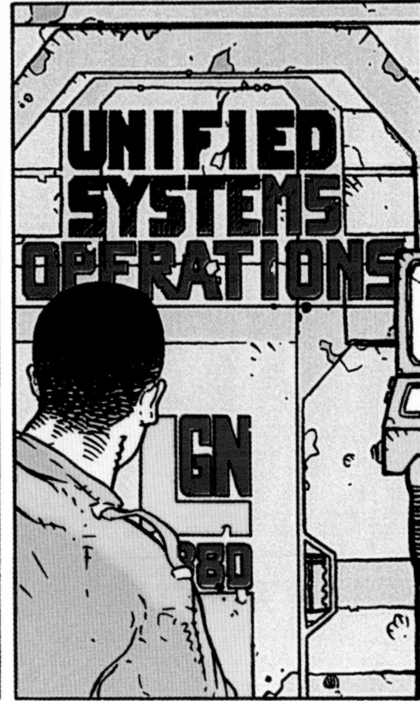
UNIFIED SYSTEMS OPERATIONS

NEEN

NOT AN EXIT

HSSSSSSSSSSSK!
HULP!
CRRRASHE
ARRRULK!
HURRSSSSSSK
YAAAAAH!
SSSSSS
FAAAH!
ZIZZZ
SSSSSSSSK

HRIEEEEENK
GASP!
WARNING
ELECTROMAGNETIC
FIELD
GENERATOR
KEEP AWAY FROM TYPE GM SUB
WEEEEEEK

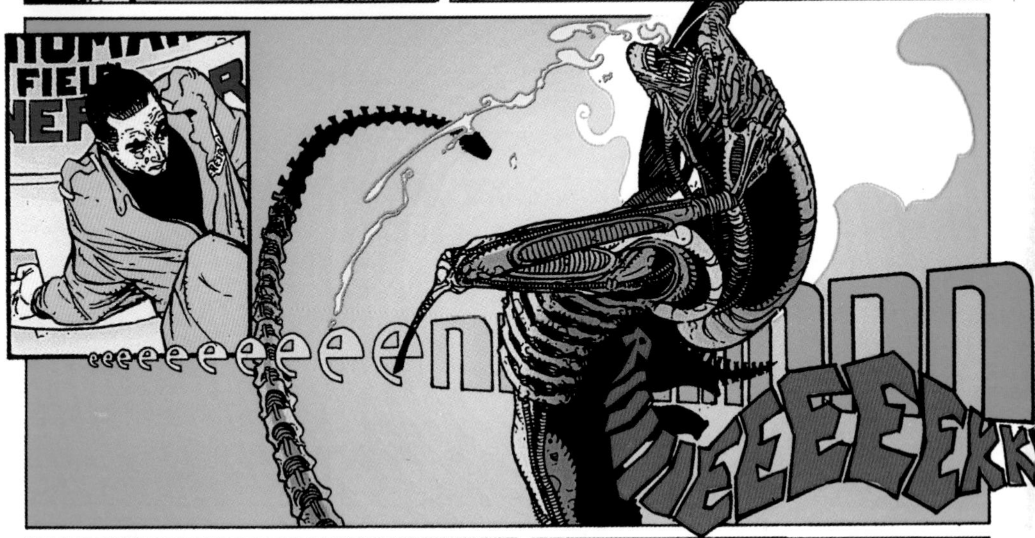
eeeeeeeeeen
WEEEEEKK

FIELD
GENERAT
WHAT TH-
COLONEL DOCTOR
CRESPI!
MY GOD!
ANOTHER ONE
GOT OUT!
TECH

STOCKDALE, WE HAVE AN ALIEN IN THE ACCENTUATOR ROOM NEAR DOC'S UNITY ROOM. IT'S BEEN ELECTRO-MAGGED, BUT YOU BETTER GET A FULL TEAM DOWN HERE IN RIOT GEAR.
IF THAT GENERATOR CONTROL PANEL HADN'T BEEN OPEN... YOU'RE A LUCKY MAN, SIR.

SIR? UH, WHERE ARE YOU GOING?
ELECTROMAGNETIC FIELD GENERATOR
DID YOU GET IT, SIR?
NO! WHAT ARE YOU DOING?
YOU SENT ME DOWN THERE TO GET LUNCHED, DIDN'T YOU? DIDN'T YOU?
STOP IT, YOU'RE HURTING ME!
I'LL HURT YOU ALL RIGHT! I'LL ... I'LL ...
GHACK ... NO ... DIDN'T ... 'TOP ... KILLING ME ...
YOU SET ME UP. YOU WORTHLESS PIECE OF FLESH TRAITOR.
NO ... NO ... GASP ...
I OUGHT TO SHOOT YOU ON THE SPOT.
NO ... IT WAS CHURCH ... I'M SURE ...

DID YOU GET THE SLATE? LET ME HAVE IT ... I'LL PROVE I'M RIGHT.
ONE CHANCE. YOU GET ONE CHANCE TO SHOW ME.
I WILL, I SWEAR I WILL. GIVE IT TO ME.
COME ON ... LET'S GET TO K LAB RIGHT NOW. CHURCH WILL BE NOTIFIED ABOUT THE ATTACK AND HE'LL COME LOOKING FOR US.
CRESPI
THIS IS ABSOLUTELY IMPASSABLE WITHOUT A KEY CODE ...
NCC.
... WHICH IS WHAT I'VE GOT HERE ...
... AND SO ... WE'RE IN!
WHAT IN THE NAME OF EVERY-THING ...
CRESPI
OH, NO ...
CRESPI

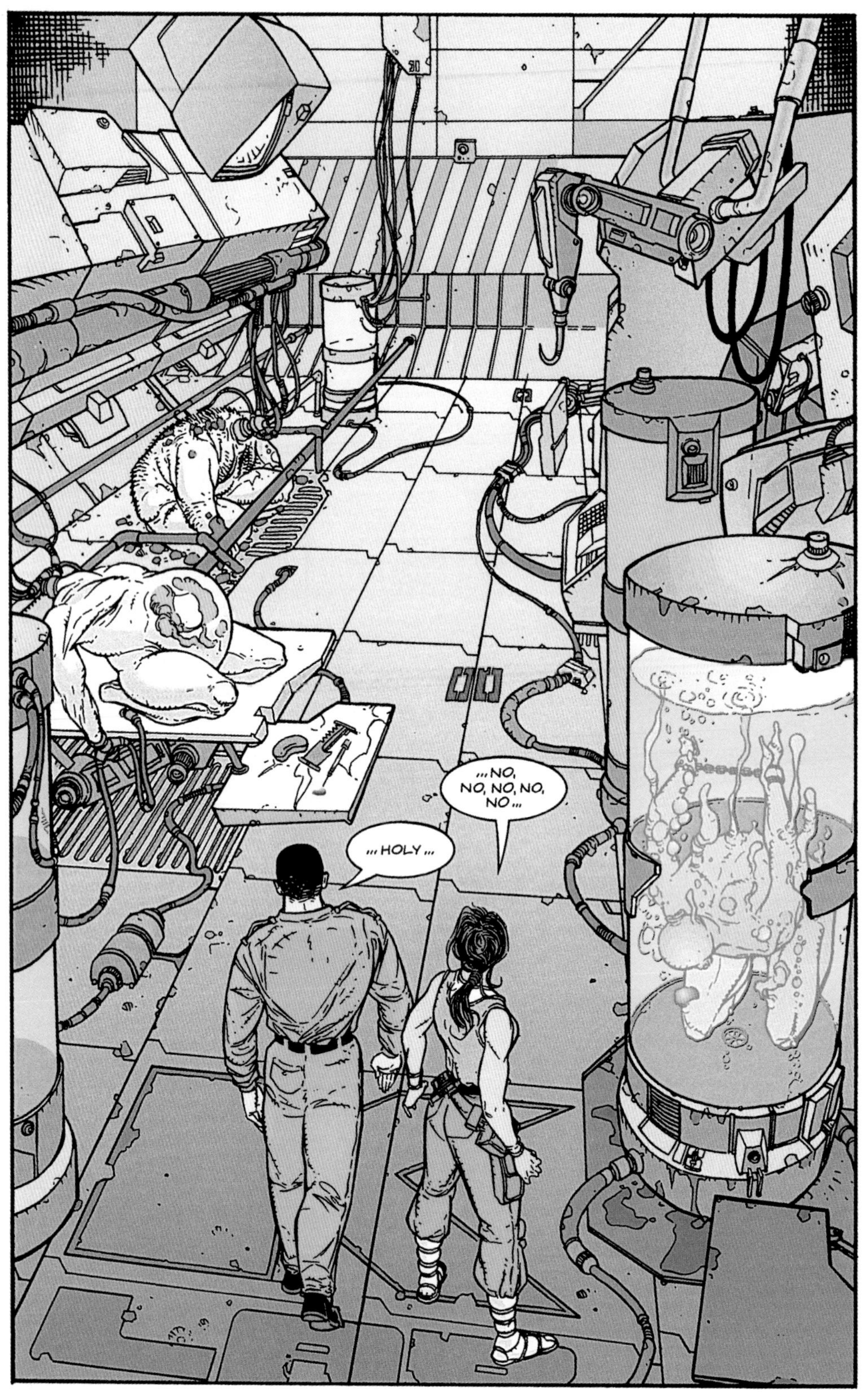
...HOLY...
...NO,
NO, NO, NO,
NO...

I ... I NEVER IMAGINED ... I DIDN'T KNOW A MAN COULD ...
CREST
... WHAT THE DEVIL HAS HE ...
NUH ... NUH ... UUUUHHHH ...
DEAR GOD, IT'S MORTENSON. HE WASN'T JETTISONED AT ALL ...
EEEEEEEEEEEEEE!
12

WHAT?! WHAT IS IT?!
OH NO! OH NO! OH NO NO NO NO NO NO NO NO!
IT'S DAVID!
LEN

HE ... HE'S ALIVE.
OH, DAVID... LOOK WHAT HE'S DONE TO YOU...
OH, YOUR POOR EYES... YOU CAN'T...
HOW COULD HEEEEEEEEEEEEEEEEEEE-EEEEEN--
FOR WHAT IT'S WORTH, HE'S FEELING NO PAIN. QUITE THE CONTRARY.
YAAAAAGH!

I'LL KILL YOU!
NO, YOU WON'T.
THEN I WILL, YOU SACK OF--
AIIEEEEERRRGH!
LET HER GO AND GET DOWN ON THE FLOOR!
GURK!
TELL HER TO BEHAVE, CRESPI.
LET HER GO AND GET DOWN ON THE DAMN FLOOR!
DON'T PRESUME TO GIVE ME ORDERS, CRESPI.
GET ON THE FLOOR! NOW!
THAT'S AN INTERESTING WEAPON...
MAY I SEE IT FOR A MOMENT?
GET DOWN!
NOW--
HMM. PRETTY LITTLE TOY...

WELL-MADE, TOO. KOREAPANESE, ISN'T IT?
YOU'RE ... YOU'RE A SYNTH!

NO, NOT A SYNTH. ASIDE FROM SEVERAL IM-PLANTS, I'M QUITE HUMAN.

YOU FOUND WHAT YOU WERE LOOKING FOR, DIDN'T YOU? ONLY YOU DON'T KNOW WHAT IT IS YOU'VE *FOUND*.
YUH-YUH-YOU KUH-KUH-KUH KILLED...

NO, I DIDN'T KILL HIM. I DIDN'T KILL ANYONE.
YOU CAN'T POSSIBLY BE EXPECTED TO UNDERSTAND WHAT YOU SEE HERE UNLESS YOU KNOW SOMETHING OF MY PERSONAL HISTORY... SO PROMISE ME THAT THERE WILL BE NO MORE OUTBURSTS...

...AND LET ME TELL YOU WHAT HAPPENED TO ME.

THIRTY-TWO YEARS AGO THIS HAPPENED. GOD, IT'S HARD TO BELIEVE. I WAS TWENTY...
JUST TWENTY...

MY PARENTS WERE TERRAFORMERS. I WAS BORN IN SPACE AND NEVER EVEN SAW EARTH UNTIL I WAS SIX. MY EARLY LIFE WAS SPENT ON SHIPS AND GENESIS CAMPS. OUR SHIP WAS THE INCUNABULUM.
INCUNAB
IT WAS AN UNNATURAL LIFE FOR A YOUNG MAN, BUT I DIDN'T MIND.
MY PARENTS AND I WERE CLOSE, AND THEIR CREW WAS LIKE FAMILY.
THE CREW CONSISTED OF THREE MEN, TAYLOR, HEWETT, AND JOHANSON, WHO DID MOST OF THE HEAVY WORK...
...AND JUDITH, A SEX SYNTH WHO KEPT TAYLOR, HEWETT, AND JOHANSON HAPPY. SHE WAS ALSO PROGRAMMED AS A BOTANIST.
QUENTIN AND LOUISE CLARK, BOTH SCIENTISTS, AND THEIR DAUGHTER, REBECCA, HAD JOINED US. WE WERE TRANSPORTING THEM TO RLW 1289.

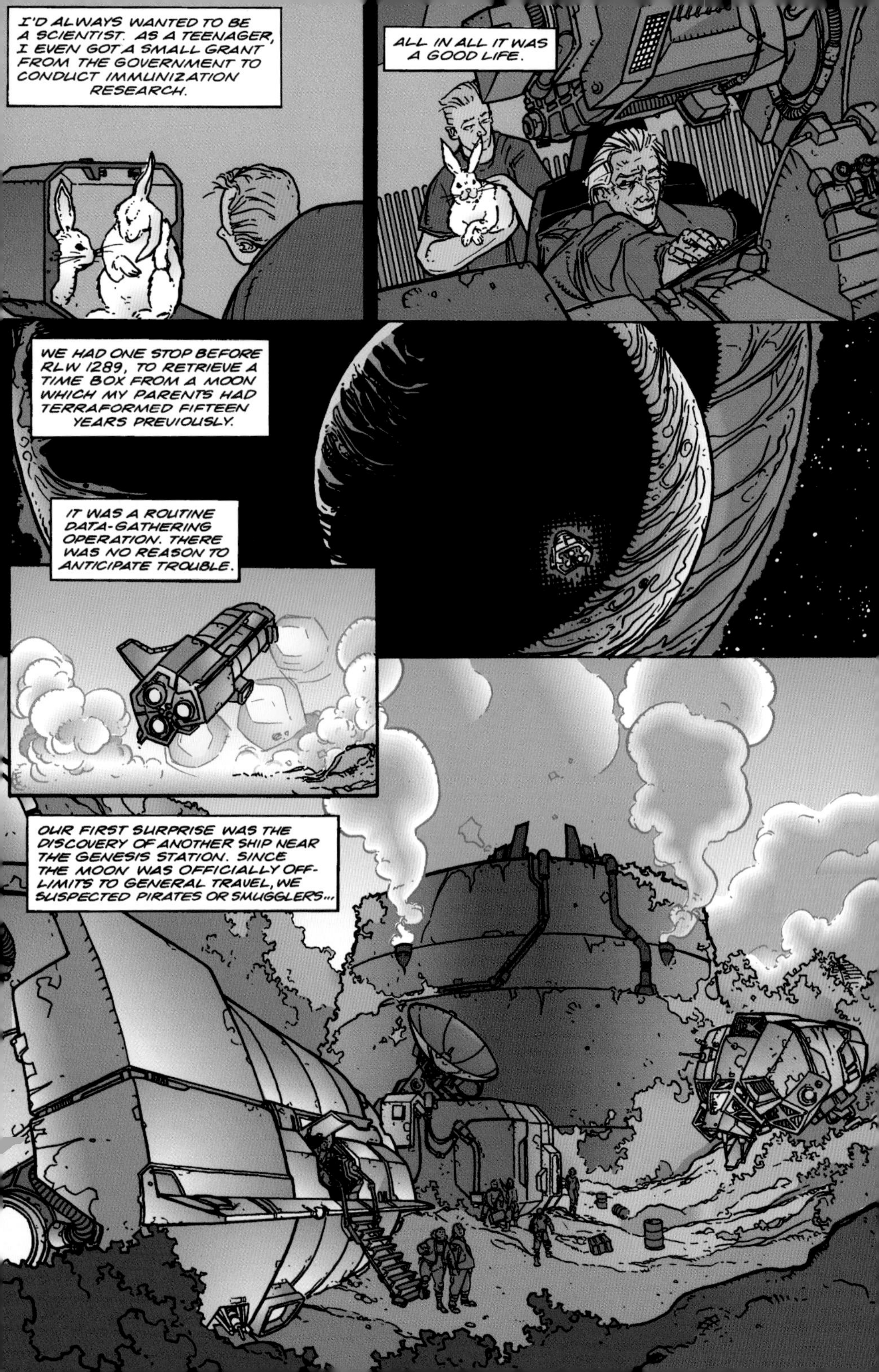
I'D ALWAYS WANTED TO BE A SCIENTIST. AS A TEENAGER, I EVEN GOT A SMALL GRANT FROM THE GOVERNMENT TO CONDUCT IMMUNIZATION RESEARCH.
ALL IN ALL IT WAS A GOOD LIFE.
WE HAD ONE STOP BEFORE RLW 1289, TO RETRIEVE A TIME BOX FROM A MOON WHICH MY PARENTS HAD TERRAFORMED FIFTEEN YEARS PREVIOUSLY.
IT WAS A ROUTINE DATA-GATHERING OPERATION. THERE WAS NO REASON TO ANTICIPATE TROUBLE.
OUR FIRST SURPRISE WAS THE DISCOVERY OF ANOTHER SHIP NEAR THE GENESIS STATION. SINCE THE MOON WAS OFFICIALLY OFF-LIMITS TO GENERAL TRAVEL, WE SUSPECTED PIRATES OR SMUGGLERS...

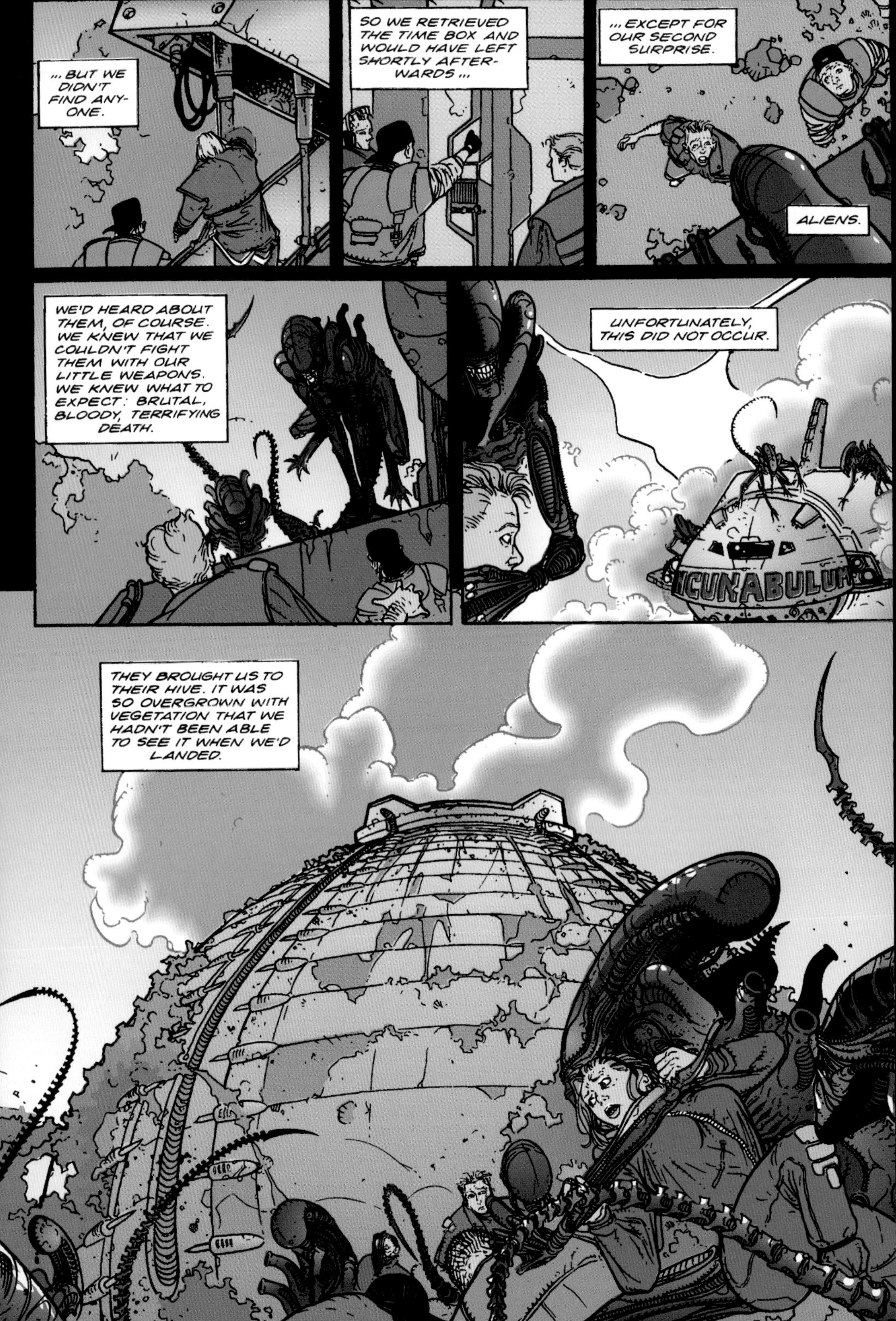
... BUT WE DIDN'T FIND ANY-ONE.
SO WE RETRIEVED THE TIME BOX AND WOULD HAVE LEFT SHORTLY AFTER-WARDS ...
... EXCEPT FOR OUR SECOND SURPRISE.
ALIENS.
WE'D HEARD ABOUT THEM, OF COURSE. WE KNEW THAT WE COULDN'T FIGHT THEM WITH OUR LITTLE WEAPONS. WE KNEW WHAT TO EXPECT: BRUTAL, BLOODY, TERRIFYING DEATH.
UNFORTUNATELY, THIS DID NOT OCCUR.
ICUNABULUM
THEY BROUGHT US TO THEIR HIVE. IT WAS SO OVERGROWN WITH VEGETATION THAT WE HADN'T BEEN ABLE TO SEE IT WHEN WE'D LANDED.

AS WE DREW NEAR THE HIVE, THE STOMACH-TURNING SMELL GREW STRONGER ...
... BUT ONCE INSIDE, IT WAS INTOLERABLE. IT WAS BEYOND STENCH. IT WAS BEYOND FOUL. IT WAS AN INCOMPREHENSIBLY LOATHSOME MIASMA THAT RAPED ONE'S SOUL THROUGH THE LUNGS.

THEY BROUGHT US TO A CHAMBER AND DUMPED US ON THE GROUND.
THEY SNIFFED US AND LICKED US AND PROBED US...
WE HAD NEVER HEARD OF ALIEN BEHAVIOR LIKE THIS. WE HAD NO IDEA WHAT WAS GOING ON.
THEN SOMETHING HAPPENED...
TWO OF THE ALIENS GRABBED HOLD OF REBECCA.
THEY SEEMED TO BE FIGHTING OVER HER.

THEY TORE HER TO PIECES AS IF SHE WERE A WET PAPER BAG.
JUDITH, WITH HER STANDARD HUMAN-DEFENSE PROGRAMMING, ATTEMPTED TO PREVENT THE SLAUGHTER.
ALIENS ARE USUALLY INDIFFERENT TO NON-ORGANIC BEINGS.
THESE ALIENS WEREN'T.
AS THEY DESTROYED JUDITH, TAYLOR ALONE MANAGED TO MAKE A MEANINGFUL PROTEST...
...WITH A GRENADE. TOOK TWO ALIENS WITH HIM, THE LUCKY BASTARD.
TAYLOR. GOD, HOW THAT MAN LOVED CIGARS.

AFTER THAT, THEY MOVED QUICKLY. WE WERE SEPARATED.
I WAS FORCED INTO THE BOWELS OF THE HIVE.
THERE, I SAW WHAT HAD HAPPENED TO THE CREW OF THE OTHER SHIP.
BLOATED, MUTILATED BODIES HUNG EVERYWHERE.
I... I THINK SOME OF THEM WERE STILL BREATHING.

I WAS ATTACHED TO THE CHAMBER WALL WITH THICK STRANDS OF WEBLIKE MUCUS...
...AND LEFT TO CONTEMPLATE MY FATE.
HOW LONG I HUNG THERE, I CAN ONLY GUESS. PERHAPS FORTY OR FIFTY HOURS.
DURING THAT TIME, MY EYES AND NOSE WERE SCOURED BY THE HIDEOUS STENCH, WHILE SOUNDS OF DISTANT HUMAN VOICES, SCREAMING AND SOBBING AND BEGGING, ASSAILED MY EARS.
WHEN THE CREATURES FINALLY RETURNED...
...I PRAYED THAT THEY HAD COME TO KILL ME...

...BUT THEY HAD COME TO DO SOMETHING ELSE.
THEY HAD COME TO FEED ME.

THE FEEDING WAS INTERRUPTED BY A HIDEOUS SCREAM. EVEN ONE OF THE ALIENS SEEMED TO SHUDDER AS THE SCREAM BECAME LOUDER ... CLOSER ...
IT WAS QUENTIN CLARK. WHAT THEY'D DONE TO HIM ... I DIDN'T WANT TO IMAGINE. HE WAS COMPLETELY OUT OF HIS MIND.
HE DIDN'T STOP SCREAMING WHEN THEY PUSHED HIM INTO A POOL OF GREEN AND GREY SLIME WHICH SWARMED WITH TINY TADPOLE-LIKE CREATURES.
HE CONTINUED TO SCREAM AS THEY GLUED HIS HEAD TO THE WALL ...
... AND HE SCREAMED AFTER THEY LEFT HIM. HE SCREAMED AND SCREAMED AND SCREAMED UNTIL HIS VOCAL CORDS WERE SHREDDED AND THEN HE MADE A HORRIBLE NOISE LIKE A GOOSE ...
... HOUR AFTER HOUR AFTER HOUR.

I SURVIVED BECAUSE I HAD NO ALTERNATIVE. I TRIED TO SWALLOW MY TONGUE, BUT FINALLY GAVE THAT UP.
ULTIMATELY MY MIND RETREATED INTO ITSELF AND I LIVED IN A REALM OF PURE DELUSION.
I WAS SO IMMERSED IN THIS DELUSIONAL REALM THAT I BARELY NOTICED WHEN THEY REMOVED ME FROM THE WALL.
IT NEVER ENTERED MY MIND TO RESIST OR FIGHT. ALL I COULD DO WAS LONG FOR DEATH AND WAIT TO SEE WHAT THEY WERE GOING TO DO.
AS I WAS CARRIED OUT I GLIMPSED QUENTIN CLARK'S FORM IN THE POOL. HE HAD BEGUN TO SWELL UP.
HE'D STOPPED SCREAMING.
AS THEY... AS WE PASSED A CHAMBER, SOMETHING INSIDE CAUGHT THEIR ATTENTION. THEY ABRUPTLY CHANGED DIRECTION AND WENT IN, DRAGGING ME WITH THEM.

I HEARD THE SOUNDS OF THIS NEW PLACE AS WE ENTERED... SOBBING, SUCKING, SLURKING NOISES... SOFT, WET MEAT NOISES...
SOMETHING CLICKED.
MY CONSCIOUS MIND BEGAN TO FUNCTION AGAIN. I WAS SUDDENLY RATIONAL, AND I REALIZED WHERE I WAS.
THEY'D BROUGHT ME TO THEIR BREEDING-PENS.

I SOMEHOW RECOGNIZED THE WOMAN: IT WAS LOUISE CLARK.
SHE WAS IMPOSSIBLY GRAVID... HUGELY, MONSTROUSLY SWOLLEN.
I WAS TORTURED BY A DESIRE TO DO SOMETHING FOR HER, BUT THERE WAS NOTHING... ABSOLUTELY NOTHING.
THEN SHE DELIVERED.
SHE SOUNDED VERY MUCH LIKE HER HUSBAND BEFORE SHE DIED.
IF THE ALIENS HAD HOPED FOR HOSTS TO BREED IN, THE... THE NEWBORN THINGS WERE OBVIOUSLY INADEQUATE. THEY DID NOT SURVIVE AN HOUR.
THAT WAS WHEN I KNEW SOMETHING WAS WRONG WITH THE HIVE. THE ALIENS WERE VULNERABLE.
A NEW RESOLVE WAS BORN IN ME.

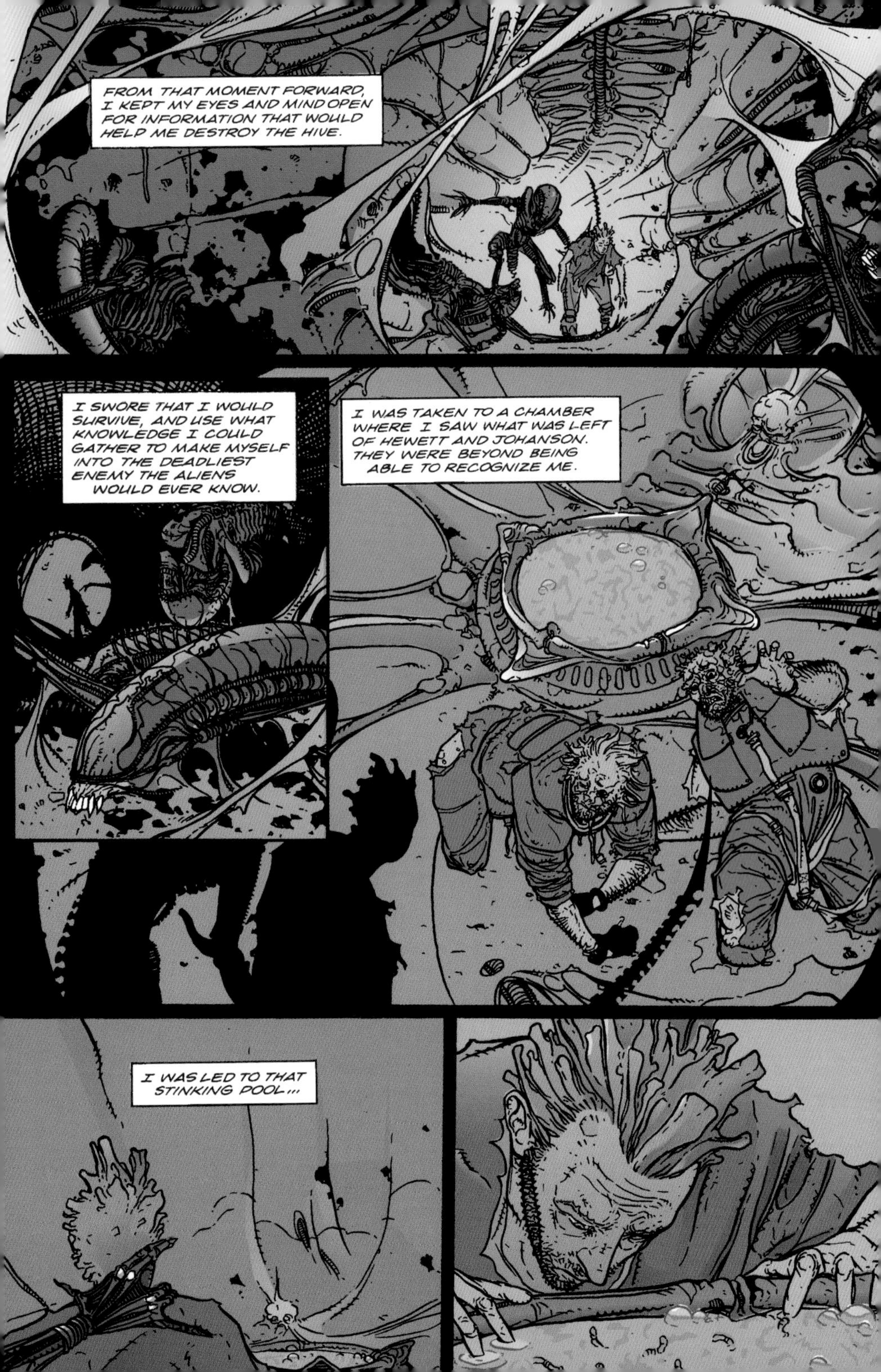
FROM THAT MOMENT FORWARD, I KEPT MY EYES AND MIND OPEN FOR INFORMATION THAT WOULD HELP ME DESTROY THE HIVE.
I SWORE THAT I WOULD SURVIVE, AND USE WHAT KNOWLEDGE I COULD GATHER TO MAKE MYSELF INTO THE DEADLIEST ENEMY THE ALIENS WOULD EVER KNOW.
I WAS TAKEN TO A CHAMBER WHERE I SAW WHAT WAS LEFT OF HEWETT AND JOHANSON. THEY WERE BEYOND BEING ABLE TO RECOGNIZE ME.
I WAS LED TO THAT STINKING POOL...

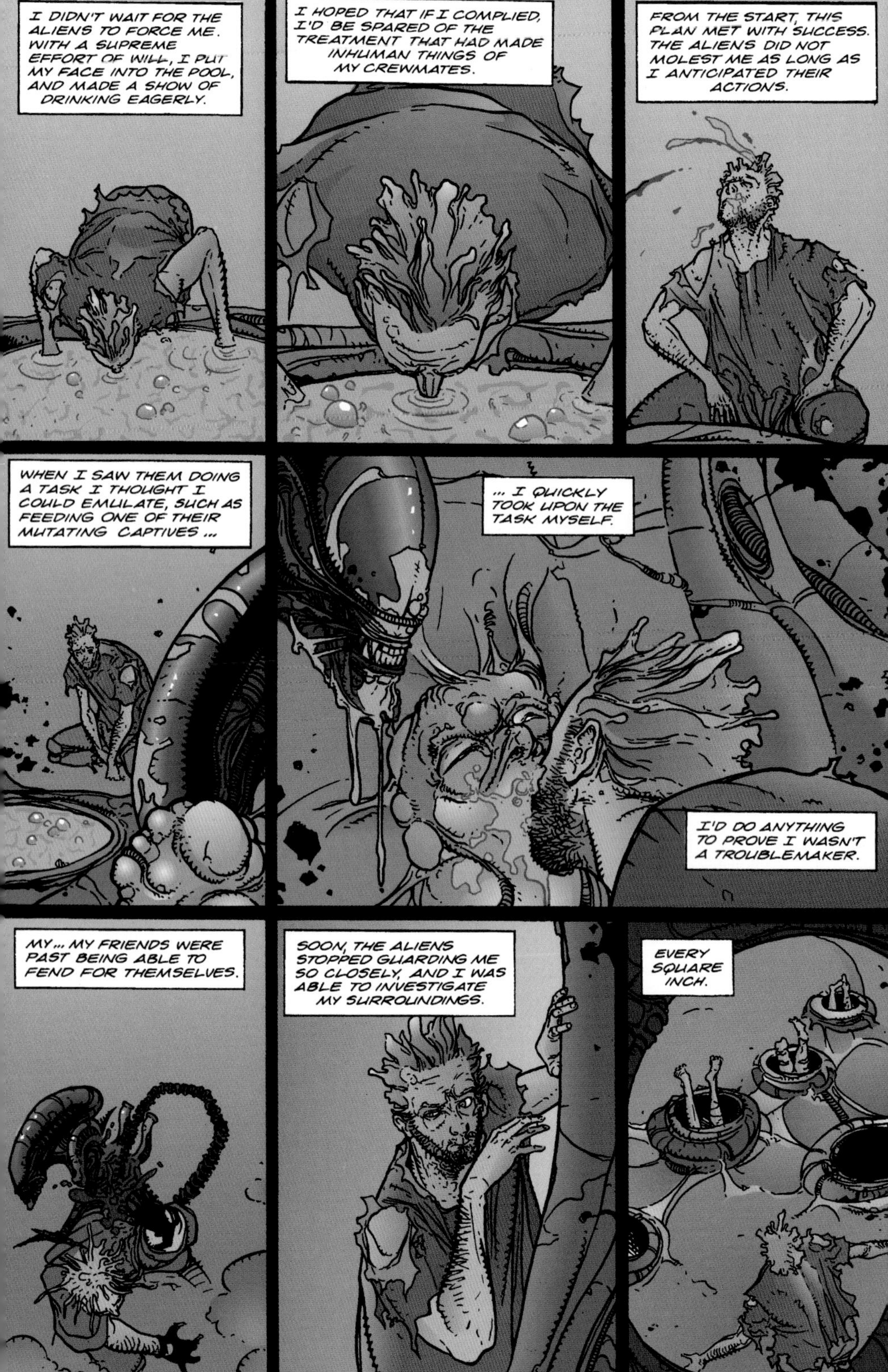
I DIDN'T WAIT FOR THE ALIENS TO FORCE ME. WITH A SUPREME EFFORT OF WILL, I PUT MY FACE INTO THE POOL, AND MADE A SHOW OF DRINKING EAGERLY.
I HOPED THAT IF I COMPLIED, I'D BE SPARED OF THE TREATMENT THAT HAD MADE INHUMAN THINGS OF MY CREWMATES.
FROM THE START, THIS PLAN MET WITH SUCCESS. THE ALIENS DID NOT MOLEST ME AS LONG AS I ANTICIPATED THEIR ACTIONS.
WHEN I SAW THEM DOING A TASK I THOUGHT I COULD EMULATE, SUCH AS FEEDING ONE OF THEIR MUTATING CAPTIVES ...
... I QUICKLY TOOK UPON THE TASK MYSELF.
I'D DO ANYTHING TO PROVE I WASN'T A TROUBLEMAKER.
MY... MY FRIENDS WERE PAST BEING ABLE TO FEND FOR THEMSELVES.
SOON, THE ALIENS STOPPED GUARDING ME SO CLOSELY, AND I WAS ABLE TO INVESTIGATE MY SURROUNDINGS.
EVERY SQUARE INCH.

I GATHERED AS MANY SAMPLES OF ORGANIC SUBSTANCES AROUND ME AS I COULD, AND KEPT THEM HIDDEN IN A SMALL RECESS.
I ACTUALLY CONDUCTED CRUDE EXPERIMENTS, TESTING THE REACTIONS OF THE SUBSTANCES ON ONE ANOTHER.
THE LEECHLIKE THINGS SECRETED A SOLVENT-LIKE COLLOID, WHICH THE ALIENS WERE CULTIVATING EVIDENTLY AS A SORT OF MEDICINE.
I OBSERVED THAT A UBIQUITOUS BLACK MOLD PRODUCED TOXINS THAT WERE DESTROYING THE ALIENS.
I HAD THE KEY TO THEIR SURVIVAL IN MY HAND.
I IMMEDIATELY PUT MY FINDINGS TO USE, USING THE TOXIC MOLD TO DE-STROY THE ALIENS' LIVING MEDICINE FACTORIES.

IT WAS AMAZING HOW WELL IT WORKED.
I MADE USE OF EVERY CHANCE I HAD TO CONDUCT THIS BIOLOGICAL SABOTAGE.
IT ALMOST SEEMED WRONG, DESTROYING THINGS WHICH I ONCE WOULD HAVE LOVED TO STUDY IN DEPTH ...
... BUT I DID THE BEST I COULD.
AT THAT POINT, ALL I WANTED WAS PROPER LAB EQUIPMENT.
I USED MY CREWMATES' SKULLS FOR DISHES, LIGAMENTS FOR STRING, ARTERIES FOR TUBING, AND SKIN FOR FORMING VESSELS.
THOUGHTS OF ESCAPE BECAME SECONDARY TO THE RESULTS OF MY EXPERIMENTS ...
... WHICH ONLY GREW IN RANGE AND COMPLEXITY.

I HAD BEEN REARED TO BELIEVE THAT ALIENS WERE ALL BUT INDOMITABLE AND ALMOST IMPOSSIBLE TO KILL...
...THAT THEY INVARIABLY DESTROYED ANY OTHER LIFE-FORM THEY CAME ACROSS, THAT THEY WERE BEYOND HUMAN COMPREHENSION.
YET HERE I WAS, SURVIVING AMONG THEM, SURREPTITIOUSLY POISONING THEM, FOOLING THEM.
LEARNING THEIR SECRETS.
TRUE, THEY WERE NOT NORMAL, HEALTHY ALIENS; BUT THEY HAD BEEN BROUGHT LOW BY NOTHING MORE THAN A COMMON MOLD.
THEY WERE VULNERABLE.
ANALYZABLE.
CONQUERABLE.
I HAD MORE KNOWLEDGE ABOUT THEM THAN ANYONE ELSE ALIVE.
AND I COULD BRING ABOUT THEIR EXTINCTION IN THE UNIVERSE.

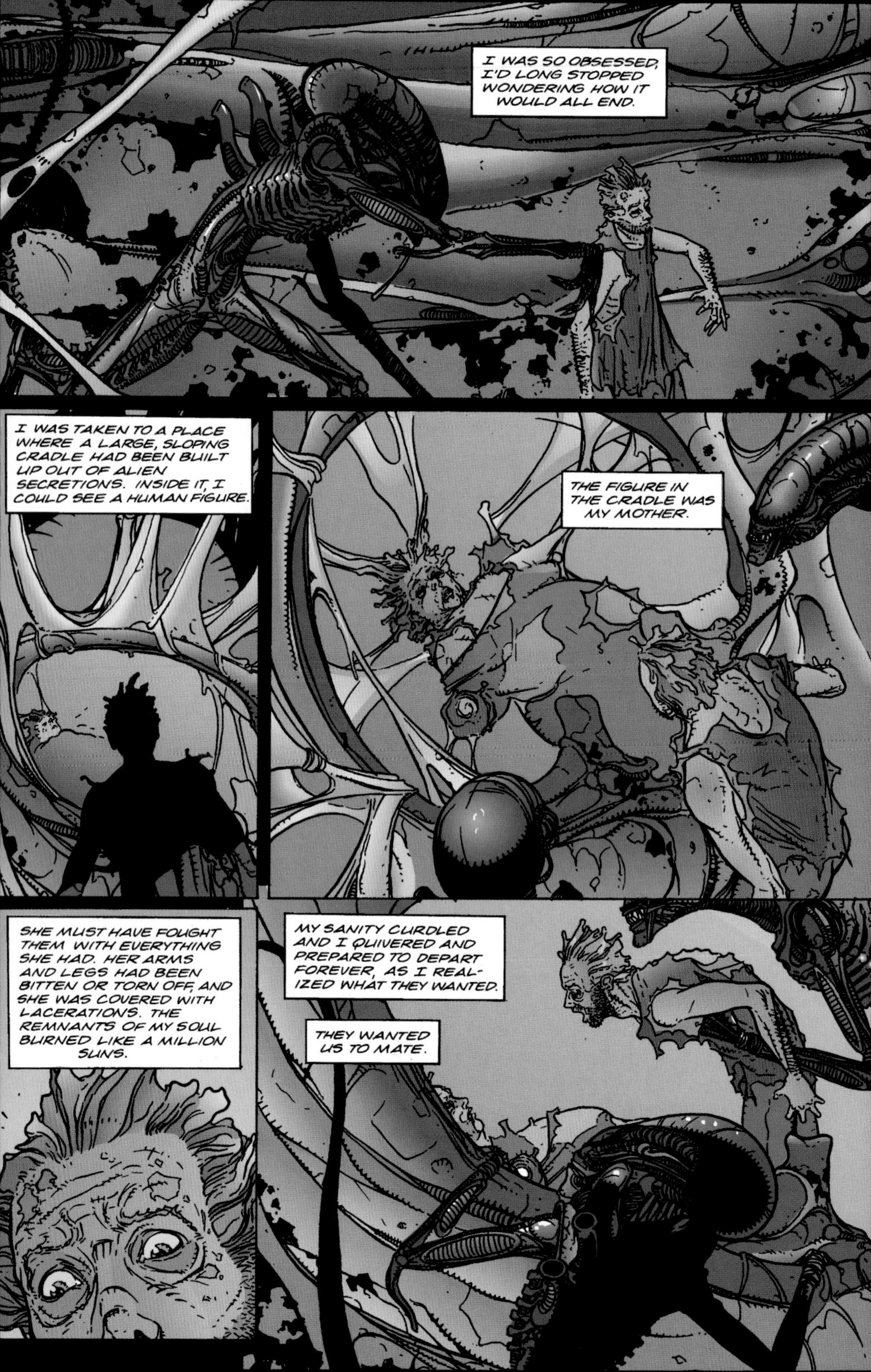
I WAS SO OBSESSED, I'D LONG STOPPED WONDERING HOW IT WOULD ALL END.
I WAS TAKEN TO A PLACE WHERE A LARGE, SLOPING CRADLE HAD BEEN BUILT UP OUT OF ALIEN SECRETIONS. INSIDE IT, I COULD SEE A HUMAN FIGURE.
THE FIGURE IN THE CRADLE WAS MY MOTHER.
SHE MUST HAVE FOUGHT THEM WITH EVERYTHING SHE HAD. HER ARMS AND LEGS HAD BEEN BITTEN OR TORN OFF, AND SHE WAS COVERED WITH LACERATIONS. THE REMNANTS OF MY SOUL BURNED LIKE A MILLION SUNS.
MY SANITY CURDLED AND I QUIVERED AND PREPARED TO DEPART FOREVER, AS I REALIZED WHAT THEY WANTED.
THEY WANTED US TO MATE.

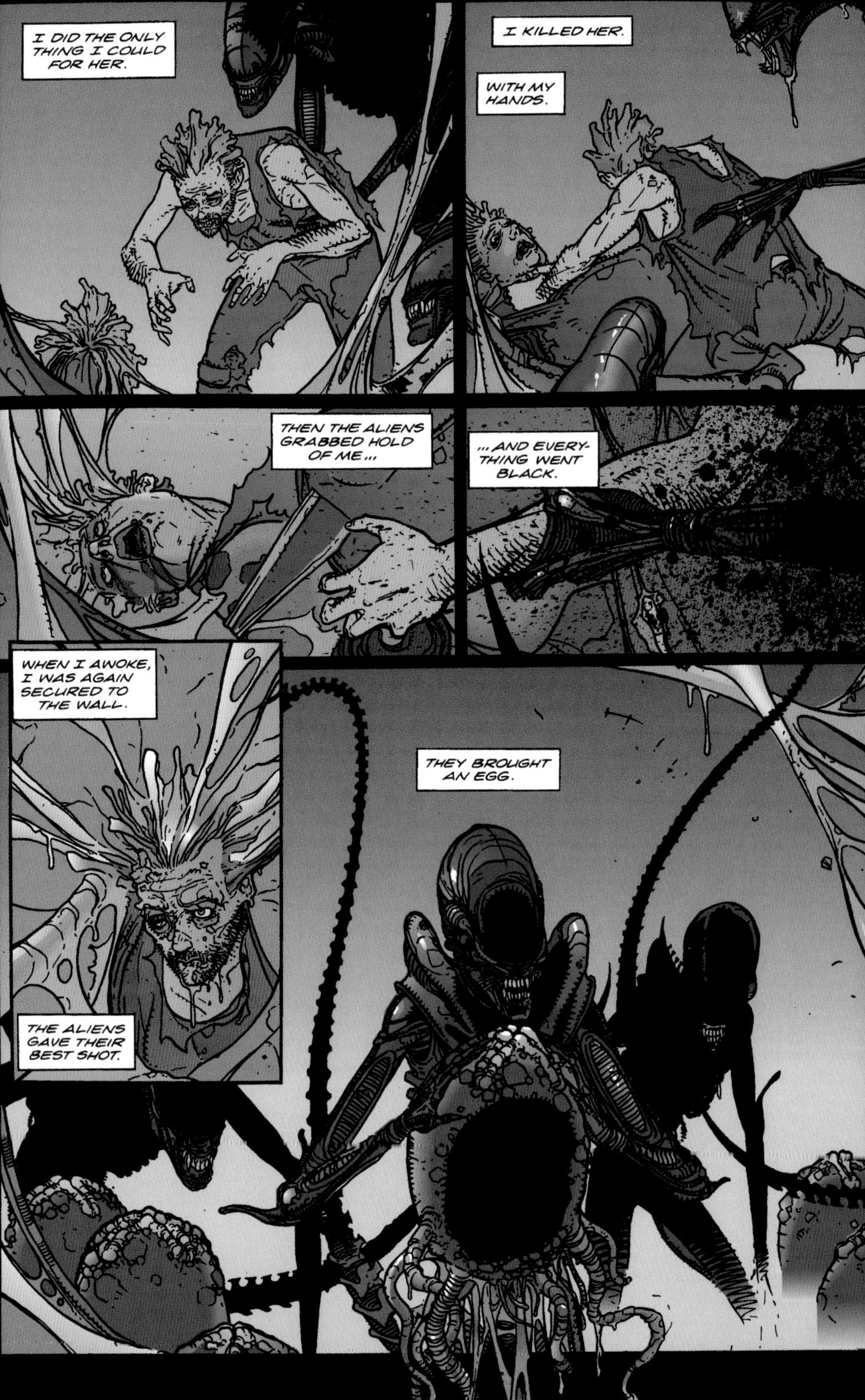
I DID THE ONLY THING I COULD FOR HER.
I KILLED HER.
WITH MY HANDS.
THEN THE ALIENS GRABBED HOLD OF ME...
...AND EVERY-THING WENT BLACK.
WHEN I AWOKE, I WAS AGAIN SECURED TO THE WALL.
THE ALIENS GAVE THEIR BEST SHOT.
THEY BROUGHT AN EGG.

WELL, THEY TRIED ANYWAY.
THE SICKNESS HAD AFFECTED EVEN THE EGGS. THEY HAD TO HELP THE FACE-HUGGER ONTO MY FACE ...
STILL, IT WAS STRONGER THAN I.
IT FORCED MY LIPS AND JAWS APART...
... AND SHOVED ITS PROBE DOWN MY TRACHEA ...
...AND INTO MY CHEST.
BUT... HOW... HOW DID YOU SURVIVE?
WHO SAYS I DID?

I THOUGHT I HAD AT LAST BEEN KILLED...
... BUT THAT MERCIFUL OBLIVION ENDED, AND I AWOKE.
AS I PULLED MYSELF FREE FROM THE WALL, I COULD FEEL THE HEAVY PARASITIC LOAD CRADLED IN MY CHEST.
THE SMELL OF DEATH WAS EVERYWHERE. THE ALIENS, THE CREW...
I DIDN'T LOOK FOR MY FATHER. I DIDN'T WANT TO SEE WHAT THEY'D DONE TO HIM.
I WANTED NOTHING MORE THAN TO DIE...
... BUT NOT INSIDE THE HIVE.
I FOUND MY WAY OUTSIDE. THE FRESH AIR, THE OPEN SPACE, AND THE LIGHT WERE SHOCKING TO MY RAVAGED SENSES.

I PASSED THE SMUGGLER'S SHIP, AND RETURNED TO THE INCUNABULUM.
IT WAS UNTOUCHED. POWER LEVELS FULL. IT HUMMED.
THIS WAS MY HOMECOMING: OUR COMFORTABLE SHIP, SWEET AND DEPENDABLE, FULL OF WARM GHOSTS THAT LOVED ME.
I SAW THE CALENDAR. I HAD BEEN IN THE HIVE FOR FORTY-THREE TERRESTRIAL DAYS.
I THOUGHT OF MY FAMILY AND THOSE ALIENS AS THEY LAY DEAD TOGETHER, ALMOST IN EACH OTHER'S ARMS.
IN DEATH, THEY WERE UNITED. I ALONE HAD EMERGED FROM THAT APOCALYPSE. PERHAPS ... FOR A REASON?
SUDDENLY, I WANTED... I WAS DESPERATE TO LIVE.
AND I SENT A DISTRESS SIGNAL.

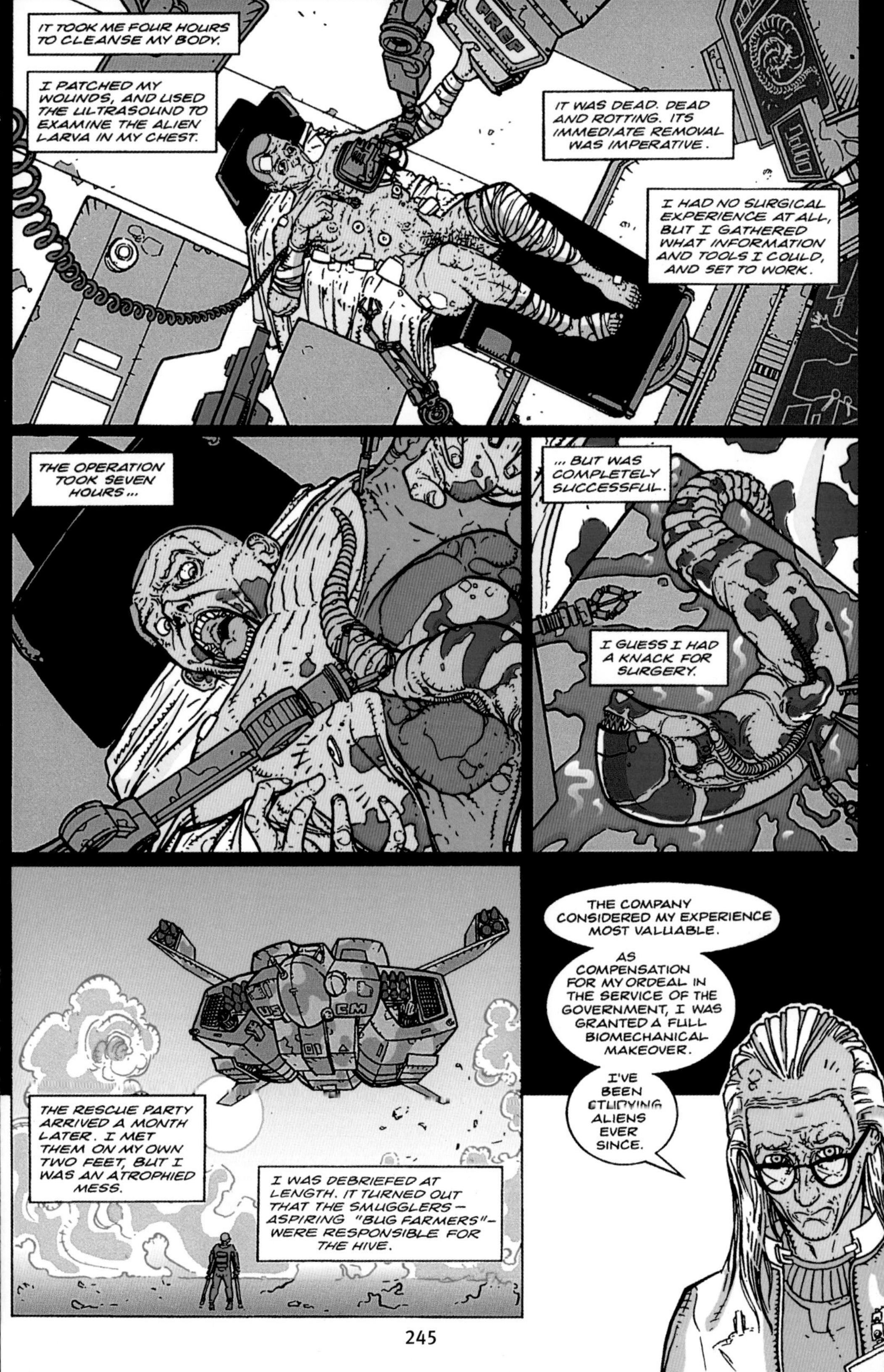
IT TOOK ME FOUR HOURS TO CLEANSE MY BODY.
I PATCHED MY WOUNDS, AND USED THE ULTRASOUND TO EXAMINE THE ALIEN LARVA IN MY CHEST.
IT WAS DEAD. DEAD AND ROTTING. ITS IMMEDIATE REMOVAL WAS IMPERATIVE.
I HAD NO SURGICAL EXPERIENCE AT ALL, BUT I GATHERED WHAT INFORMATION AND TOOLS I COULD, AND SET TO WORK.
PREP
THE OPERATION TOOK SEVEN HOURS...
...BUT WAS COMPLETELY SUCCESSFUL.
I GUESS I HAD A KNACK FOR SURGERY.
THE RESCUE PARTY ARRIVED A MONTH LATER. I MET THEM ON MY OWN TWO FEET, BUT I WAS AN ATROPHIED MESS.
I WAS DEBRIEFED AT LENGTH. IT TURNED OUT THAT THE SMUGGLERS— ASPIRING "BUG FARMERS"— WERE RESPONSIBLE FOR THE HIVE.
THE COMPANY CONSIDERED MY EXPERIENCE MOST VALUABLE.
AS COMPENSATION FOR MY ORDEAL IN THE SERVICE OF THE GOVERNMENT, I WAS GRANTED A FULL BIOMECHANICAL MAKEOVER.
I'VE BEEN STUDYING ALIENS EVER SINCE.

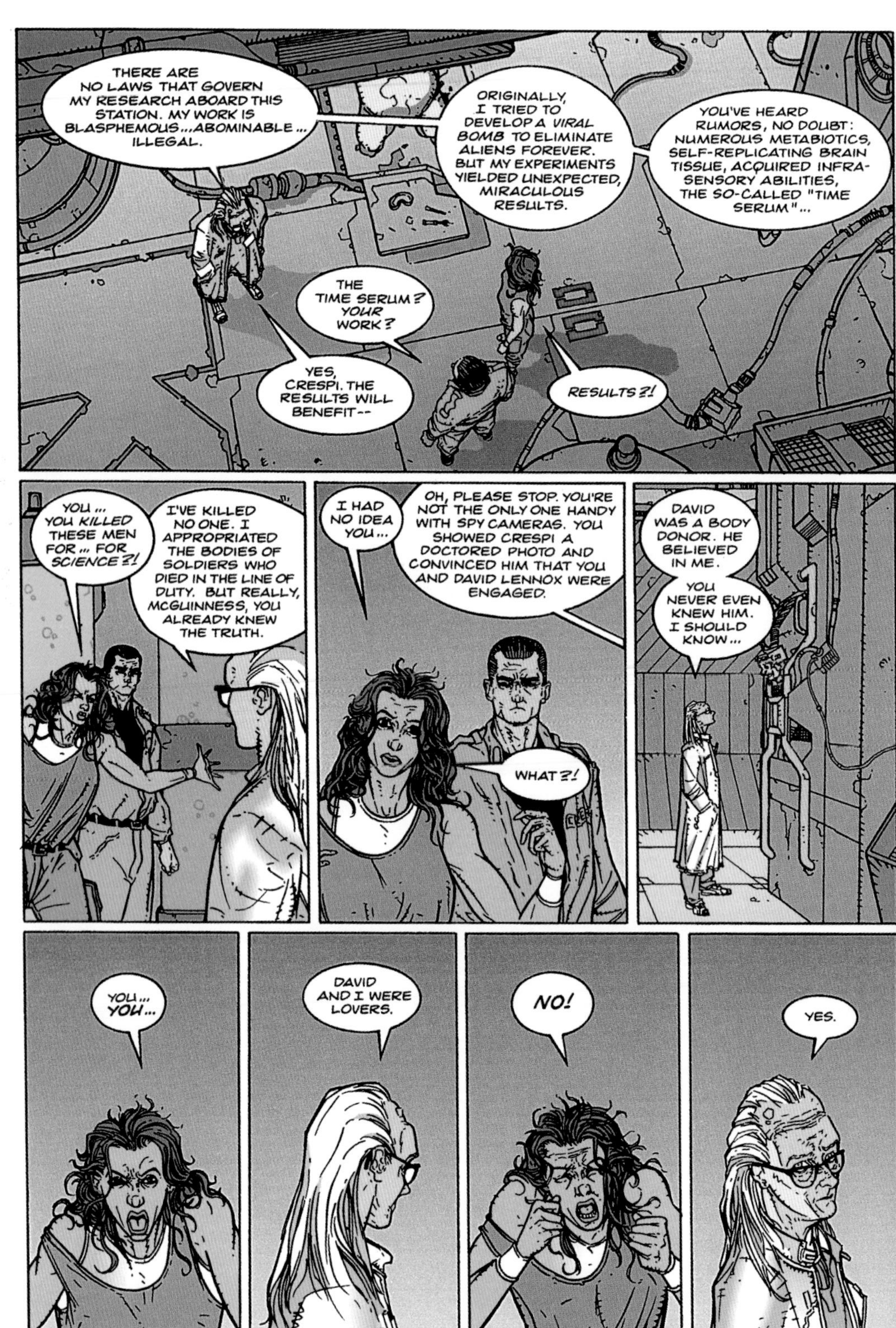
THERE ARE NO LAWS THAT GOVERN MY RESEARCH ABOARD THIS STATION. MY WORK IS BLASPHEMOUS...ABOMINABLE ... ILLEGAL.
ORIGINALLY, I TRIED TO DEVELOP A VIRAL BOMB TO ELIMINATE ALIENS FOREVER. BUT MY EXPERIMENTS YIELDED UNEXPECTED, MIRACULOUS RESULTS.
YOU'VE HEARD RUMORS, NO DOUBT: NUMEROUS METABIOTICS, SELF-REPLICATING BRAIN TISSUE, ACQUIRED INFRA-SENSORY ABILITIES, THE SO-CALLED "TIME SERUM"...
THE TIME SERUM? YOUR WORK?
YES, CRESPI. THE RESULTS WILL BENEFIT--
RESULTS?!
YOU ... YOU KILLED THESE MEN FOR ... FOR SCIENCE?!
I'VE KILLED NO ONE. I APPROPRIATED THE BODIES OF SOLDIERS WHO DIED IN THE LINE OF DUTY. BUT REALLY, MCGUINNESS, YOU ALREADY KNEW THE TRUTH.
I HAD NO IDEA YOU...
OH, PLEASE STOP. YOU'RE NOT THE ONLY ONE HANDY WITH SPY CAMERAS. YOU SHOWED CRESPI A DOCTORED PHOTO AND CONVINCED HIM THAT YOU AND DAVID LENNOX WERE ENGAGED.
WHAT?!
DAVID WAS A BODY DONOR. HE BELIEVED IN ME.
YOU NEVER EVEN KNEW HIM. I SHOULD KNOW...
YOU... YOU...
DAVID AND I WERE LOVERS.
NO!
YES.

HE'S LYING, CRESPI! DON'T LISTEN TO HIM!
SEE HERE, CRESPI. MORTENSON WAS A SPY FOR GRANT CORPORATION.

ADMIRAL THAVES PEGGED MORTENSON. WE PUT HIM ON SHIP'S ORDERS TO KEEP HIM UNDER CONSTANT SURVEILLANCE. McGUINNESS WAS HIS PARTNER.
IT'S A LIE!

THAT'LL BE FOR A TRIBUNAL TO DECIDE. NOW, CRESPI, IF YOU'LL BE SO KIND AS TO ARREST THIS WOMAN--
CRESPI... PLEASE! HE'LL KILL ME!

I...

I'M SORRY, McGUINNESS, BUT I...
YOU MONSTERS.

McGUINNESS!

AFTER HER! I CAN CONTROL EVERY DOOR IN THE STATION FROM HERE! WE'LL CORNER HER IN THE PIT!
RIGHT!
AAAAGH!
GIVE IT UP, MCGUINNESS.
STUPID... STUPID...
CLANG
HE'S GOT US.

YOU REALLY SHOULD HAVE LISTENED TO HER, CRESPI.
CHURCH?! WHAT THE DEVIL ARE--

OH, PLEASE. YOU FLATTER YOURSELF BY BEING SURPRISED AT HOW EASILY YOU'VE BEEN DECEIVED.

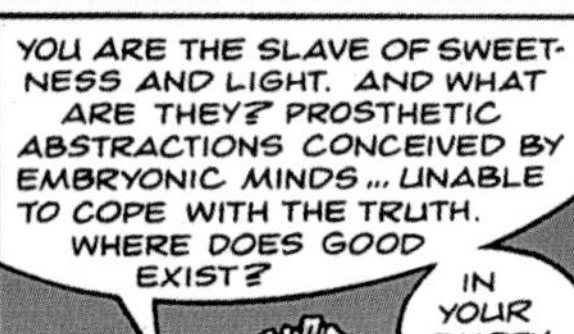

YOU ARE THE SLAVE OF SWEETNESS AND LIGHT. AND WHAT ARE THEY? PROSTHETIC ABSTRACTIONS CONCEIVED BY EMBRYONIC MINDS... UNABLE TO COPE WITH THE TRUTH. WHERE DOES GOOD EXIST?
IN YOUR EMPTY SKULL.

YOU CAN BE BOUGHT WITH A COOKIE... FOOLED WITH THREE WORDS. GOD, IF YOU ONLY KNEW HOW I SEE YOU... HUMANS.

BUT **YOU'RE** HU--
DO SHUT UP, CRESPI. MUST YOU ALWAYS BELIEVE IN APPEARANCES?

I DIDN'T SURVIVE THE HIVE. I *AM* THE HIVE. WHEN I LOOK THE COSMOS IN THE EYE, IT BLINKS.
AND YOU... THE GOOD SOLDIER, SO PROUD OF YOUR BRAINS AND COURAGE. TEN-HUT! YOU'RE NOTHING BUT A FATUOUS RAH-RAH BOY. I CANNOT HATE YOU ENOUGH.
BUT THERE'S HOPE FOR YOU YET.

YOU HAVE THE HONOR OF CONTRIBUTING TO MY RESEARCH.
ALTHOUGH YOU WON'T BE IN ANY CONDITION TO APPRECIATE IT, YOU WILL HAVE ASSISTED IN THE CREATION OF AN EVOLUTIONARY BRIDGE TO THE TRUE CROWN OF CREATION.
THE PINK POETRY OF MAN WILL BE SUBSUMED BY THE BLACK BLANK GENIUS OF THE ALIEN AND THE RESULT WILL BE THE ORIGINAL AND FINAL CREATURE.
IT WILL FEED AND LIVE OFF OF ITSELF. AND I WILL JOIN IT.
THERE WERE MOMENTS WHEN I THOUGHT YOU WERE ON THE VERGE OF BEGINNING TO UNDERSTAND...
SO I'M GIVING YOU A CHANCE... A CHANCE TO SEE THE TRUTH BEFORE YOU DIE.
GO THROUGH THE DOOR. BOTH OF YOU.
GO TO HELL!
BEEN THERE.
MUUUUUUHHHHN
STOHHHHHP!
WHERE'S YOUR SENSE OF SPORT? MAKE IT THROUGH THE LABYRINTH AND I MIGHT EVEN LET YOU LIVE.
YOU ALL RIGHT?
NO.
COME ON. LET'S GO.
WATCH YOUR FIRST STEP...

...IT'S A LULU!
NOW I'M REALLY SORRY, McGUINNESS--
BEGGING YOUR PARDON, SIR, BUT ... IT'S A LITTLE LATE FOR THAT.
MOVE ALONG NOW, CHILDREN, OR I'LL FRY YOU WHERE YOU STAND.
CRESP

HISSSSSSSSSSSSSSSS
THE DOOR!
WAIT! IT'S HARNESSED! IT CAN'T REACH US.
UN--UNTIL CHURCH WANTS IT TO!
I'M GOING TO KILL THAT BASTARD.
THERE HAS TO BE A WAY OUT OF HERE!

QUICK! THIS WAY!

SEE ANY-THING?
NO... JUST IT'S DARK.

WAIT... THERE'S LIGHT. IT'S ...

HISSSSSK
EEEEEEEEEEEEEE!

SHARON!
GO BACK! GO BACK!

UNF!

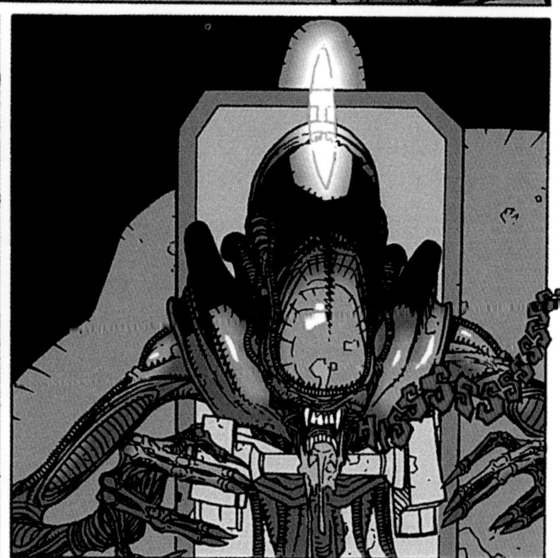

WH-WH-WHY DON'T THEY G-GET IT OVER WITH?!
IT'S LOOSE!
THEY... THERE'S SOMETHING WRONG WITH THEM.
CHURCH'S EXPERIMENTS HAVE WEAKENED THEM.
CRESPI
WHICH MEANS...?
WE MIGHT HAVE A CHANCE!
THE DOOR! MOVE!
RRRRRAUGH!
HURNT!
HORSSK
AAAAAAAAAAHH!
CRESPI?!

OH, MY GOD, CRESPI, YOU'RE REALLY HURT!
I'M ... I'M FINE. AND I'M GOING TO GET US OUT OF HERE!
CHURCH WANTED TO SHOW US ...
... BUT I'LL SHOW --
HISSSSSSSSSSSSS

HURRRAAAGH!
AAAAURGH!
NO!
CHUSK
CRESPI! DON'T MOVE! LET ME--
HUIERGH!

YUH-YUH
YOU D-DON'T HAVE TO T-TELL ME.
SOMETHING... I'M COLD... THIS IS REALLY... IT...

OH GOD, CRESPI! I CAN'T DO ANYTHING FOR YOU--
YES, YOU CAN... DON'T LET THEM... DON'T LET HIM... PLEASE... KILL ME...

NO! I CAN'T! DON'T MAKE ME--
AND... THEN... KILL CHURCH... PLEASE... SHARON...

PLEASE... PLEASE... PLEASE...

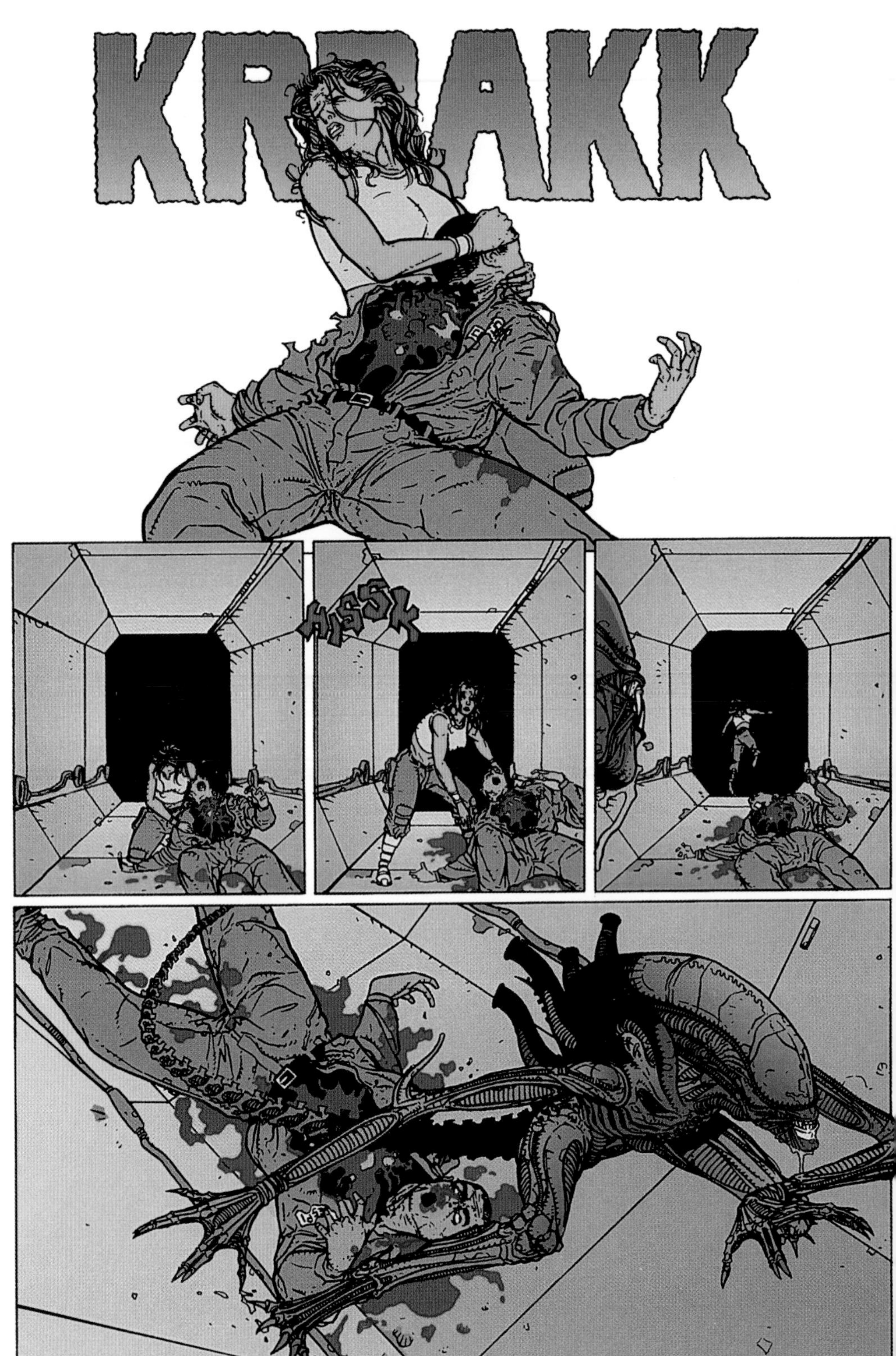
KRRAKK
HISSK

CHURCH!
I'M GOING TO KILL YOU, YOU BASTARD!
HURSSSK
BASTARD!
UHHN!

MCGUINNESS!
I AM SURPRISED.
YOU ARE GOING TO GIVE ME SOME VERY BEAUTIFUL CHEMICALS.
AND THEN, I THINK I'LL ARRANGE FOR YOU AND LENNOX TO SPEND SOME QUALITY TIME TOGETHER.
YAUUUUUUUUGH!
BZZZZXXX
UH-OH. HERE COMES YOUR DANCE PARTNER.
CAREFUL, TRIXIE. MUSTN'T GRAB. MCGUINNESS MIGHT GIVE YOU A PIECE OF HER MIND!

YOU UGLY MOTHER--
AARRRRGH!
YOU'RE DEAD, CHURCH! DEAD!
WHAT? BUT... THERE'S NO TELEPATHINE IN YOUR--
SCREW TELEPATHINE! I WANT YOU...
BIZZZZZZZZZEXXX
...DEAD!

YOU ... YOU BROKE THE FORCE FIELD!
YOU REALLY ARE UPSET, AREN'T YOU?
UCK!
RRRRRLLLL!
HURNT!
FREEZE!
LLLLLL!
NO!

I SAID FREEEEZE!
LLLLLL!
AAAAGH!
DOCTOR CHURCH! GET AWAY FROM IT! I CAN'T GET A CLEAN SHOT!
UNNH!
HELLO, TRIXIE.
MISS ME?
HISSSSSSK

COLONEL DOCTOR CHURCH STILL NEEDS REST, ADMIRAL THAVES, SIR.
IT'LL JUST TAKE A FEW MINUTES.
YES, SIR.
HOW ARE YOU FEELING, DOCTOR?
BETTER, ADMIRAL. ACTUALLY, I'M QUITE WELL ENOUGH TO GET BACK TO WORK, AND--
FORGET IT. THE MEDS SAY YOU NEED ANOTHER WEEK. EVERYTHING OKAY?
I... I KEEP THINKING OF McGUINNESS.
HELL, YOU SAW THE RECORDINGS, THE WAY SHE LED CRESPI INTO THE LAB... KILLED HIM WITH HER BARE HANDS!
THE MARINES PICKED HER UP LAST WEEK. DON'T WORRY ABOUT HER COMING BACK--
IT'S NOT THAT...
SOME OF THE THINGS SHE SAID... ABOUT ME. IT HAS ME THINKING WHETHER MY WORK HERE IS... WRONG.
SHE WAS A CRAZY SABOTEUR! DOCTOR CHURCH... PAUL... YOUR RESEARCH HAS SAVED COUNTLESS LIVES. HECK, IF IT WEREN'T FOR YOUR VIRAL TENT, MY OWN DAUGHTER WOULDN'T BE ALIVE TODAY.
YOU'RE A GOOD MAN, PAUL.
THINK WHERE IT GOT CRESPI.
I'M... SORRY ABOUT CRESPI. YOU TWO SEEMED TO HIT IT OFF.
ED
AY
I'LL SEE YOU TOMORROW. GET SOME REST.

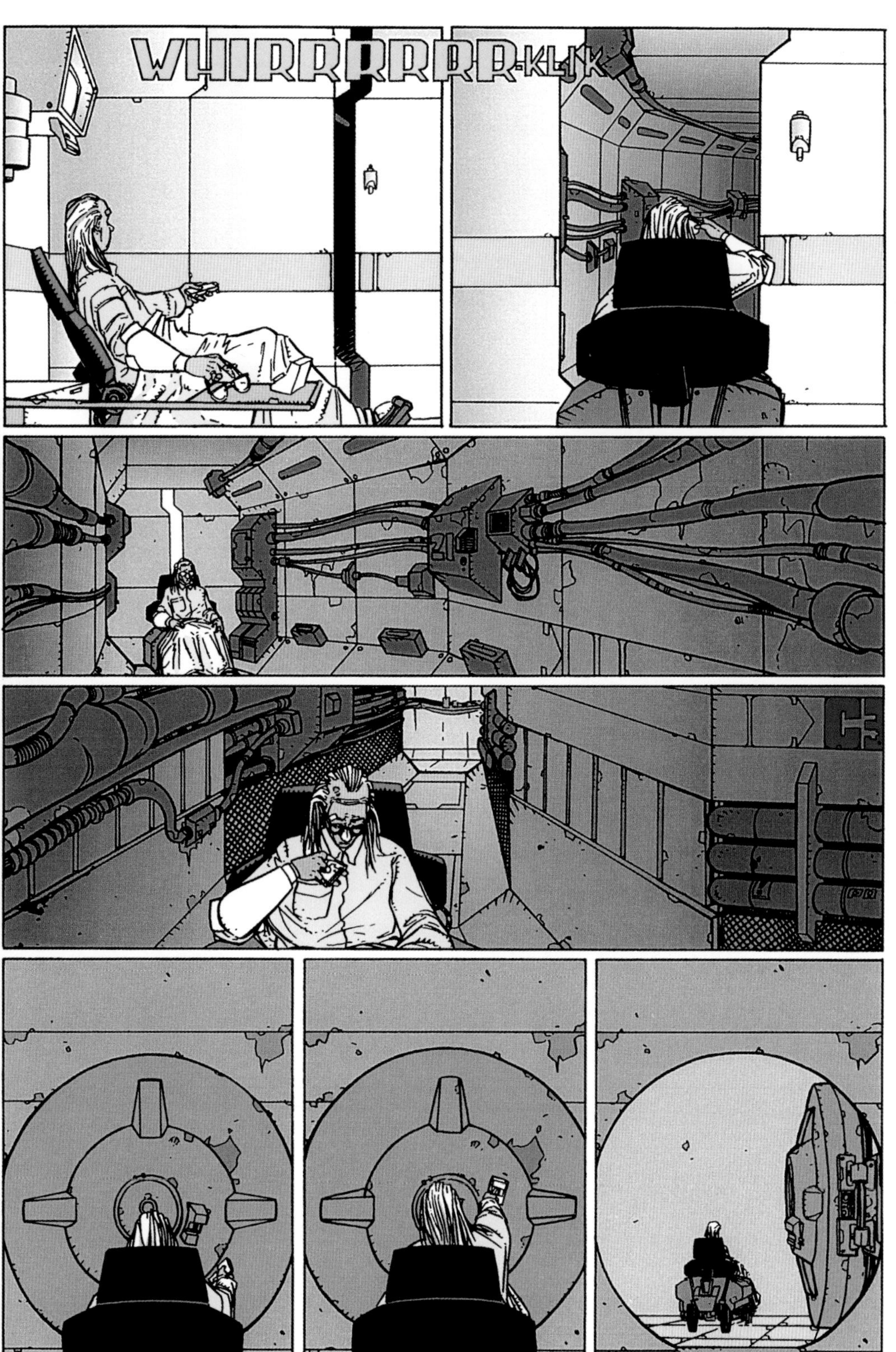
WHIRRRRRRR-KLIK

I...
I HOPE YOU KNOW, TONY...
...NONE OF THIS IS PERSONAL.

SALVATION

script
DAVE GIBBONS

pencils
MIKE MIGNOLA

inks
KEVIN NOWLAN

colors
MATT HOLLINGSWORTH

lettering
CLEM ROBINS

title illustration
MIKE MIGNOLA with **DAVE STEWART**

MIGNOLA

I KNOW THAT YOU CAN SEE ME, LORD...

I KNOW THAT YOU CAN READ MY HEART...
I...I PRAY THAT YOU WILL FORGIVE MY SINS.
FOR I HAVE SINNED.
I HAVE DONE TERRIBLE THINGS.
TERRIBLE THINGS.
NNNGH. SHIT.

CAREFUL MY LEG, YOU HICK BASTARD.
BUT WHAT FOSS DID WAS WORSE.

I KNOW THAT'S NO EXCUSE, BUT...
HNNG DAMN YOU.
SON OF A BITCH.
WELL, HE WAS THE CAPTAIN.

HE COULD HAVE SAVED THEM ALL. HE COULD HAVE...
BUT HE DIDN'T.
HE JUST SAVED HIMSELF.
NOVA MARU

AND ME.

MORE WATER, YOU GOD-BOTHERIN' BASTARD...

BUT THAT WAS YOUR DOING, WASN'T IT, LORD?
PART OF YOUR PLAN. TO TEST MY FAITH.
I SEE IT ALL, NOW.

THE NOVA MARU. THE COMPANY, RECRUITING US FROM THE BACKWORLDS.
NO QUESTIONS, NO ANSWERS. JUST MONEY.

TO ME, IT MEANT A FREEHOLD ON SOME FARM PLANET.
WHAT DID IT MEAN TO THE OTHERS?
FOSS, STUTZ, LEE, BOYD...?
YES, AND DEAN...

WHAT IS THIS CRAP, SELKIRK?
WHERE'D YOU LEARN TO COOK, FOR GOD'S SAKE? A PIGSTY?
LORD'S NAME IN VAIN, STUTZY. TUT, TUT.

OOH, I FORGOT. HE'S WATCHING US, AIN'T HE?
GOTTA BELIEVE IT. LOOK, THERE'S HIS EYEBALL, STARING RIGHT AT US!

OH, AMEN. AMEN.
SO, DEAN, WHAT'S THE POOP? THIS OUR DESTINATION? ONE BIG ISLAND IN ONE BIG SEA?
WHAT THE HELL KINDA CARGO HAS TO BE HAULED HALFWAY 'ROUND THE UNIVERSE JUST TO END UP HERE?

YOU DON'T NEED TO KNOW, BOYD. JUST TAKE YOUR PAY AND--
EMERGENCY STATIONS. EMERGENCY STATIONS. MALFUNCTION IN CARGO HOLD FOUR. MALFUNCTION IN --

HOLD FOUR? THAT'S YOURS, STUTZ--
ALL CREW TO EMERGENCY STATIONS. ALL CREW --
HEY, I CHECKED IT ALREADY!

CHECKED IT, MY ASS!
FOSS...!

YOU STUPID, LAZY--
BRAKA
BRAKA

YOU, SELKIRK. OVER HERE...
FOSS! GET A GRIP--
CONDITION RED. CARGO HOLD MAIN BULKHEAD BREACHED. EMERGENCY STATIONS.

WE CAN FIX THIS. THE SHUTTLE--
TOO LATE FOR THAT, DEAN.
SEAL THE DOOR!

CONDITION RED.
CREW TO CARGO
JETTISON STATIONS.
CONDITION RED.
C-CAPTAIN? THE OTHERS--
SCREW 'EM ...DEAD ANYWAY. ONLY... ONE LIFEBOAT ON THIS BUCKET...

TWO SEATS. NO HYPERSLEEP OR... AUTOCONTROL--
DAAMN! DAMN, MY LEG! HNNGH...

NEED A ... PILOT. YOU... GOT LUCKY, SELKIRK...
WHERE'S... NNG... GODDAMN MED POUCH...?

CARGO 6A
CARGO
NO. HNNGH. HELL.
BURNING... HELL, CAN'T...
FOSS COULD HAVE SAVED THEM ALL.
HE COULD HAVE.
MAYBE THAT'S WHY YOU MADE HIS PAIN SO BAD.
SO HE WOULDN'T FORGET.

NO. BURNING.
ACID. HNNN.
TOO MANY. NNNNO!
AND YET, THAT FIRST LONG NIGHT, I PLEADED FOR YOUR MERCY UPON HIM...

UPON US BOTH.
THIS CRAP'S SPOILED!
CHEAP COMPANY BASTARDS.

BETTER HOPE TO GOD YOUR... FISHING'S BETTER THAN... YOUR FLYING, SELKIRK.

I TRIED NOT TO THINK ABOUT HOW LITTLE FRESH WATER WE HAD.

OR WHAT FOSS MIGHT DO WHEN HIS DRUGS RAN OUT.

I JUST PRAYED FOR COURAGE...

SQUUAARRK
...AND PATIENCE.

AND YOU COMFORTED ME.
PROMISED ME THAT SALVATION WOULD COME.
'BOUT... TIME, HOLY JOE.

I KNEW FOSS WOULD NEED ME UNTIL THEN. HE WAS TOO BADLY INJURED TO FEND FOR HIMSELF.
...TRULY THANKFUL. AMEN.
TASTES LIKE DIRT.

AND EVERYTHING ON THIS PLANET WAS AGAINST US.
BASTARD... H-HHRUUULK. BAST--
RR-URRKHH...
EVERY-THING.

TRYING TO POISON ME, YOU SON OF A BITCH?
N-NO, CAPTAIN ...NO! IT--IT MADE ME SICK, TOO...
I THOUGHT THAT I WOULD DIE THEN, LORD. I BEGGED FOR YOUR HELP...

AND...AND THE SKY FILLED WITH FIRE AND THUNDER.

EVEN AS IT FADED, I KNEW IT WAS A SIGN.
FOR US BOTH.
DAMN YOU, MARU. DAMN YOU.

AT DAWN, FOSS ORDERED ME TO REMOVE EVERYTHING USEFUL FROM THE LIFEBOAT.
HE WAS AFRAID THAT A SUDDEN STORM MIGHT WASH IT AWAY.

I WAS TRYING TO GET THE COMM-LINK WORKING WHEN I HEARD GUNFIRE...
BRAKABRAKA

BRAKA BRAKA BRAKA BRAKA
DEAD! DAMN YOU, BASTARD ...DEAD!
FOSS HAD DRAGGED HIMSELF TO THE SHORE.

ALL DEAD!
BRAKA BRAKA BRAKA
HE'D SEEN SOMETHING IN THE SURF.

DEAD, HEAR ME? DEAD! SO DIE, DAMN YOU, BASTARD!
DIE!
SOMETHING ALIEN.
BRAKABRAKA

C-CAPTAIN? CAPTAIN--
DIE!!

OFF! GET OFF ME. TOO MANY!
IT--IT'S DEAD, CAPTAIN. BEEN BURNT...EATEN BY F-FISHES...

SELKIRK. YES. FISHES. DEAD.
SAVE AMMO. OTHERS. OTHERS MIGHT HEAR.
BASTARD CARGO.

THEN I KNEW JUST WHAT THE NOVA MARU HAD BEEN CARRYING.
BASTARD COMPANY.
KILL US ALL. BASTARDS!

FOSS HAD LOST HIS REASON.
BUT I HAD FOUND HOPE.

THAT NIGHT, FOSS TOOK THE LAST OF HIS DRUGS AND WAS SOON SLEEPING.
BUT I WAS TOO EXCITED TO REST.

YOU HAD ANSWERED MY PLEAS FOR SALVATION.

FOR IF THE... THING ON THE BEACH WAS PART OF THE NOVA MARU'S CARGO, THEN THE SHIP ITSELF MUST HAVE LANDED, TOO.

THE FIRE AND THUNDER WE'D SEEN IN THE NIGHT WAS THE MARU ENTERING THE ATMOSPHERE.
UNLESS IT HAD BEEN DESTROYED ON IMPACT, OR SUNK, THERE WOULD BE FOOD AND WATER.

AND A DEEP-SPACE DISTRESS BEACON.
BADEEP BADEEP

I FELL TO MY KNEES IN THANKS. WE WERE SAVED.
BUT THEN...
KKKIKT

BASTARD. KNOW YOU'RE IN THERE. BASTARD!

ALIEN BASTARD!
CAPTAIN, NO! IT'S ME, SELKI--

BAAAASTARDD!
BRAKA BRAKA BRA
SPANG
KTIIING
PTWEEE

THEN YOU HELPED ME AGAIN, LORD.
DAMN. JAMMED. DAMN.
KKKTCHKK

IT'S ME, CAPTAIN! SELKIRK, THE COOK...
TRICK. ALIEN TRICK!
HNNN! GOT IT. BASTARD.

ABRAKABRA
I HAD TO STOP HIM.
HE WAS POSSESSED.

HE WOULD HAVE KILLED ME.
BRAKABRAKABRAKABR

NO! CAPTAIN--
BRAKABRAKABRAKABR
ALIEN BASTARD!

SATAN WAS IN HIM. I HAD NO CHOICE.

HE KILLED THE OTHERS-- KILLED THEM ALL.
HE WOULD HAVE KILLED ME, TOO. HE WOULD HAVE.
I HAD TO. I HAD TO DO IT.

I KNOW IT WAS A TERRIBLE THING, LORD.
AND WHAT I DID NEXT WAS WORSE.

BUT IF I WAS TO SURVIVE...
...I HAD TO EAT.

FOSS HAD KILLED SO MANY.
NOW HE WOULD HELP ME TO LIVE.

IT WAS PART OF YOUR PLAN. I KNOW THAT NOW.

BUT, THOUGH MY BELLY WAS COMFORTED, MY MIND WAS NOT...

AND YET, BY YOUR MERCY, I SLEPT THAT NIGHT WITH-OUT DREAMING.

AT FIRST LIGHT, I GAVE THANKS...

AND PRAYED THAT FOSS'S SOUL MIGHT ALSO FIND REST.

THEN I SET OFF TO FIND THE NOVA MARU.

DEEP IN THE JUNGLE, I FELT LOST AS NEVER BEFORE.

THE BACKWORLDS WERE LONELY, BUT AT LEAST THERE, THE STARS IN HEAVEN WERE REMINDERS OF DISTANT HUMANITY.

HERE, STRANGENESS PRESSED IN ON ME FROM EVERY SIDE, WITH ONLY MY COMPASS TO GIVE DIRECTION.

TIME, TOO, WAS LOSING ITS MEANING.

WHEN I REALIZED THAT IT WAS YOUR HOLY SABBATH...

...I STOPPED AND GAVE THANKS FOR ALL YOUR CREATION.
FOR HUMANKIND. FOR ANIMALS. FOR PLANT-LIFE. INSECTS.
EVEN FOR--

BRAKAB
WAS THIS WHAT HE FEARED SO MUCH?

BRAKAB

KRAAASH
NO. TOO LATE, I SAW THE CREATURE FOR WHAT IT REALLY WAS.

IT WASN'T LIKE THE THING ON THE BEACH, PART OF OUR CARGO. IT WAS JUST A SIMPLE NATIVE OF THIS WORLD.
FRIGHTENED AND INNOCENT.

AND I HAD KILLED IT.
ON YOUR SABBATH.

AFTER THAT THE DAYS GREW EVEN LONGER, AS MY FOOD SUPPLY GOT SHORTER...
...AND TASTED WORSE THAN EVER.

I WAS BITTEN, AND STUNG, AND CUT, A THOUSAND TIMES.
ONCE I THOUGHT I SAW SOME WRECKAGE FROM THE MARU, BUT DECIDED IT WAS A FEVER DREAM.
I TRIED NOT TO THINK OF OUR CARGO AT ALL.

AS THE SABBATH DAWNED AGAIN, I DRANK MY LAST DROPS OF WATER.
THEN PLEADED FOR SALVATION AS NEVER BEFORE.

AND YOU DID NOT FAIL ME, LORD.
IT MUST HAVE BEEN THE FOLLOWING EVENING WHEN I SAW ANOTHER SIGN IN THE SKY...

FAINT WITH HOPE, I CRAWLED TO THE CREST OF THE NEXT HILL.

AND MY HEART LEAPT WITH JOY AND GRATITUDE.

FOR THERE SHE LAY...
THE NOVA MARU, FALLEN FROM HEAVEN.

I WAS OVERCOME WITH RELIEF AND EXHAUSTION.
EVEN THOUGH SALVATION WAS AT HAND, I HAD TO REST...

SO MUCH HAD HAPPENED SINCE FOSS AND I HAD LEFT HER...
I HAD SEEN SO MANY THINGS...
...SO MANY TERRIBLE THINGS...

LOOK. HE'S WATCHING US.
EYE-BALL'S STARING RIGHT AT US.

CAPTAIN FOSS. NOVA MARU.
NO QUESTIONS.

COULD HAVE SAVED THEM ALL. COULD HAVE.
HAVE TO EAT. HAVE TO EAT.

TERRIBLE THINGS. TERRIBLE THINGS.
HAD NO CHOICE.
NO CHOICE. FORGIVE ME, LORD. NO...
oh please no...

NOOO!
IT WAS A DREAM. JUST A DREAM.
A DREAM OF HELL.
THEN I SAW THAT MY GUN WAS GONE...
NO! WHO--?
SHH, TAKE IT EASY. TAKE IT EASY...

FOR A MOMENT, I THOUGHT I HAD WOKEN UP IN HEAVEN.
IT'S OVER.

OH, FORGIVE ME! FORGIVE ME.
HE WOULD HAVE KILLED ME. HE WOULD HAVE.
I HAD TO--

SELKIRK, IT'S ALL RIGHT.
JUST SHUT UP.
BUT IT WAS NO ANGEL THAT SPOKE TO ME.

IT WAS DEAN. FIRST OFFICER DEAN.
WHERE'S FOSS?
DID HE MAKE IT DOWN?

F-FOSS? YES, HE... BUT...
HE'S DEAD. WENT MAD. I HAD TO...
HE WOULD HAVE KILLED ME.

Hmm. LOOKS LIKE YOU'RE THE ONLY SURVIVOR, THEN, SELKIRK.
I MEAN, APART FROM ME.
YOU HUNGRY...?

OHHH.
I GET IT.
DEAN KNEW...

HERE, WASH THE TASTE OUT OF YOUR MOUTH.
...BUT SHE DIDN'T CARE.

AND THAT WATER WAS SO SWEET.
C'MON, SELKIRK... PLENTY OF TIME FOR PRAYING ONCE WE GET OFF OF THIS WORLD.

MY HEAD WAS FULL OF QUESTIONS.
I'LL CARRY YOUR GUN. DON'T WANT ANY MORE ACCIDENTS...
THE... MARU. YOU LANDED IT... ALONE?!

YES. TOOK SOME TIME, BUT I KNOW A FEW EMERGENCY ROUTINES...
COMPUTER GOT US DOWN IN ONE PIECE, MORE OR LESS.

THE OTHERS. HOW ...HOW DID THEY DIE? AND THE CARGO. WHAT--
LATER.

D-DEAN, THEY'RE--
I KNOW. SHUT UP.
IT WAS MORE NATIVES.

A...A FAMILY.
FRIGHTENED.
HUNTED.

DEAN, DON'T SHOOT. THEY--
SHUT UP.
THEN I HEARD IT. COMING THROUGH THE JUNGLE, TOWARDS US.

VERY FAST.

OUR CARGO HAD SURVIVED, TOO.

DEAR GOD! NOOO--
SHUT UP, MAN! SHUT

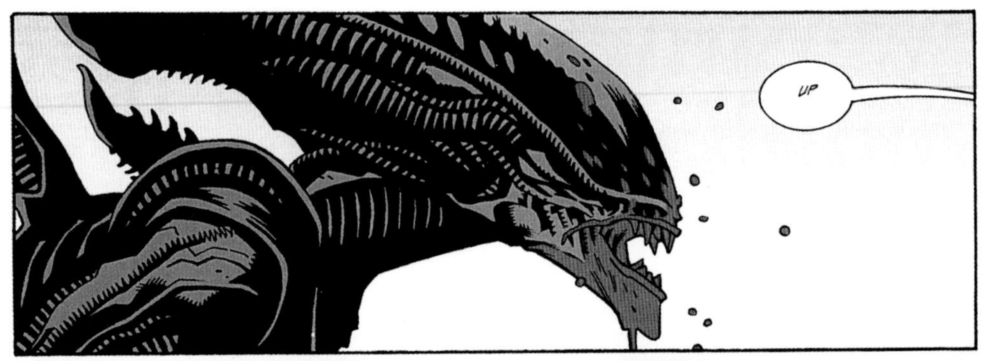
UP

SSSSCCHHHHH

DEAN! IN THE TREES!
BUDDA BUDDA BUDDA

TAKE THIS.

SHOOT ANYTHING THAT MOVES!
AND RUN! THIS WAY...

THE JUNGLE CLAWED AT ME.
BRAKA BRAKA BRAKA
BUDDA BUDDA BUDDA

GUNFIRE NUMBED MY EARS.
BUDDA BUDDA
BRAKA

THEN I RAN OUT OF AMMUNITION.
BUDDA BUDDA

BUDDA BUDDA
COME ON!
NEARLY THERE!
DEAN WAS SO FAST...

AND SO STRONG.
BUDDA
JUUUMMP!
BUDDA

SPLAASH
I PRAYED I HAD NOT COME THIS FAR JUST TO DROWN...

THEN I FELT DEAN'S BODY AGAINST MINE. SHE HELD ME UP, GUIDING ME TO SAFETY.

AS BREATH RETURNED, SO DID MY QUESTIONS...
SHIP'S ABOUT FOUR KLICKS, THAT WAY.
W-WAIT, DEAN, THOSE...THOSE DEMONS. WHY DID THE MARU BRING THEM HERE? WHAT--

COMPANY BUSINESS, SELKIRK. YOU DON'T NEED TO KNOW.
LET'S JUST CONCENTRATE ON GETTING OUT OF HERE.

DEAN WOULD ONLY TELL ME THAT THE MARU'S SHUTTLE WAS STILL SERVICEABLE...
...AND THAT THE WAY TO IT WAS PAST MORE OF THE DEMONS.

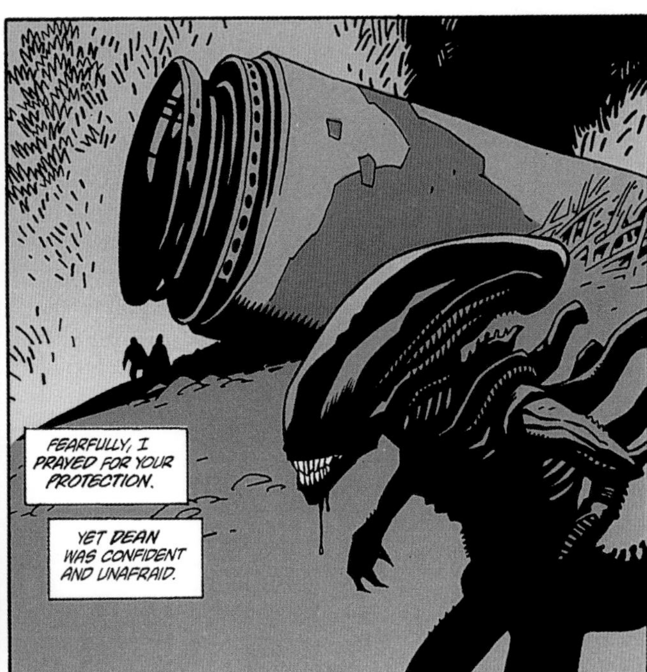
FEARFULLY, I PRAYED FOR YOUR PROTECTION.
YET DEAN WAS CONFIDENT AND UNAFRAID.

AND...AND I BEGAN TO THINK SHE MIGHT... LIKE ME.
HIDE IN HERE. I'LL BE A COUPLE OF MINUTES.
KEEP YOUR EYES OPEN...
...AND KEEP QUIET.

THAT ONE DAY, WE MIGHT EVEN--

NO.
IT WAS JUST ANOTHER TEST. I KNOW THAT NOW.

I PLEADED ONCE MORE FOR SALVATION FROM THIS HELL.
HSST-- SELKIRK.

TAKE THIS. AND REMEMBER...
...WE'RE IN THIS TOGETHER, OKAY?

WHEN WE GET TO THE SHUTTLE, WE'RE HOME FREE.
STAY CLOSE AND DON'T FIRE UNLESS YOU HAVE TO.

I'VE FIXED A DIVERSION.
LIQUID OXYGEN TANKS.

ANY SECOND...
00.03

KAWHOOMPH

I SAW DEMONS DANCING IN THE FLAMES.

I PRAYED THAT I COULD KEEP UP WITH DEAN.

I DIDN'T SEE THE WIRE.

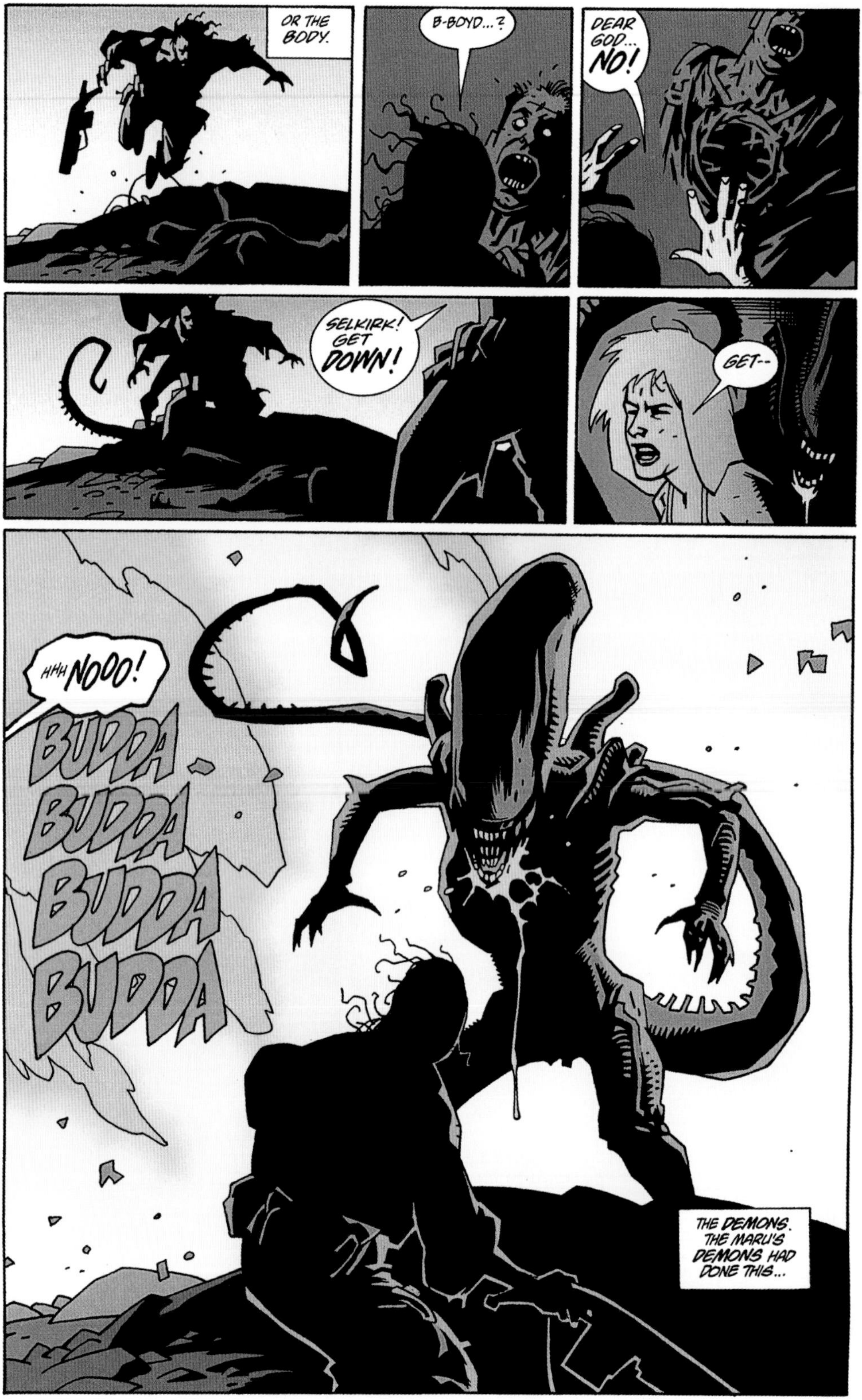

HHH NOOO!

BUDDA BUDDA BUDDA BUDDA

THE DEMONS. THE MARU'S DEMONS HAD DONE THIS...

SCHREEECCHH
BUDDA
BUDDA
BUDDA
DEMONS! DEMONS!!

DEAN!
WHERE-- WHERE ARE YOU?
BUD
BUDDA
BUDDA

IN MY LONG FALL FROM GRACE, I HAD SEEN MANY THINGS.
MANY TERRIBLE THINGS.
BUDDA
BUDDA
NOOOoo

BUT WHAT I SAW NEXT WAS THE WORST.

I HAD DREAMT OF HELL...

...SURELY THIS WAS THE PIT OF HELL ITSELF.

WITH SATAN AT ITS CENTER, SPAWNING DEMONS.
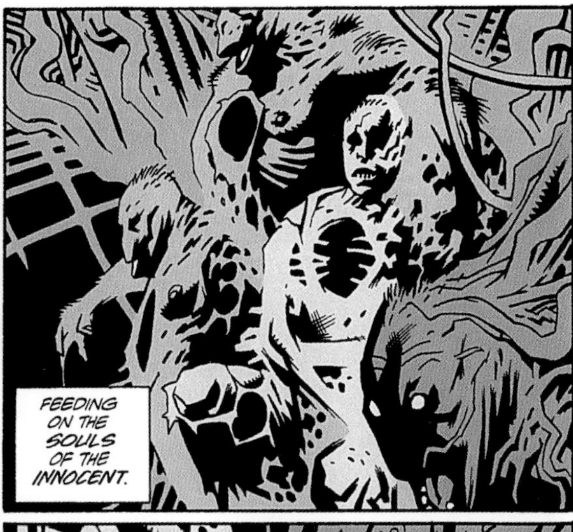
FEEDING ON THE SOULS OF THE INNOCENT.

I WONDERED IF THIS WAS TO BE MY FATE, AS WELL...

IF THE LAST DAYS HAD BEEN BUT PURGATORY...
...PREPARATION FOR THIS.

NO.
WHILE I CLUNG TO LIFE, I MIGHT STILL HOPE FOR SALVATION.
THERE WAS STILL THE SHUTTLE... AND DEAN.

THE WRECK OF THE MARU WAS LIKE A MAZE, DARK AND HAUNTED.
I DREADED DEATH AT EVERY TURN. SILENTLY, I BEGGED FOR GUIDANCE.

AGAIN, YOU SHOWED ME THE WAY.
ANGER
ENCY DESTRUCT
I RECOGNIZED THE CENTRAL SYSTEMS CONSOLE, JUST AFT OF MY GALLEY.

SILENTLY, I DISABLED THE PRESSURE SEALS ON THE GALLEY WASTE CHUTE.
BUT THE WAY TO THE SHUTTLE WAS OVER OPEN GROUND...
...AND I HAD TO REACH IT WITHOUT DEAN.

YET STILL YOU DID NOT DESERT ME...
SKREE
BUDDA
BUDD
BUD

AND SOON I HEARD THE HUM OF THE SHUTTLE'S LIFE-SUPPORT SYSTEM.
I PRAYED THAT DEAN WAS SAFE INSIDE.

THEN I HEARD HER VOICE...
SEL...KIRK? THOUGHT YOU...

...WERE... DEAD.
IT WAS SLOWER, STRANGELY THICKER.
AS I OPENED MY MOUTH TO REPLY...

...I NOTICED SOMETHING BRIGHT ON THE FLOOR.

IT WAS STARING RIGHT AT ME.

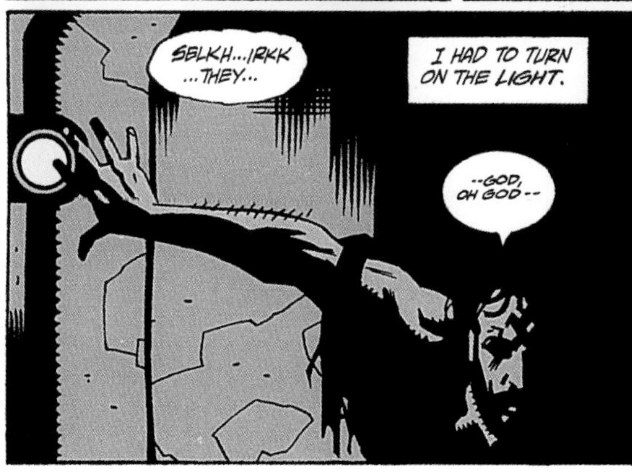
SELKH...IRKK ...THEY...
I HAD TO TURN ON THE LIGHT.
--GOD, OH GOD--

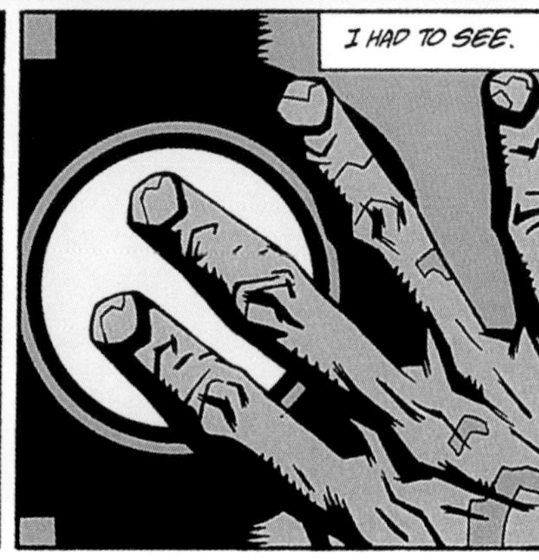
I HAD TO SEE.

WHAT I SAW WASN'T...
...DEAN WASN'T... HUMAN.
THEY... C...CAUGHT ...ME...

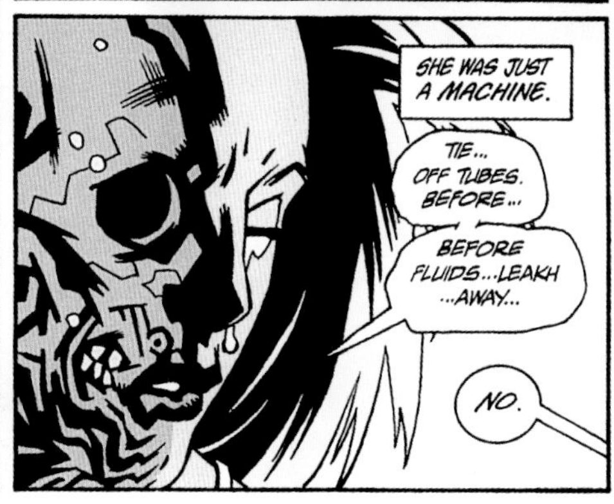

JUST A MACHINE. NOT ALIVE. NOT REALLY.
N-NOT UNTIL-- UNTIL YOU TELL ME WHY.
"WHY?"
SELH...KIRKH... I'M... I'M DYING...

DEAN WAS JUST TUBES AND CIRCUITS...
...AND INFORMATION.

WHY THE MARU WAS CARRYING THOSE DEMONS. WHY WE BROUGHT THEM HERE. WHY--
COMPANY... BUSINESS. Y...YOU DON'T...

I DO... I HAVE TO KNOW.
TELL ME NOW, OR I'LL...I'LL LET GO.
KLUNKT

O...OKAY...NO TIME TO...ARGUE...

THE MILITARY... WANTS THOSE CREATURES... ERADICATED FROM... GALAXY.
BUT THE...COMPANY BELIEVES...BELIEVES IT'S PRUDENT TO KEEP... RESERVES. IN CONTROLLED ...CONDITIONS. IMPORTANT... BIO-WEAPONS.

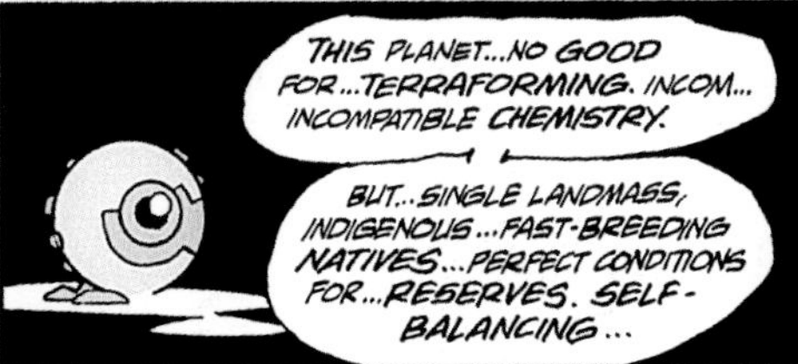

THIS PLANET...NO GOOD FOR...TERRAFORMING. INCOM... INCOMPATIBLE CHEMISTRY.
BUT...SINGLE LANDMASS, INDIGENOUS...FAST-BREEDING NATIVES...PERFECT CONDITIONS FOR...RESERVES. SELF-BALANCING...

NOVA MARU...TO LAND ALIENS. CREW...CREW LEAVE...IN SHUTTLE... BEFORE RELEASE...
BUT...STUTZ SCREWED...UP. STASIS FIELDS ...FAILED.

ONLY FOSS...AND I KNEW ABOUT...CARGO. LOST HIS...NERVE. TRIED TO...SAVE HIMSELF.
OTHERS DIDN'T STAND... CHANCE...

BUT ALIENS NOT...INTER...ESTED IN MACHINES LIKE...ME...
AND ME? WHY COME LOOKING FOR ME?
A MACHINE HAD NO COMPASSION.

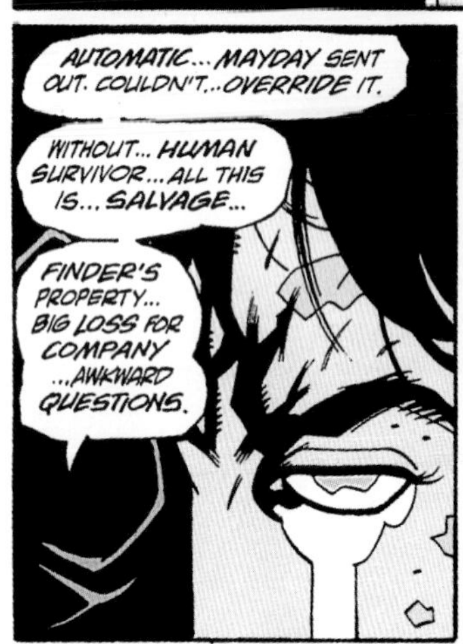
AUTOMATIC...MAYDAY SENT OUT. COULDN'T...OVERRIDE IT.
WITHOUT... HUMAN SURVIVOR...ALL THIS IS... SALVAGE...
FINDER'S PROPERTY... BIG LOSS FOR COMPANY ...AWKWARD QUESTIONS.

BUT IF...FLY SHUTTLE INTO ORBIT...SIT TIGHT... HYPERSLEEP CAPSULES...
THEN...MISSION ACC...ACCOMPLISHED. INVESTMENT... SECURE...
GOD.

DEAR GOD.
PULL YOUR...SELF TOGETHER, SELK...IRK. THIS ... PLANET...MICROBES ...TOXINS. CON...FUSING YOU...

NOW...PATCH ME...UP...
VALUABLE PROPERTY... YOU'RE STILL...COMPANY EMPLOYEE. MAY MEAN A...A BONUS FOR...YOU...
MONEY. THAT WAS ALL THIS WAS ABOUT.

A BONUS...

SSEL...SELLH... KHIRKK...GGK... HHHELLP M...ME...
THAAGSS... KKGK... ORDER...

A BONUS?!
BUDDA BUDDA BUDDA

HH..HELL..HPP...
KLIK KLIK
I DIDN'T KILL HER, LORD. SHE WAS NEVER ALIVE.
NOT REALLY. NO SOUL. JUST A... A PUPPET...

A PUPPET.
IN THAT MOMENT, YOU SHOWED ME WHERE SALVATION LAY.
TOLD ME HOW I COULD DEFEAT SATAN...

GAVE ME A CHANCE TO REDEEM MY SINS.
TSSSSSTT

SSST

I PRAYED FOR STRENGTH.
AIRLOCK
OPEN

I HAD COME SO FAR.
SUFFERED SO MUCH.

SALVATION WAS SO CLOSE.
I COULD NOT FAIL NOW.
KWUMP

THE ALIENS WERE JUST LIKE DEAN.
INHUMAN, SOULLESS PUPPETS.
SATAN WAS NOT IN THE MARU.
BUDDA
BUDDA
BUDDA
FWOOOOOOSSCH

THE REAL EVIL WAS MUCH LARGER, MUCH MORE POWERFUL.
BUDD BUDDA BUDDA
SKREECH SKREECH

IT SAT IN SAFETY, FAR AWAY, COUNTING ITS MONEY AND PULLING THE STRINGS OF ITS PUPPETS.

LIFE WAS JUST SOMETHING IT BOUGHT AND SOLD.
FWOOOSH
BUDDA BUDDA BUDDA

IT DIDN'T CARE ABOUT ANYONE.
IT NEVER HAD.
IT WAS THE TRUE SATAN.

MEN CALLED IT THE COMPANY.
FWOOOSH

I COULDN'T STOP IT.
IT WAS TOO BIG.
BUDDA
BUDDA
SKREEEEK

BUT I COULD HURT IT.

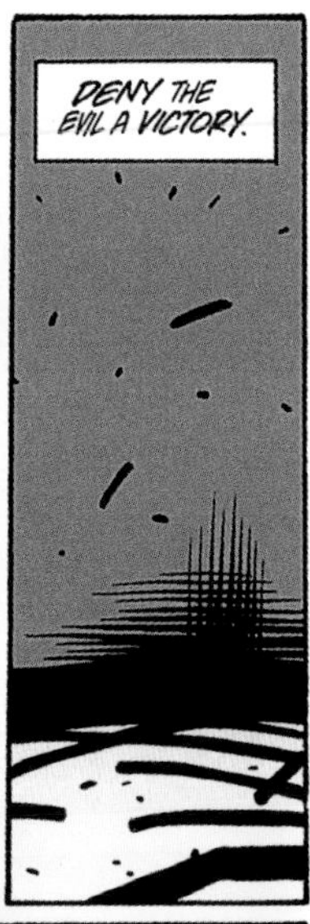
DENY THE EVIL A VICTORY.

THE COMPANY WANTED TO BREED THE ALIEN DEMONS HERE.
TURN THIS PLANET INTO HELL.
CONDEMN ITS INNOCENT NATIVES TO A LIVING DEATH.

DANGER
KILLING THEM ALL WOULD BE A TERRIBLE THING.
DANGER
EMERGENCY DESTRUCT

09:53:03
A TERRIBLE THING...
Danger. The emergency destruct system is now activated. The ship will automatically detonate in T minus ten minutes. No override possible.

BUT LETTING THEM LIVE WOULD BE WORSE...
... will automatically detonate in T minus one minute.

00:43:06
HEAR MY CONFESSION, LORD...
...AND IN YOUR MERCY, FORGIVE ME MY SINS.

T minus twenty seconds.
DELIVER ME FROM EVIL...
AND GRANT ME YOUR ETERNAL SALVATION.

FOR THINE IS THE KING-DOM...
...THE POWER AND THE GLORY...
Seven.

FOR EVER AND EVER...
Two.

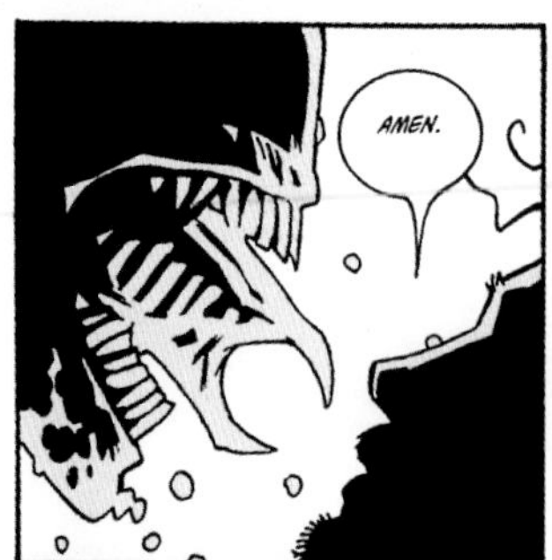
AMEN.

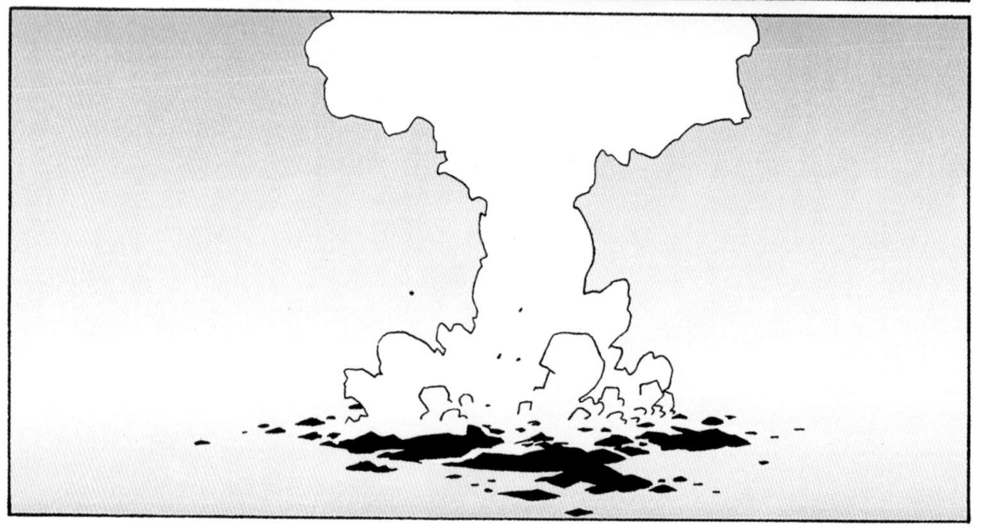

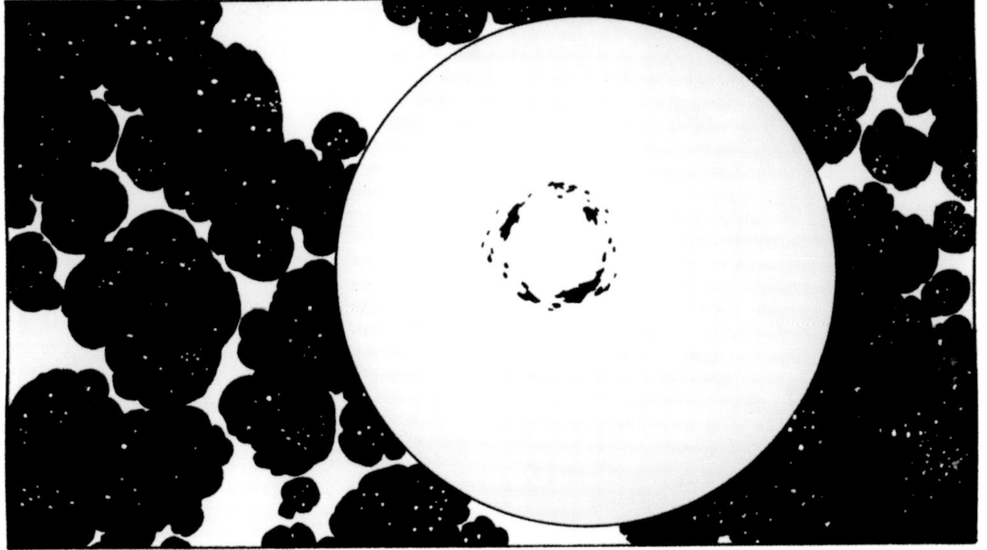

REPORT OF MISSIONARY VESSEL ST. PETER:
It is now more than four years since distress signals from planet PCW9512 ceased abruptly. Under Intersystem Law it has been our sad duty, as nearest manned craft, to investigate.
With deep regret, we can confirm that our probes reveal no sign of life upon its much diminished landmass.
Whether the disaster which claimed the freighter NOVA MARU and its crew was of human or divine origin, we are unable to determine.
Accordingly, we shall now resume our Mission, to spread the Word of God throughout the Galaxy. Our thoughts and prayers are with the souls of the departed...
ST. PETER
923N
May the Lord grant them true salvation.

END

ADVENT / TERMINUS

script
ANINA BENNETT and **PAUL GUINAN**

art
PAUL GUINAN

colors
RACHELLE MENASHE

lettering
WILLIE SCHUBERT

title illustration
KILIAN PLUNKETT

"THEY SAY THERE'S NOTHING NEW UNDER ANY SUN. WE'VE BREACHED THE 'FINAL FRONTIER' AND COME FACE-TO-FACE WITH OUR OWN PAST. ANOTHER NEW WORLD BRINGS ANOTHER GOLD RUSH-- ONLY THIS TIME, THE PROSPECTORS ARE ARMED TO THE TEETH AND SCOURING THE LANDSCAPE IN HI-TECH LO-FLIERS™.
"IF NOT FOR THIS PARCHED PLANET'S STORMY MAGNETOSPHERE, WE'D ALL BE SITTING COZILY IN AN ORBITAL STATION PINPOINTING ARCHAEOLOGICAL SITES VIA REMOTE SCAN. SCRATCH THAT.. I PROBABLY WOULDN'T BE HERE AT ALL. REAL-LIFE ADVENTURE IS SCARCE THESE DAYS. SO SCARCE THAT IT QUALIFIES AS NEWS.
"A PHYSICAL FORAY INTO ONE OF THESE EDIFICES IS BIG NEWS THESE DAYS. EXPEDITIONS INTO PYRAMIDS ELSEWHERE ON THIS PLANET HAVE YIELDED PRECIOUS GEMS AND METALS, UNFAMILIAR ALLOYS, INSCRIBED TABLETS, AND A WEALTH OF OTHER ARTIFACTS OF SOME LONG-EXTINCT RACE.
"THEY'VE ALSO REPORTED FINDING ALIEN EGGS."
ALIENS
PART ONE
ADVENT

"SEVERAL TEAMS HAVE ALREADY GONE MISSING, AND THERE'S NO TELLING WHICH SITE CLAIMED THEIR LIVES.
"FOR ALL WE KNOW, IT COULD HAVE BEEN THIS ONE.
"BUT NONE OF THIS FAZES THE MAN BEHIND OUR MISSION-- WELLINGTON FRICK, THE ONE-TIME PLAYBOY WHOSE RECENT BANKRUPTCY MADE INTERPLANETARY HEADLINES."
BELLE, WE'RE ABOUT TO BUY A LIFE-LONG MEAL TICKET.
I'M VERY HAPPY FOR YOU, WELLIE. BUT YOU KNOW I DON'T NEED TO EAT...
IT'S JUST AN EXPRESSION, YOU SYNTHOID BIMBO. NOW QUIT YOUR YAMMERIN'.
"OUR TEAM IS MINIMAL-- FRICK AND HIS 'SECRETARY,' BELLE, WITH HIRED GUN EMIL ZORN LEADING THE WAY.
"ZORN, THE ONLY KNOWN SURVIVOR OF A 'CHEST-BURSTER,' IS ABOUT 15% HUMAN.
"RUMOR HAS IT THAT AFTER THE TECHIES FITTED ZORN WITH AN ARTIFICIAL TORSO, HE DEMANDED THAT HIS UNDAMAGED LIMBS BE REPLACED AS WELL.
"I'M NOT SURE WHICH MAKES ME MORE NERVOUS-- ZORN, OR THE UNKNOWN CONTENTS OF OUR PYRAMID.
"NERVOUS OR NOT, I NEED THIS STORY. IT'S WORTH AT LEAST $60,000 FROM KOLCHAK. WONDER IF I CAN PARLAY THIS INTO A REGULAR CORRESPONDENT GIG...?"
TEN TO ONE SAYS THIS PLACE HAS BEEN SUCKED DRY ALREADY.
THAT'S WHAT I LIKE ABOUT YOU, ZORN--YOUR OVERWEENING OPTIMISM.
NO. NO, I'VE GOT A FEELING ABOUT THIS ONE...
COME ON. LET'S GET IN THERE.

SEEMS STUPID TO BUILD SOMETHING SO HUGE UP TOP IF HE'R GONNA PUT ALL THE GOODIES IN THE BASEMENT.
ACCORDING TO CURRENT THEORY, STRUCTURES SUCH AS THIS ONE REPRESENT A SPIRITUAL FOCAL POINT FOR COMMUNION WITH THE SACRED.
OF COURSE, THAT THEORY IS GROUNDED IN HUMAN EXPERIENCE, AND--
BELLE, SWITCH TO RESPONSE MODE. NO UNSOLICITED LECTURES, PLEASE.
SPEAK WHEN SPOKEN TO, eh, FRICK? SEEN BUT NOT HEARD. HOW PROGRESSIVE OF YOU

YOU'RE NOT HERE AS ETHICAL ADVISOR, POSADA-- JUST TO DOCUMENT MY DISCOVERIES.
AS SOON AS YOU DISCOVER SOMETHING, I'LL BE CERTAIN TO DOCUMENT IT.
BELLE, WHAT DO THOSE INSCRIPTIONS SAY?

THEY PROBABLY SAY, "NO FEMALES ALLOWED BEYOND THIS POINT."
I CAN'T GUARANTEE 100% ACCURACY. ROUGHLY TRANSLATED IT READS "SACRED IS THE SLEEP OF THE AGES, AND SAFE WITHIN THE SECOND WOMB..." "...DEATH FOLLOWS UPON BIRTH..."
THAT'S ALL I CAN TRANS-LATE.

"AS WE DESCEND TOWARDS THE MAIN CHAMBER, MY VAGUE FEARS COALESCE INTO A STOMACH-CURDLING KNOT. OUR 'LEADER' AND OUR 'PROTECTOR' ARE BOTH OUTCLASSED AND OUTSMARTED BY OUR ANDROID SIDEKICK.
"I FIND MYSELF WONDERING IF THIS IS HOW ADVENTURE IS SUPPOSED TO FEEL."

THE SEAL'S BEEN BROKEN.
LET'S HOPE THEY LEFT A FEW TRINKETS BEHIND FOR THE ALSO-RANS.

"FINALLY, OUR GOAL IS IN SIGHT-- A TOMB EVEN THE ANCIENT PHAROAHS WOULD HAVE APPRECIATED.

"I ONLY WISH MY STOMACH WOULD STOP TRYING TO DIGEST ITSELF."

WOW.

NICE DIGS!

HOY, FRICK--
I THINK I FOUND THE LAST EXPEDITION.
THESE GUYS MADE FOR A NICE HATCHERY. POSADA WAS RIGHT--THERE'S GOTTA BE THREE ADULTS IN HERE SOMEWHERE.
ZORN, COVER US WHILE I GO FOR THEIR LOOT BAGS.
COME ON, POSADA. UP CLOSE AND PERSONAL, JUST LIKE YOU WANTED IT.
"THIS IS OUR TEST OF FIRE. NO ADVENTURE WOULD BE COMPLETE WITHOUT A TREASURE OF SOME SORT."
WHERE'RE YOU HEADED, SYNTHETTE?
THE INSCRIPTIONS ALONG THIS DAIS ARE MOST INTRIGUING...
...THE TOMB-BUILDERS WERE DEFINITELY NOT OF THE SAME RACE AS THESE EGGS.

IN FACT, THIS ENTIRE STRUCTURE BEARS A REMARKABLE RESEMBLANCE TO--
LOOK OUT!

STOP WHINING AND HEAD FOR THE DOOR!
AND YOU PICKED THE WRONG BUNCH OF SUCKERS, BUCKO!
THAT UGLY HIDE OF YOURS AIN'T QUITE TOUGH ENOUGH, IS IT?

BELLE! OMIGOD, BELLE!
NO. OH, NONONONO. I KNEW IT, I KNEW IT...

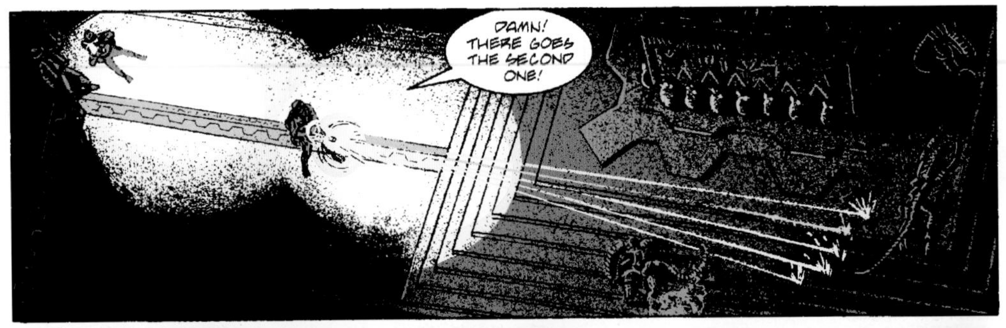
DAMN! THERE GOES THE SECOND ONE!

CLOSE THE DAMN DOORS!
WHAT DOES IT LOOK LIKE WE'RE DOING?!

A COUPLE EXTRA GUNS WOULD'VE BEEN HELPFUL IN THERE, FRICK-FACE.
YEAH? TELL ME AGAIN HOW YOU ONCE FOUGHT OFF A HALF-DOZEN OF THOSE THINGS SINGLE-HANDED!
SAY, WHY DON'T WE ALL BEAT A HASTY RETREAT WHILE WE'VE GOT THE CHANCE?

BECAUSE, POSEY, WE LEFT TWO LIVE ALIENS IN THERE--
AND A FORTUNE...
--AND YOU WANT ANOTHER CHANCE AT EXCLUSIVE FOOTAGE OF ME KICKING ALIEN BUTT!
YEAH, WELL... THAT IS PART OF WHY I CAME ALONG.
AFTER ALL, THE NETWORKS WON'T PICK UP A STRINGER REPORT UNLESS IT'S GOT A STRONG ACTION SEQUENCE...

"OUR VARIOUS GOALS HAVE WON OUT OVER OUR INSTINCT FOR SELF-PRESERVATION, AND SO WE TURN BACK INTO THE MAW OF 'ADVENTURE.' ONE LAST TRY FOR THE BRASS RING.

"AS WE RE-ENTER THE MAIN BURIAL CHAMBER OF THIS E.T. PYRAMID, I CONSIDER RETREATING TO THE SHIP WHILE I'VE GOT THE CHANCE. WE'VE ALREADY LOST FRICK'S ANDROID, *BELLE*, TO ONE OF THE GUARDIAN ALIENS IN HERE--AND *SHE* WAS THE MOST *RELIABLE* MEMBER OF OUR CREW.

"THEN I PICTURE MYSELF TRYING TO SELL THIS FOOTAGE TO THE NETWORKS WITHOUT THE REQUISITE 'BIFF-BANG-POW.' FAT CHANCE.

"I KNEW GOING IN THAT GLORY CAME WITH A STEEP PRICE TAG. I JUST HAVE TO KEEP TELLING MYSELF IT'S WORTH IT."

ALIENS PART TWO TERMINUS

NO MOVEMENT ON THE TRACKER YET.

LOOK ALIVE--I'M READING TWO NASTIES ON THE MOVE.
THEY'RE FLANKING US! MAKE SURE YOU GET THIS ALL IN FRAME, POSADA.

SNEAKY BASTAAARRRD--

LOOK OUT, ZORN-- THE ONE YOU WINGED IS COMIN' AT YA!

KEEP 'EM BUSY, ZORN--JUST ANOTHER MINUTE AND WE'LL BE RICH!
CHEW ON THIS, BUCKWHEAT!
ZORN! BEHIND YOU!
UNH
FRICK, I NEED BACKUP!
FRICK, DAMMIT!!
ARRRR

HOLD ON FOR ONE MORE SECOND, ZORN.

I-- OH, SH--!

NONONONONO... NOT WHEN I'M THIS CLOSE...

=uff= YOU...AIN'T =ungg=
...SO...
...TOUGH!
YARRRRRRR
"THAT WASN'T QUITE THE WRAP-UP I'D EXPECTED.
=ulp= ZORN...
"BUT AT LEAST I'LL GET TOP DOLLAR OUT OF THIS-- THE GREATER THE SHOCK VALUE, THE FATTER THE FEE."

HEY! YOU'RE NOT LEAVING ME BEHIND, FRICK!
YOU RAT! YOU COULD'VE HELPED HIM!
HEY, WE BOTH KNEW ZORN WAS CANNON FODDER--
--AND WE'RE ALIVE ONLY BECAUSE HE WAS SUCH DURABLE, TENACIOUS CANNON FODDER.
SAVE YOUR BREATH, POSADA. IT'S A LONG SPRINT TO THE SHIP.

I'LL SHOW YOU "CANNON FODDER."
=whuff=

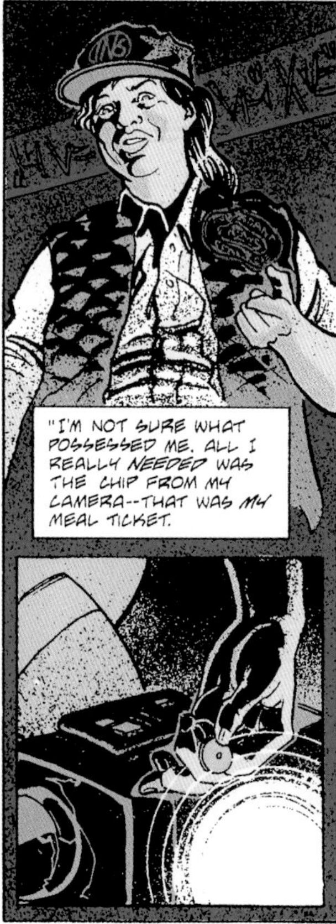
"I'M NOT SURE WHAT POSSESSED ME. ALL I REALLY NEEDED WAS THE CHIP FROM MY CAMERA--THAT WAS MY MEAL TICKET.

"MAYBE I JUST FELT THE NEED FOR SOME POETIC JUSTICE. DO THE GALAXY A FAVOR FOR A CHANGE."
THANKS FOR THE BONUS, FRICK!

=mmmff=
...OH, HELL!! WHAT DID THAT BITCH DO TO ME?
HA! SO SHE COULDN'T CARRY BOTH BAGS, eh? SERVES HER RIGHT.
WAIT'LL SHE FINDS OUT THAT THE SHIP'S CONTROLS ARE KEYED TO MY THUMB-PRINTS.
I'D LOVE TO SEE THE LOOK ON HER--
FWAAAA
"WHAT WAS IT KOLCHAK SAID? SOMETHING ABOUT HAPPY ENDINGS...
"OH, YEAH: 'IF TWO PEOPLE ARE ALIVE AT THE END OF YOUR PIECE, IT'S A HAPPY ENDING. IF ONE PERSON SURVIVES, IT'S A COMEDY. COMEDY ALWAYS PLAYS BETTER.'
"MAYBE THERE AREN'T ANY REAL ADVENTURES LEFT TO BE HAD-- JUST TRAGEDIES AND FARCES TO BE PLAYED OUT."

"WELL, AT LEAST THE CLOSING MONOLOGUE IS MINE.
"I'D HATE FOR SOMEONE ELSE TO HAVE THE LAST WORD."

I'M AFRAID WE'RE NOT THE FIRST ONES HERE, JUNCO. TAKE A LOOK.
OH, THIS PYRAMID HASN'T EVEN BEEN CHARTED YET. I'M SURE THERE'S PLENTY LEFT TO GO AROUND.

BY ALL ACCOUNTS, ONE OF THESE THINGS HOLDS ENOUGH TO MAKE EARTH A RICH PLANET AGAIN.
AND IF OUR PREDECESSORS AREN'T WILLING TO SHARE, WELL...

...GREED IS A LOSING PROPOSITION, ISN'T IT?
END

REAPERS

script
JOHN ARCUDI

art
SIMON BISLEY

colors
CHRIS CHALENOR

title illustration
SIMON BISLEY

PUKE

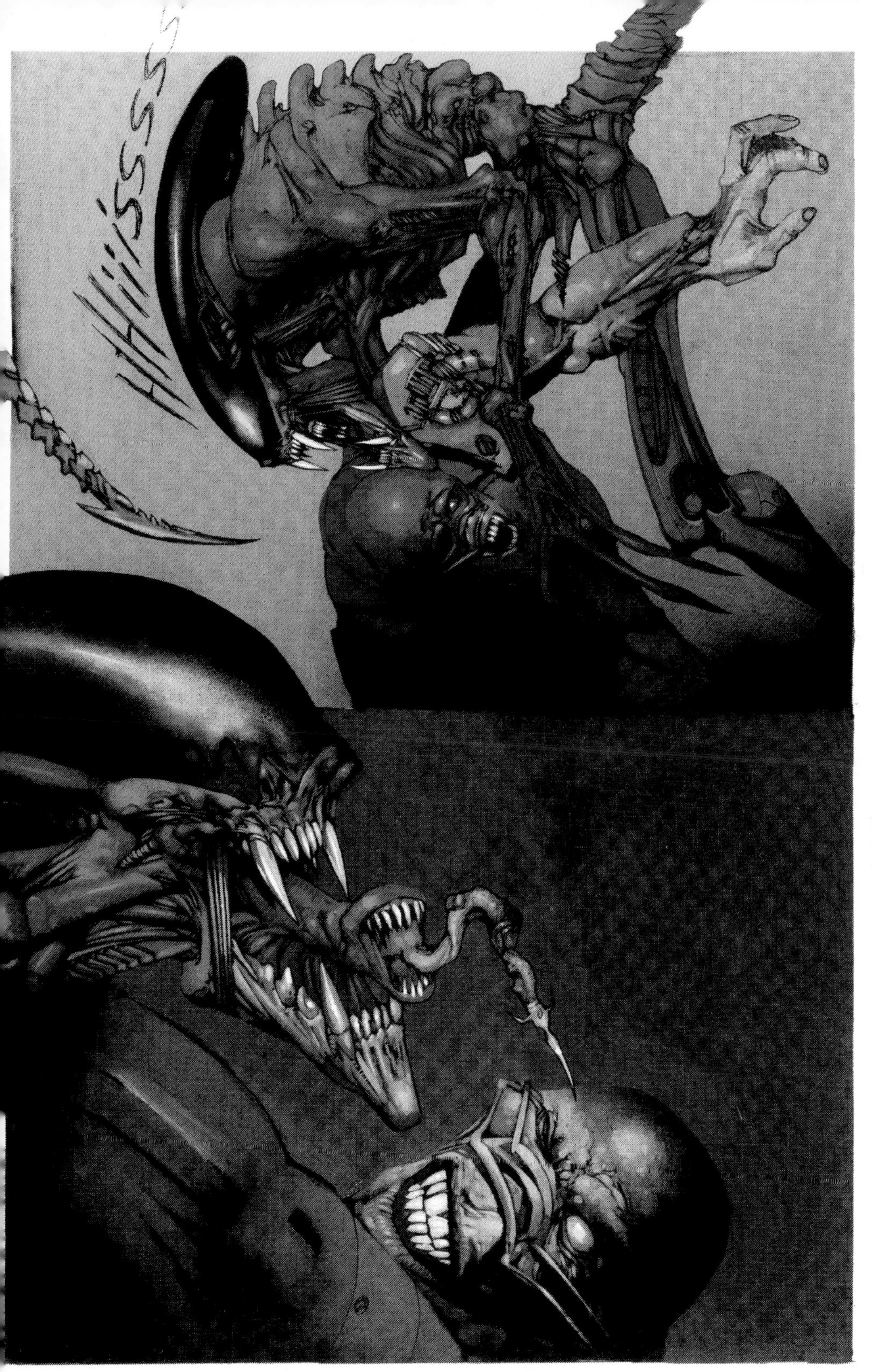
HIISSSSS

WHACK

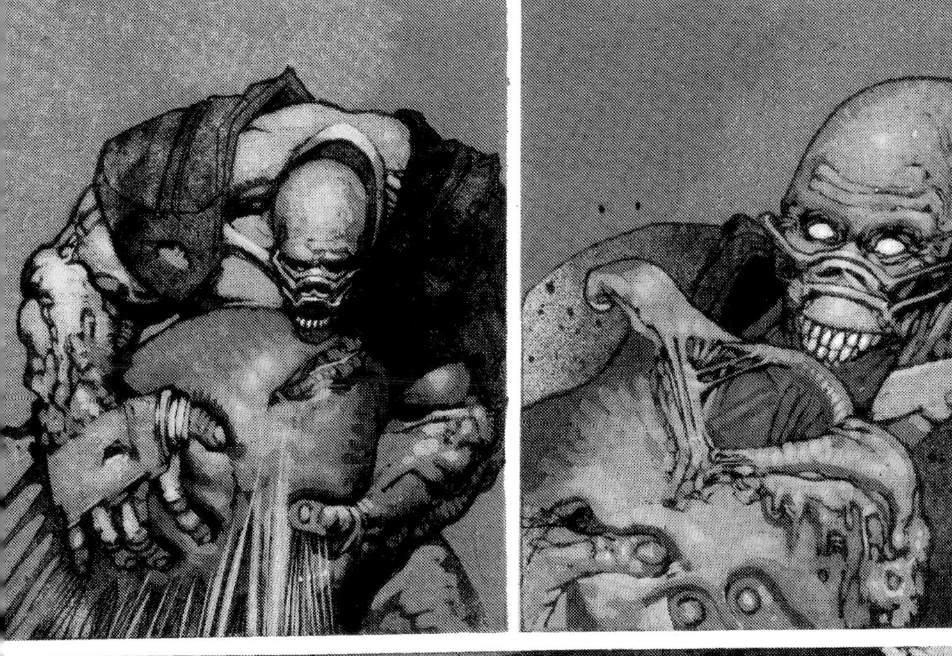

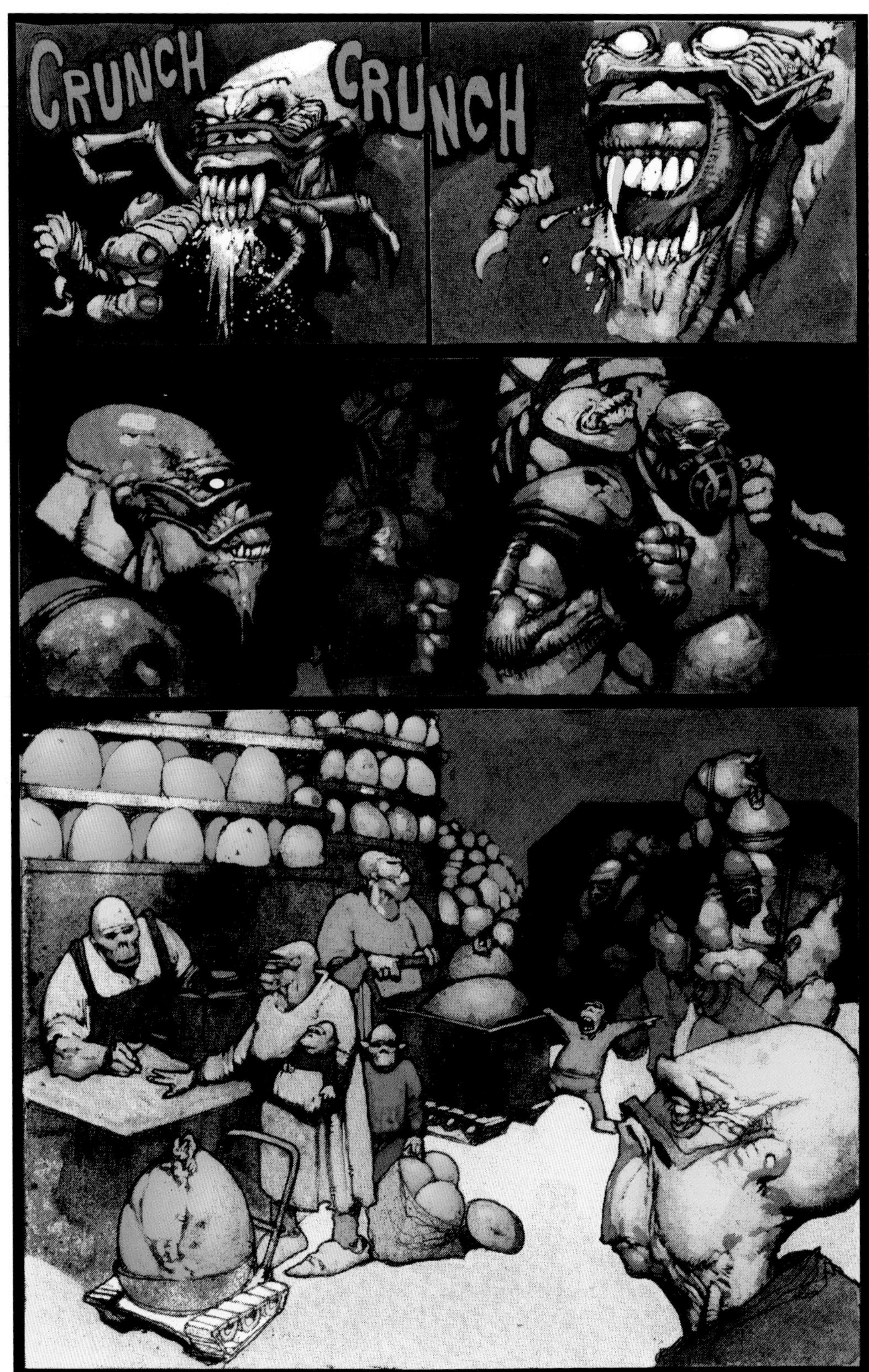
CRUNCH
CRUNCH

HORROR SHOW
DORMAN

script
SARAH BYAM

art
DAVID ROACH

colors
ALEX WALD

lettering
PHIL OWEN

title illustration
DAVE DORMAN

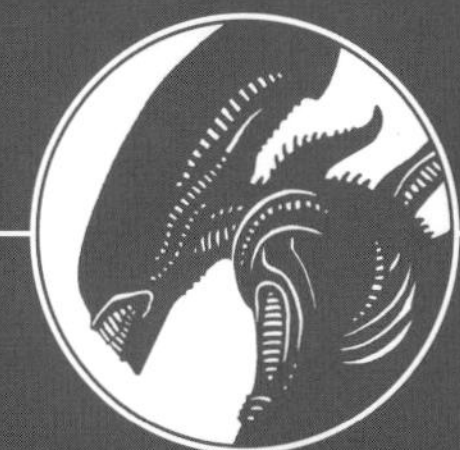

ALIENS
Horror Show: Part 1

LUNA CITY IS A SLEEPY TOWN. AND PEOPLE LIKE IT THAT WAY, NOW. BACK IN THE '20s, IT WAS A ROARING PLACE: VIBRANT... ENERGIZED... BECAUSE IT WAS THE HOME OF ORSON MASCH ENTERTAINMENT INDUSTRIES, LUNA BECAME A CITYWIDE THEME PARK, A PLAYGROUND FOR ADULTS...
...UNTIL THE INFESTATION.
NOW THE PEOPLE FEEL A LITTLE BIT GUILTY ABOUT THEIR FRIVOLOUS HISTORY, WHAT WITH THE ENTIRE HUMAN RACE PERISHING DOWNSIDE. WE DON'T TAKE TRANSMITS FROM THE SURFACE ANYMORE, AND NO ONE WOULD EVEN THINK OF SHUTTLING DOWN FOR A LOOK.
QUIETLY, METHODICALLY, WE TERRAFORM LUNA ONE MILE AT A TIME. AND IF POSSIBLE, WE DON'T TALK ABOUT THEM.

I SAW THEM, JUST BEFORE I SQUEEZED ONTO THE LAST OUTBOUND SHUTTLE. I WAS SIX.
I DON'T TALK ABOUT 'EM EITHER.
BUT I DREAM...
ORSON MASCH RULES THE WORLD NOW, WHAT THERE IS LEFT OF IT, BECAUSE ENTERTAINMENT IS THE ONLY CHALLENGE WE'LL BE ABLE TO RISK IN THE NEXT GENERATION OR TWO.

ME, I WORK FOR THE OMEI TESTING THEIR NEW VID-LINE.
IT'S A CHEAP THRILL, BUT SOMEBODY'S GOTTA DO IT...

WHAT ARE THESE?
HERE, JUST SWALLOW AND GET IT OVER WITH.
MILD HALLUCINOGENS -- NOTHING DANGEROUS. I PROMISE.
I HAD A GIRLFRIEND WHO SAID THAT ONCE.

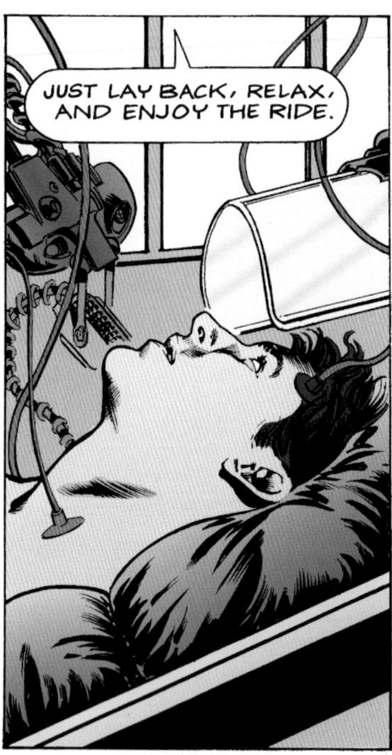
JUST LAY BACK, RELAX, AND ENJOY THE RIDE.

WARM, SHALLOW -- OKAY, THE BOYO GETS THE "SENSORY DEPRIVATION TEST" ON DOWNERS.

THIS OUGHT TO BE A PIECE OF CAKE.

OH-MY-GOD-OH-MY-GOD.

THMP!

ROBYN?

ROBYN?
HONEY...

NO, YOU SUNNUVA --

GILLS... GOTTA REACH THE...

LOSE A LEG, GAIN A... SOMETHING, PLEASE...

OH BABY, TAKE ME OUTTA THIS NIGHTMARE.

PLEASE, I'M SO GLAD IT'S...
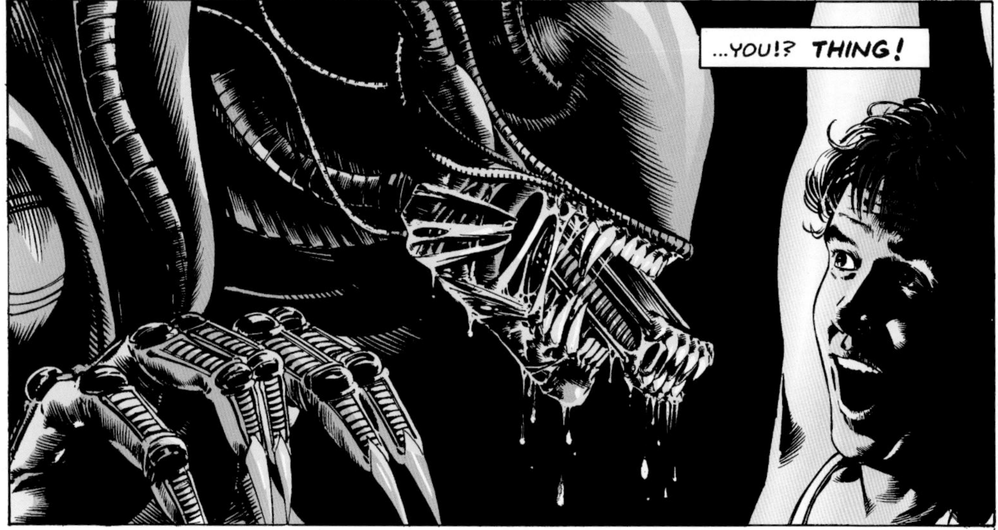
...YOU!? THING!

AAHH! NO! NO!
AAAAHH!!

NO #$*!% WAY YOU BASTAAA--
SUBJECT INTO OVERLOAD.
CODE RED! CODE RED!
DAMMIT, RAY. HURRY UP WITH THAT SEDATIVE.
NOW!

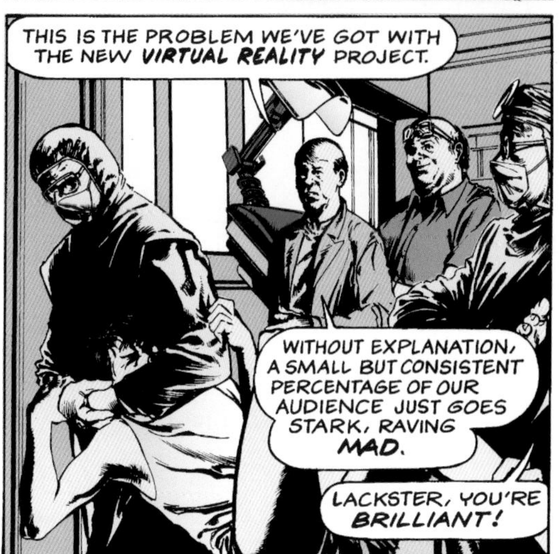
THIS IS THE PROBLEM WE'VE GOT WITH THE NEW VIRTUAL REALITY PROJECT.
WITHOUT EXPLANATION, A SMALL BUT CONSISTENT PERCENTAGE OF OUR AUDIENCE JUST GOES STARK, RAVING MAD.
LACKSTER, YOU'RE BRILLIANT!

I DON'T BELIEVE YOU UNDERSTAND THE SITUATION, SIR.
UNDERSTAND!? ORSON MASCH NEVER MISSES A TRICK, MY BOY. YOU'VE INVENTED THE GOLDEN GOOSE!

I'VE MANAGED TO CONTROL THIS LITTLE COLONY BY PROVIDING PEOPLE WITH THE MOST BANG FOR THEIR BUCK.
SENSIBLE PEOPLE RUN FROM WHAT THEY'RE AFRAID OF UNLESS YOU TELL 'EM THEY CAN'T HANDLE IT.

THEN THEY'LL PAY YOU DOUBLE FOR THE PRIVILEGE OF PROVING YOU WRONG.

WE'LL START THE PROMO CAMPAIGN FIRST THING TOMORROW--
-- BUT, MR. MASCH, IT NEEDS MORE TESTING.
TEST. TEST. BY ALL MEANS. BY THE TIME WE RELEASE IT...

...THEY'LL BE DROOLING FOR IT.

PICKED IT UP THIS MORNING--
--LIKE IT?

SO TELL ME HOW IT WORKS -- JUST THE BASICS, Y'UNDERSTAND.
DON'T HAVE TIME FOR LOTS OF USELESS DETAILS.
UH, WELL, IN SIMPLE LANGUAGE, WE PROVE AN ELECTROCHEMICAL STIMULATION OF THE HYPO-THALAMUS AND THE PINEAL ORGAN WHILE ARTIFICIALLY INDUCING DEEP HYPNOSUGGEST-IBILITY WITH OLFACTORY AND VISUAL STIMULI...

IN ENGLISH, SON.

IT'S A NIGHTMARE, SIR. EXCEPT YOU CAN TASTE IT, SMELL IT, FEEL IT, SEE, HEAR...
...AND YOU CAN'T WAKE UP.

WHAT YOU NEED IS THE NAME AND THE MATERIAL.
WE'LL CALL IT "THE GENRE" AND START WITH THE HORROR LINE.
THEN SKIN FEELIES AND ADVENTURES FOR THE KIDS.

YOU'RE GONNA BE RICH, LACKSTER
I WANT SIX FEATURES BY FEBRUARY.

DISMISSED, LACKSTER.

BUT YOU'VE GOT TO HELP ME, DOCTOR--
I NEED SIX MORE NIGHTMARE FEATURES --OR THE OLD MAN IS GONNA FEED ME TO THE ALIENS.
DIDN'T I TAKE YOUNG MR. FRED PRESTON OFF YOUR HANDS WITHOUT QUESTION?
JUST AS I'VE CARED FOR EVERY OTHER UNFORTUNATE VICTIM OF YOUR PROFESSIONAL EXPERIMENT? I DO HAVE OTHER RESPONSIBILITIES.

JUST REMEMBER, KAF, YOUR PRECIOUS NON-PROFIT CLINIC WILL LOSE THE SUPPORT OF OMEI INDUSTRIES--

--IF I LOSE THE SUPPORT OF ORSON MASCH...
FITZ-KLIK
PHILISTINE!

LET'S CONTINUE THE TOUR, SHALL WE?
DADDY?
IT'S OKAY, ROBYN-HONEY. DR. KAF IS THE BEST THERE IS.

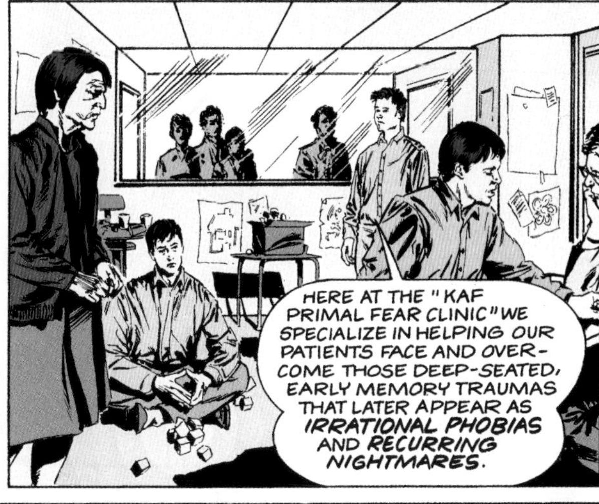

HERE AT THE "KAF PRIMAL FEAR CLINIC" WE SPECIALIZE IN HELPING OUR PATIENTS FACE AND OVERCOME THOSE DEEP-SEATED, EARLY MEMORY TRAUMAS THAT LATER APPEAR AS IRRATIONAL PHOBIAS AND RECURRING NIGHTMARES.

IT HAS BEEN SUGGESTED, FOR EXAMPLE, THAT ALL HUMAN BEINGS FEAR SPIDERS AND MULTI-LEGGED CREATURES...
... BECAUSE THE LAST THING THAT ANY OF US SEE IN THE WOMB JUST BEFORE OUR BIRTH TRAUMA IS A KNOT OF UMBILICAL VEINS-- PULSING, CONTRACTING VEINS --AGAINST THE WALL OF THE UTERUS AS WE ARE SQUEEZED INTO THE PAIN OF THIS MORTAL...

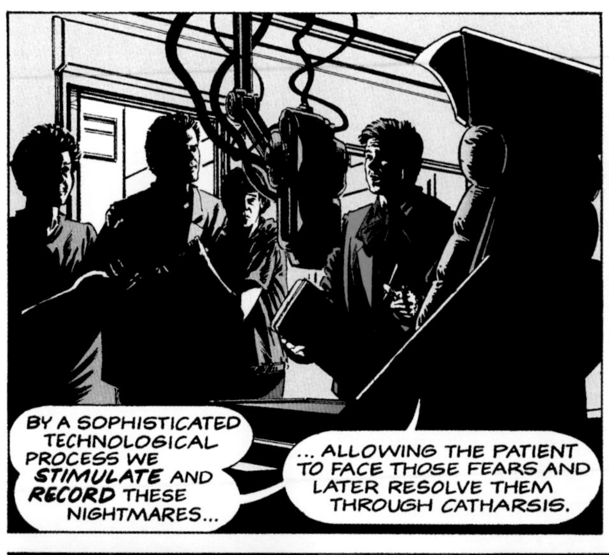
BY A SOPHISTICATED TECHNOLOGICAL PROCESS WE **STIMULATE** AND **RECORD** THESE NIGHTMARES...
... ALLOWING THE PATIENT TO FACE THOSE FEARS AND LATER RESOLVE THEM THROUGH CATHARSIS.

AND WE'LL LEAVE HER HER PRIVACY THIS FIRST TIME--MOST PATIENTS SHOW SOME EMBARRASS-MENT AT HAVING THEIR INNER SELVES EXPOSED...

CRYING FOR DADDY DIDN'T HELP.

"WE'RE LEAVING YOU HERE TO CURE YOU OF THOSE IRRATIONAL FEARS, ROBYN."

"YOU **KNOW** THIS DOESN'T HURT YOU NEARLY AS MUCH AS IT HURTS ME."

RIGHT.

FIVE YEARS OF BEING TRAPPED IN THE LIMESTONE MINES.
FIVE YEARS OF HIDING FROM THOSE...
...MONSTERS.

FIVE YEARS OF TORTURE...

...AND YOU LEARN A FEW THINGS.

HOW TO HIDE.
HOW TO FIGHT.

WHEN TO RUN.
WHERE TO STRIKE.
OF COURSE, IN THE END, THEY ALWAYS WIN.

ALMOST ALWAYS.

THIS IS MY MOST AMBITIOUS PLAN YET.
SHE KILLED MY RACE, SO I'LL TURN THE FAVOR BACK, I FIGURE.

DADDY WOULD HAVE BEEN PROUD, I GUESS.
AND EVEN IF HE ISN'T, I **AM.**

ROBYN MILES, ALIEN IMPERSONATOR, RECLAIMS THE PLANET EARTH FOR THE HOMOSAPIENT RACE.

THERE WERE SEVEN PRIMARY NESTS ON **THIS** CONTINENT.

NOW THERE ARE THREE.

THIS IS A BORROWED TIME GAME...

...THOUGH AIN'T NO WAY I'LL MAKE IT THROUGH TO THE END.

BUT SO FAR THEY HAVEN'T CAUGHT ON TO THIS PARTICULAR SCAM. AND THAT'S SOMETHING.

SNEAK IN AS ONE OF THEM. PLANT THE BOMB UNDER THE QUEEN'S LAP.

REVEAL YOURSELF.

THE STRATEGY'S SIMPLE --IT'S THE EXECUTION THAT'LL KILL YA...
... EVERY TIME.

THE "DO-IT-OR-DIE-TRYIN' GIRL"..
THAT'S ME.

NO. GOD, NO.
NOT NOW.

DON'T LET
THEM
CATCH ME.

DON'T LET
THEM--

--PENETRATE.

ALIENS?! ORSON MASCH IS GONNA KILL ME.
YOU'VE RECORDED HUNDREDS OF NIGHT-MARES AT A COST OF MILLIONS OF CREDITS...

...AND ALL YOU CAN GIVE ME ARE MORE ALIEN FEATURES?
DON'T YOU HAVE A FEW WET DREAMS? ...ANYTHING?

MY GOOD MAN, AUTO SUGGESTION ONLY WORKS SO FAR.
THE ENTIRE EARTH WAS ABANDONED AFTER THE INFEST-ATION--

WHAT DO YOU EXPECT PEOPLE TO DREAM ABOUT?

IRONICALLY, WE'RE BEGINNING TO SEE SOME EVIDENCE THAT THESE POOR SLOBS...
...ARE MORE LIKELY TO SURVIVE AN ACTUAL ALIEN ATTACK THAN YOU OR I WOULD.

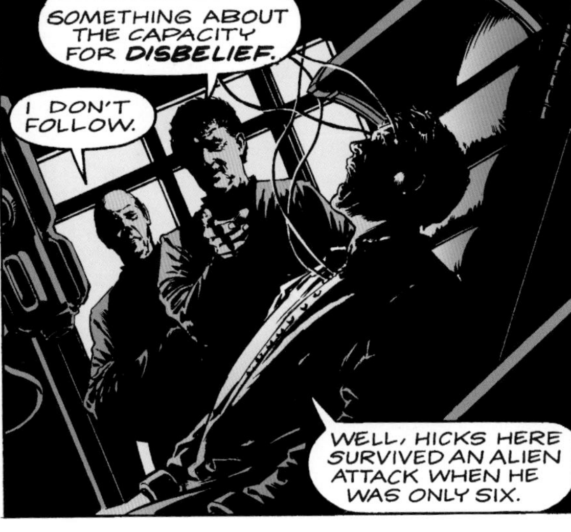
SOMETHING ABOUT THE CAPACITY FOR DISBELIEF.
I DON'T FOLLOW.
WELL, HICKS HERE SURVIVED AN ALIEN ATTACK WHEN HE WAS ONLY SIX.

DON'T RESIST ME, MY DEAR.
M-M-R-R-R!

UNLESS YOU WANT ANOTHER DOSE OF THERAPY.

THAT GOES FOR ALL OF YOU!
GROVELING, COWARDLY EXCUSES FOR HUMAN PSYCHES --

THAT'S IT, MR. HICKS, FLINCH!

YOU HAVEN'T BEGUN TO UNDER-STAND THE DEPTH OF YOUR OWN FEAR.

HE WAS ONE OF THE LAST CHILDREN TO MAKE IT TO THE LUNAR ESCAPE SHUTTLE...
...BECAUSE HE TRUSTS HIS SENSES.

BUT HE WENT MAD DURING YOUR LITTLE VIRTUAL REAL-ITY TESTS BECAUSE HIS SENSES WERE LYING TO HIM.

THE CYNICISM NEEDED TO SURVIVE IN MODERN SOCIETY...
...WOULD BE DEATH IN THE JUNGLE.

"THE PRICE...

...OF CIVILIZATION, MR. LACKSTER."

YOU'VE HAD MY DAUGHTER IN YOUR PRECIOUS INSTITUTION FOR FIVE YEARS, DR. KAF.
WE HAD HOPED TO BREAK THROUGH HER CATATONIA BY NOW, BUT THESE THINGS... WELL, THEY HAPPEN SOMETIMES.
ALIENS
Horror Show: Part 3

NOT TO MY DAUGHTER, THEY DON'T.
I BROUGHT YOU A FRIGHTENED CHILD, AND YOU TURNED HER INTO A VEGETABLE.
I KNOW YOU'VE BEEN SELLING THEIR BRAIN SCANS TO ORSON MASCH ENTERTAINMENT INDUSTRIES.

OMEI GENEROUSLY FUNDS OUR RESEARCH HERE.
YOUR DAUGHTER WAS IN YOUR CUSTODY FOR EIGHTEEN YEARS BEFORE YOU PLACED HER DAMAGED PSYCHE ON MY DOORSTEP.
DO NOT PUNISH ME FOR YOUR PATERNAL GUILT.

YOU'VE GOT ONE HELL OF A NERVE, OLD MAN--
--I WILL CLOSE DOWN THIS LITTLE HOUSE OF HORRORS.

OH, YOU WILL TRY. AND YOU WILL WASTE A GREAT DEAL OF MONEY.
YOU SEE, THE LUNA CITY COUNCIL SUPPORTS OUR WORK HERE--AS DO A NUMBER OF OUR MORE FINANCIALLY INFLUENTIAL CITIZENS.

"IT'S SOCIAL DENIAL, MY GOOD MAN. SINCE WE LOST THE PLANET TO THE ALIENS, EVERYONE IS AFRAID--
"--BUT NO ONE WANTS TO ADMIT IT. BETTER TO HIDE THE EXTREME CASES--
"--TOO MUCH LIKE THE DEMONS IN OUR OWN BELLIES. BELIEVE ME, SIR--
"--THERE'S NOTHING YOU CAN DO."

WAKE UP, HONEY.
ROBYN--WAKE UP.
KOFF KOFF!

THE NIGHTMARE'S OVER.

KOFF KOFF KOFF!
HURRY WITH THAT SUCTION--
-- SHE'S GONNA DROWN!

HER PULSE IS RETURNING TO NORMAL.
I THOUGHT --OH GOD--
--THEY WERE EVERYWHERE.
I KNOW, ROBYN. BUT IT'S OVER NOW.
YOUR FATHER HELPED US--WE TOOK CONTROL OF THE LAB THIS MORNING.

DR. KAF HAS RETREATED TO THE TOP CUBE OF THE EAST WING IN HIS PRECIOUS SENSORY LAB.
YOU'VE TRAPPED HIM IN THE NIGHTMARE ROOM?!
YOU GOT IT.

HOW MUCH LONGER BEFORE THEY'RE FINISHED DOWNSTAIRS?

TWENTY MINUTES, EASY.

ALL RIGHT. ROBYN AND I WILL BREACH THE EMERGENCY HATCH IN FIFTEEN MINUTES. THEN CUT THE CORRIDOR OFF AND JOIN THE OTHERS IN THE SHUTTLE.

IF ANYTHING GOES WRONG...

...**LEAVE** WITHOUT US.

YOU MISERABLE SON OF A...

I'M--I'M GLAD TO WITNESS YOUR--
--REMARKABLE, UH, RECOVERY--
SHUT IT!
YOU'RE LUCKY YOU'RE NOT DEAD ALREADY!

PLEASE, YOU MUST LET ME GO!
NO, I DON'T THINK SO.

YOU KNOW, THIS IS QUITE A DEVICE YOU'VE CREATED, DR. KAF.
EDUCATES, STIMULATES, TRAINS REFLEXES, BUILDS CHARACTER.
--YEAH LOOK HOW WE TURNED OUT.
WE THOUGHT **YOU** SHOULD TRY IT.

THERE'S ONLY ONE CATCH.
REMEMBER YOUR DISCOVERY, DOCTOR?
WE FOUND CERTAIN PATIENTS, SENSITIVE ONES, OR SURVIVORS, WHO COULD NOT COPE WITH "THE GENRE"--
--BECAUSE THEY REACTED TO THE STIMULUS AS THOUGH IT WERE REAL. YES, **THAT'S** THE ONE.

WELL, HERE'S **YOUR** PSYCHE TEST. IF WHAT YOU SEE IN THAT BOX IS **NOT** REAL...
...YOU WILL SURVIVE AS LONG AS YOU REMAIN CALM AND CONNECTED TO YOUR LIFE SUPPORT.
THE POLICE WILL DISCOVER YOUR ABSENCE AND THEY WILL SHUTTLE YOU BACK TO LUNA IN A FEW HOURS... OR A FEW DAYS.

IF WHAT YOU SEE IN THAT BOX **IS** REAL...
...YOU MIGHT SURVIVE BY DISCONNECTING YOUR LIFE SUPPORT AND FIGHTING IT--WITH **WHATEVER** YOU HAVE AT YOUR DISPOSAL.

"IT WAS HARD TO ACQUIRE, AND EXPENSIVE, BUT ROBYN'S FATHER HAS A LOT OF OF MONEY, AND HE WAS VERY ANGRY.
"YOU ONLY HAVE TO ANSWER ONE QUESTION.
"IS IT LIVE?
"OR IS IT THE GENRE?
"ONE THOUGHT SHOULD COMFORT YOU WHILE YOU DECIDE.
"YOU TRAINED US WELL, DR. KAF. WE'VE DEVELOPED A UNIQUE CAPACITY FOR SURVIVING ALIEN ENCOUNTERS. AND WHILE WE THINK OF YOU HERE, SUFFERING YOUR LACK OF COURAGE.
"WE WILL BE RECLAIMING THE BIRTHRIGHT YOU WILL NEVER SEE --
"--EARTH!"

ALIENS™
NOVELS FROM DARK HORSE BOOKS®
DARK HORSE BOOKS
darkhorse.com

In China, the art of carving and engraving "chops," devices used to imprint a personal seal of identity, dates back over 3,000 years. Nowadays, seals are still widely used, and the art of seal engraving has become more, not less, popular than ever before.

AVP
ALIEN VS. PREDATOR™

Carrying on this tradition, Dark Horse has created two deluxe chops in honor of two of the most widely recognized monsters of the Dark Horse comics universe—the Alien and Predator. The symbol on the bottom of each is taken from the hieroglyphics seen in Twentieth Century Fox's *Alien vs. Predator* film. Designed by Curt Chiarelli.

Each chop stands 5.5" tall and features a beautiful stone texture finish. $29.99 each

AVAILABLE AT YOUR LOCAL COMICS SHOP OR BOOKSTORE!
To find a comics shop in your area, call 1.888.266.4226. For more information or to order direct: •On the web: darkhorse.com •E-mail: mailorder@darkhorse.com •Phone: 1.800.862.0052 Mon.–Fri. 9 A.M. to 5 P.M. Pacific Time. *Prices and availability subject to change without notice.